CULTURAL
ANTHROPOLOGY

CULTURAL ANTHROPOLOGY

A CHRISTIAN PERSPECTIVE

Second Edition

Stephen A. Grunlan
and
Marvin K. Mayers

with a foreword by Eugene A. Nida

ZondervanPublishingHouse
Grand Rapids, Michigan

CULTURAL ANTHROPOLOGY: A CHRISTIAN PERSPECTIVE
Copyright © 1979, 1988 by Stephen A. Grunlan and Marvin K. Mayers.

Requests for information should be addressed to:
Zondervan Publishing House
Grand Rapids, Michigan 49530

First edition, 1979; second edition, 1988.

Library of Congress Cataloging in Publication Data

Grunlan, Stephen A.
     Cultural anthropology : a Christian perspective / Stephen A.
  Grunlan and Marvin K. Mayers : with a foreword by Eugene A. Nida.
       p.   cm.
     Bibliography: p.
     Includes indexes.
     ISBN 0-310-36381-0
     1. Christianity and culture.   2. Anthropology.   I. Mayers. Marvin
  Keene, 1927–   II. Ttile.
  BR115.C8G76 1988
    306—dc 1987-27083
  ISBN 0-310-36381-0

The Scripture text used is that of the *Holy Bible: New International Version* (North American Edition), copyright © 1973, 1978, 1984 by the International Bible Society, used by permission of Zondervan Bible Publishers.

Printed in the United States of America

98 99 00 / DH / 17 16 15 14 13 12

To our parents

Magnus Arthur and Esther Lenea Grunlan

Homer Douglas and Irma Hope Mayers

CONTENTS

FIGURES

FOREWORD

This volume on cultural anthropology by Stephen Grunlan and Marvin Mayers presents precisely what its subtitle indicates, namely, "a Christian perspective." Stephen Grunlan, who formerly taught at Moody Bible Institute and at St. Paul Bible College, is now senior pastor at the Appleton Alliance Church, Appleton, Wisconsin. He first studied anthropology under Dr. Marvin Mayers at Wheaton College and later was engaged in work among Chicanos in California and the Chicago area. Dr. Mayers engaged in field work among the Pocomchi of Guatemala under the sponsorship of the Wycliffe Bible Translators before teaching for nine years at Wheaton College, during which time he also had some field experience in the Philippines. He was director of the program for the Summer Institute of Linguistics in Dallas, Texas, and professor of linguistics at the University of Texas at Arlington for many years. He is currently dean at the School of Intercultural Studies at Biola University.

Cultural Anthropology: A Christian Perspective is addressed primarily to Bible school students of conservative evangelical backgrounds, with the hope that a sympathetic approach to the problems of cultural diversity throughout the world will help young people overcome typical North American cultural biases and make them more able to understand and appreciate the diversities of behavior and thought that exist in a culturally heterogeneous world.

Grunlan and Mayers take the position of "functional creationism"; and though they discuss some of the problems implied in traditional interpretations of the age of the world and especially of the creation of the human race, they do not attempt to deal with either physical anthropology or the origins of man. They do, however, attempt to deal meaningfully with the problems posed by biblical absolutism and cultural relativism, and their practice of concluding chapters with a series of thought-provoking questions should prove to be of real help to the nonprofessional teacher of anthropology, who has been specifically in mind as they prepared this text.

Some readers may be disappointed in not finding full-scale discussions of some of the crucial issues in contemporary anthropology, but I am confident that most of those for whom this volume has been written will be pleased with the sincere and sensitive manner in which the authors have tried to be both constructive and helpful to those who seek to relate their faith to the problems of cultural diversity and change.

EUGENE A. NIDA

PREFACE TO THE SECOND EDITION

Both of us authors were engaged in teaching cultural anthropology in missionary training programs, and this book grew out of our need for a text. The actual project began when one of us was teaching cultural anthropology at Moody Bible Institute and the other was teaching anthropology at Wheaton College. When neither of us could find a satisfactory text for our purposes, we decided to write one of our own.

Because there are so many theological positions being espoused today and different people are using the same terms to mean different things, it is very important to know the theological position of writers. We consider ourselves to be in the theological mainstream of evangelical Christianity. We believe the Bible is the inspired and authoritative Word of God (2 Tim. 3:16). We believe God is the Creator of the universe and that humans came into being as the result of a special creative act of God (Gen. 1:1, 27).

Anthropology is the study of humanity, and we view human beings as the apex of God's creative work. Hence we see anthropology as a discipline that helps us to better understand the central object of God's creation. A better understanding of people will lead to a more effective ministry to them.

In evangelical circles today, a suspicion of the behavioral sciences still lingers. This is understandable, since many behavioral scientists have been non-Christian or even anti-Christian. Some of the positions they have taken have been contrary to the teachings of biblical Christianity. However, these positions have been based on interpretations of the data. The data alone do not contradict Scripture.

In light of the Lausanne Conference on World Evangelization, Evangelicals have become more aware of the multicultural world in which they are serving. The consensus of many evangelical missiologists is that the only effective approach to this multicultural world is that of cultural relativism. We also see cultural relativism as an important element in formulating effective missionary strategy. *Relativism* is one of those words that make Evangelicals uncomfortable. The problem is that many Evangelicals do not distinguish between the various types of relativism. It's true that

xiv   CULTURAL ANTHROPOLOGY

ethical relativism finds the principles for behavior within the social situation, but we advocate cultural relativism coupled with biblical absolutism. Thus the culture defines the situation, but the principles for behavior are found in God's Word. Indeed the Bible is the absolute authority for all cultures, but it must be applied to specific and relative cultural forms.

It is our purpose to introduce the reader to the discipline of cultural anthropology, not only as an academic discipline, but also as an effective tool for the missionary, pastor, and layman in their task of presenting the gospel of Jesus Christ.

The principles that guided us as we worked on this project were our love for the Lord Jesus Christ, our conviction that the Bible is the inspired Word of God, and our commitment to the task of world evangelization. We wanted to prepare a text that would help present and prospective missionaries to better understand both their own culture and the culture in which they will minister and thus facilitate the crosscultural communication of the gospel.

Putting together a textbook involves the efforts of many people. We especially appreciate the contributions made by our colleagues and students. John Snarey, who was Dr. Mayers' graduate teaching assistant at Wheaton College, contributed many of the ideas in chapter 10.

We also want to recognize our wives, Sandra Grunlan and Marilyn Mayers, who have helped us with the bibliography and indexing. Their support and cooperation made this project possible.

Portions of chapters 1, 6, and 14 are taken from material written by Dr. Grunlan for *Christian Perspectives on Sociology* (Zondervan, 1982), a book that is now out of print.

It is our prayer that this book will contribute to the advance of the gospel of Jesus Christ.

INSTRUCTOR'S INTRODUCTION

We realize that while many who use this text in the classroom are professional anthropologists or have advanced training in anthropology, many others who use it are not anthropologists nor have they had much, if any, advanced work in anthropology.

We also realize that this text is being used in Bible colleges and Bible institutes, as well as seminaries, where anthropology is taught as an applied science rather than as an academic discipline.

This text was written so that it might be used by an instructor who has a minimal background in anthropology as well as by the professional. It was also written with the Bible college, Bible institute, and seminary curriculum aims in mind. Therefore we have attempted to keep the technical and theoretical concerns to a minimum and to emphasize the practical aspects of the discipline (see student's introduction). We have also geared our applications and illustrations to a broad range of Christian ministries.

For those teaching a course in cultural anthropology with a limited background in the broader subject of anthropology, the annotated suggested readings at the end of each chapter may prove helpful for further research in areas of weakness. These listings should also prove useful to your students for further research.

We have included study questions at the end of each chapter. These have been written to allow the student to apply or relate the material in the chapter to his or her broader experience. They are essay or thought questions rather than short-answer or objective questions. They may be used as homework assignments, in classroom discussion, in small-group discussion, or in any other way that is in keeping with your teaching needs.

Finally, we commend a book that you may want to consider using in conjuction with this text or in a follow-up course—*Christianity Confronts Culture* (Mayers:1987 [2nd ed.]). This work applies the anthropological perspective to a strategy of crosscultural evangelism.

It is our hope and prayer that this text will better enable you to teach anthropology to your students.

STUDENT'S INTRODUCTION

We realize that most of you who use this text will not go on to obtain a degree in anthropology, in fact, for many of you this will be your only anthropology course. We have written this text with that in mind.

We have purposely kept the technical vocabulary to a minimum and have emphasized the practical rather than the theoretical. However, as with all disciplines, there is a certain amount of technical vocabulary you must master. You will discover that this vocabulary often consists of everyday words that have been given very narrow and specific meanings. This is important so that two individuals in the same discipline may communicate technical information to each other with precise meaning. Ideally, this vocabulary is not meant to be memorized; rather, you should work with it until you are familiar with it and are able to use it in a variety of contexts.

Although we emphasize the practical aspect of this study, we also present some theory. The value of the theoretical is that from it we can develop principles that we may then apply in a variety of situations.

We recognize that many of you who use this text are either involved in or are planning to become involved in missions or other forms of Christian ministry. With this in mind, we have included many illustrations and applications in these areas.

We have added an annotated list of suggested readings at the end of each chapter. These lists include works that are usually available in the average library. We suggested these specific readings because we felt they were the best sources for you to use to begin further research in this subject, should you have occasion to do so. These lists are not exhaustive but are only starting points.

It is our hope and prayer that this text will contribute to your understanding of culture and that it will enable you to communicate the gospel more effectively.

1

Anthropology and Missions

A young missionary had just arrived in the interior of Kalimantan, Indonesia, fresh from language training. She was glad to be working among the Dayak people. She had heard about the explosive growth of the church in this area. She was excited about being part of this dynamic church planting ministry.

However, as time passed and she observed how the church was growing, she began to be bothered. The Dayak were not coming to Christ as individuals, but as households. It appeared to her to be a communal decision rather than an individual decision. This disturbed her because she had always been taught that conversion was an individual choice. One had to respond personally to the gospel.

This young missionary began to question if the Dayak Christians were truly born again. She began to wonder if the missionaries who had worked with the Dayak for years were more interested in "church growth" than true conversions.

What is the role of cultural anthropology in Christian missions? Is it the answer to all that ails missions or a secular tool some missionaries use instead of relying on the Holy Spirit? These are two extremes. The role of cultural anthropology in missions is neither of these.

Cultural anthropology is not a cure-all for missions. It is just one tool of a well-prepared missionary. Neither does cultural anthropology replace the Holy Spirit. No real missionary work takes place apart from the Holy Spirit. However, many Christians misunderstand the role and place cultural anthropology can have in effective ministry.

Imagine a missionary couple working among a group of tribes located along a jungle river. To reach these scattered tribes they need a boat to travel the river. They have found some scrap iron and other materials left behind by an oil-exploration crew. Using these materials, they begin to build a boat, but they know little about physics and boat building. In the end the boat turns out to be heavier than the water it displaces.

Anyone who has studied elementary physics knows that an object that is heavier than the water it displaces will sink. "Oh, but in this case the Holy Spirit will overrule, and the boat will float. After all, it was built for God's work," some might say. No. The missionaries were foolish. They should have built the boat in keeping with the laws of nature.

This same principle applies to presenting the gospel to people of another culture. Since we do not expect God to overrule when we go against natural laws, why do we expect Him to overrule when we go against cultural or behavioral laws?

Just as there is underlying order in nature, so there is underlying order in human behavior. The behavioral sciences are concerned with discovering the underlying order in human behavior just as the natural sciences are concerned with discovering the order in nature.[1] True science, natural and behavioral, is concerned with discovering the order in God's creation.

The missionary who uses cultural anthropology as a tool in developing a missionary strategy is not trying to work apart from the Holy Spirit but in harmony with Him. Peter Wagner of the School of World Mission at Fuller Theological Seminary points out the need for strategy:

The Holy Spirit is the controlling factor in missionary work, and the glory for the results go to Him. But, for reasons we have not been informed of, God has chosen to use human beings to accomplish His evangelistic purposes in the world. These human beings, missionaries in this particular case, may well become obstacles to the work of the Holy Spirit, just as they may well be effective instruments in God's hands. . . .

[1] Cultural anthropology is one of the behavioral sciences. The behavioral sciences are further discussed in chapter 2.

Missionary strategy is never intended to be a substitute for the Holy Spirit. Proper strategy is Spirit-inspired and Spirit-governed. Rather than competing with the Holy Spirit, strategy is to be used by the Holy Spirit (1971:15).

James F. Engel and H. Wilbert Norton of the Wheaton Graduate School of Theology in discussing the biblical pattern of evangelization say:

One theme that consistently runs throughout the New Testament is that the Holy Spirit works by renewing our *mind* (see Eph. 4:23; 1 Pet. 1:13; Rom. 12:2). We are expected to analyze, to collect information, to measure effectiveness—in short, to be effective managers of the resources God has given us. Unless we undertake this discipline . . . we effectively prevent the Holy Spirit from leading us! The ever present danger is that "a man may ruin his chances by his own foolishness and then blame it on the Lord" (Prov. 19:3, *Living Bible*) (1975:40).

As we have said, cultural anthropology is not a cure-all for missions nor a human effort working apart from the Holy Spirit. What, then, is the role of cultural anthropology in missions? Cultural anthropology may contribute in at least four ways to an effective missionary strategy:

1. It gives the missionary understanding of another culture.
2. It aids the missionary in entering another culture.
3. It facilitates the communicating of the gospel in another culture.
4. It aids in the process of planting the church in another culture.

Understanding Another Culture

A distinction should be drawn between *mission* and *missions,* according to missions scholar George Peters (1972). Mission is the total biblical mandate of the church of Jesus Christ. Missions is local assemblies or groups of assemblies sending authorized persons to other cultures to evangelize and plant indigenous assemblies. Missions is one aspect of mission. Basically, missions is the church in one culture sending workers to another culture to evangelize and disciple.

The preceding definition emphasizes moving from one culture to another, not from one nation to another.[2] National boundaries

---

[2] The Great Commission, as found in Matthew 28:19-20, exhorts the Christian to "make disciples of all nations." The word translated *nations* in the English is the Greek word *ethnē* from which such words as *ethnic, ethnos,* and

are artificial lines drawn on maps by politicians; cultures are realities in geographical localities. Someone from New York who ministers to the Pima Indians of the American Southwest is just as much involved in a crosscultural ministry as the New Yorker who ministers to the Mapuche Indians of Chile.

One who intends to minister to another culture needs to become familiar with the other culture. Although basic behavioral laws or universals underlie all human behavior, this behavior takes various forms in different cultures. In order to function in another culture, a person must understand that culture. Cultural anthropology provides the conceptual tools necessary to begin that process.[3]

Entering Another Culture

To minister in another culture, one must enter the culture. When an individual leaves his or her own culture with its familiar customs, traditions, social patterns, and way of life, the individual quickly begins to feel like a fish out of water and must either begin to adjust to the new culture or be tossed and buffeted by it until he or she finally succumbs to exhaustion and suffocation.

A person will respond to the new culture in one of two ways: with empathy, acceptance, and identification, which will result in adjustment and success, or with culture shock and ultimate failure. Often culture shock is

> precipitated by the anxiety that results from losing all our familiar signs and symbols of social intercourse. These signs or cues include the thousand and one ways in which we orient ourselves to the situations of daily life: when we shake hands and what to say when we meet people, when and how to give tips, how to give orders to servants, how to make purchases, when to accept and refuse invitations, when to take statements seriously and when not. Now these cues which may be words, gestures, facial expressions, customs, or norms are acquired by all of us in the course of growing up and are as much a part of our culture as the language we speak or the beliefs we accept.
>
> Now when an individual enters a strange culture, all or most of these familiar cues are removed. . . . No matter how broadminded or full of good will you may be, series of props have been knocked from under you, followed by a feeling of frustration and anxiety (Oberg 1960:177).

---

ethnology are derived. The concern of the Great Commission is not only with political units but also with cultural units.

[3] This process is further discussed in chapter 13.

Culture shock comes in three stages. First is the fascination, or tourist stage, which comes when the person first enters the new culture. There are new and fascinating sights and sounds. There are exciting things to see and experience. There are usually friendly, English-speaking people to help and see to one's comforts. The tourist, or short-term visitor, usually never goes beyond this stage before leaving the host culture.

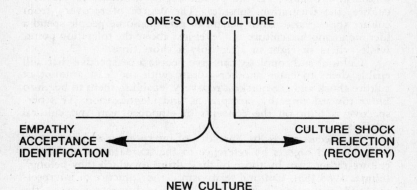

ONE'S OWN CULTURE

EMPATHY
ACCEPTANCE
IDENTIFICATION

CULTURE SHOCK
REJECTION
(RECOVERY)

NEW CULTURE

Figure 1-1. TWO REACTIONS TO A NEW CULTURE. When people leave their own culture and move into a new culture, they can move in one of two directions—either toward empathy, acceptance, and identification or toward culture shock and rejection (and possible recovery).

The second stage is the rejection stage. The fun and fascination of the new culture begin to fade, and the newcomer meets head-on the difficulties involved in living in the new culture. But now the "rules" of living are different, and the newcomer is not "in" on most of them. The way of doing things in the person's own culture may have been neat and logical, but the ways of doing things in the new culture may seem capricious, without design or purpose. The newcomer becomes frustrated in attempting to function in the new culture by applying the "rules" of his or her own culture. When these "rules" do not accomplish the desired results, the person blames the new culture; and he or she begins to reject the new culture.

This rejection may take several forms, such as stereotyping members of the new culture, making derogatory and joking remarks about the people, dissociating oneself as much as possible from members of the new culture, and associating as much as possible with members of one's own culture. Most people make at least a partial recovery from culture shock. Those not able to accommodate themselves to the new culture eventually withdraw from it completely.

The third stage, recovery, begins as the person starts to learn the language or dialect of the new culture and some of the "rules" of the new culture. As the person begins to adjust to the new culture, the frustration subsides. The degree of recovery from culture shock varies from person to person. Some people spend a lifetime in another culture at a level just above the toleration point, while others fit right in after only a short time.

Cultural anthropology can give people a perspective that will enable them to enter another culture with the least amount of culture shock and the quickest recovery, enabling them to begin to move toward empathy, acceptance, and identification. This perspective is built on the concepts of ethnocentrism and cultural relativism.

Ethnocentrism is the "practice of interpreting and evaluating behavior and objects by reference to the standards of one's own culture rather than by those of the culture to which they belong" (Himes 1968:485). Cultural relativism is the "practice of interpreting and evaluating behavior and objects by reference to the normative and value standards of the culture to which the behavior or objects belong" (484).

These definitions show that ethnocentrism is a way of viewing the world in terms of one's own culture. An action is right or wrong as defined by one's own culture. Other ways of doing things in different cultures make sense or do not make sense, depending on how they are viewed in one's own culture. Cultural relativism is a way of viewing the world in terms of the relevant culture, that is, in terms of the culture in which one finds oneself. An action is right or wrong as defined by the relevant culture.[4]

People entering another culture should recognize their own ethnocentric tendencies and become cultural relativists. Peter Wagner gives the following excellent advice to one entering a new culture:

> Make a conscious effort to detach yourself from the old culture. In order to do this, you must realize that all cultures are relative and that in no sense is your old culture any more

---

[4]Cultural relativism should not be confused with moral or ethical relativism. It is cultures that are relative not biblical morality. See chapter 14 for an in-depth discussion of this issue.

right than the new one. Accept it as different but not better (1971:94).

The following excerpt from *Christianity Today* illustrates the problem of ethnocentrism and the need for cultural relativism:

"Lord," Jojo began, "we thank you so much for sending Ron and Linda to us . . ."

While the bamboo trees creaked like doors on rusty hinges, nineteen Filipinos and three foreigners sat around a large open shed, praying. Tonight we were concentrating on one another's needs. " . . . for their careful Bible teaching. Their beautiful personal lives. Their warm home. Their enthusiasm and energy in serving you." Ron and Linda and I were the only foreigners on the staff. "And now, Lord," Jojo continued, "we beg you to deliver them from tensions . . ."

I was a little surprised. Tension? In their capable, efficient ministry? Well, yes, I suppose I had seen them tense, when they were weak from hepatitis, tired of wading around dead rats floating through the flooded market, charged full of adrenalin for a dozen meetings crammed into the week ahead and then let down when people forgot to show up for a crucial planning session. Yes, maybe they could relax a little more.

A gecko swiveled down from the roofbeam. The prayers murmured on. Then I heard Arturo praying for *me*.

" . . . and, our Father, we ask you to deliver her from tension . . ."

Tension—again! What was this all about? Were we foreigners so much more tense than everybody else?

As a matter of fact—yes. We liked efficiency. So sometimes we got uptight about lagging schedules, while the Filipinos adjusted calmly to a land where natural or political typhoons could demolish any system. As a result, peace characterized pagan Filipinos more than it did many of us missionaries.

On the other hand, some cultures with little Christian heritage do seem outstanding in some areas. When I looked around at my Filipino neighbors, for example, I saw strong families. Warm hospitality. Lots of time lavished on children. Enduring loyalties. The ability to live graciously on little money. A heritage of economic freedom for women. Creativity in music. Sauces that deliciously extended a little meat to many people. A delight in sharing. Skill in the art of relaxation. Lithe, limber bodies. The ability to enjoy being with a large number of people continuously (Adeney 1975:11–12).

The attitude exhibited by the missionary in the above account is an excellent example of a person practicing cultural relativism. The missionary was able to see the values in another culture and did not try to judge that culture by her own culture's standards.

Crosscultural Evangelism

The central task of missions is to present the gospel of Jesus Christ, the redemptive act of Christ through which individuals may enter into a personal relationship with God. The gospel message is exclusive. There is no other way, according to God's Word:

> Jesus answered, "I am the way and the truth and the life. No one comes to the Father except through me" (John 14:6).

> For there is one God and one mediator between God and men, the man Christ Jesus, who gave himself as a ransom for all men (1 Tim. 2:5–6).

We have an imperative to present the gospel of Jesus Christ to all people. We have no imperative to present our culture to anyone. Because we have learned the gospel within the wrappings of our own culture, we tend to assume that our culture is the biblical culture.

When a person has been raised in one culture as a Christian and enters another culture to bring the gospel, the person brings more than just the gospel. The person is bringing his or her cultural understanding of the gospel and cultural manifestation of it. In other words the gospel has been contextualized in the culture of the Christian. Buswell defines *contextualization* as

> theology done from inside a system, rendering the supracultural Christian absolutes not only in the linguistic idiom but also within the particular forms that "system" takes within the system: concepts of priority, sequence, time, space, elements of order, customs of validation and assertion, styles of emphasis and expression (1978:90).

As we introduce the gospel in another culture, we must attempt to lay aside our own cultural understanding and manifestation of the gospel and allow understandings and manifestations of the gospel to develop in the light of the host culture, that is, to become contextualized.

Cultural anthropology is a useful tool in separating our culture from the gospel and putting it in terms of the new culture. Speaking of the role of cultural anthropology in crosscultural evangelism, Dr. Eugene Nida says,

Of course, a study of cultural anthropology will not guarantee that a message communicated to any group of people will be accepted. Far from it! Cultural anthropology only helps to guarantee that when the message is communicated, the people are more likely to understand (Smalley 1967:310–11).

At this point we might ask, Is there not only one gospel and is it not the same for all cultures? This question has been dealt with by the contributors to the *Willowbank Report:*

it is important to identify what is at the heart of the gospel. We recognize as central the themes of God as Creator, the universality of sin, Jesus Christ as Son of God, Lord of all, and Saviour through his atoning death and risen life, the necessity of conversion, the coming of the Holy Spirit and his transforming power, the fellowship and mission of the Christian church, and the hope of Christ's return.

While these are basic elements of the gospel, it is necessary to add that no theological statement is culture-free. Therefore, all theological formulations must be judged by the Bible itself, which stands above them all. Their value must be judged by their faithfulness to it as well as by the relevance with which they apply its message to their own culture (1978:12–13).

In order to be effective in ministering crossculturally, we must be cultural relativists as well as advocates of biblical authority. It is important to realize that the members of any culture are going to emphasize some facets of the gospel while the members of another culture will tend to emphasize other facets of Scripture. As the *Willowbank Report* emphasizes so well:

The Bible proclaims the gospel story in many forms. The gospel is like a multi-faceted diamond, with different aspects that appeal to different people in different cultures. It has depths we have not fathomed. It defies every attempt to reduce it to a neat formulation (1978:12).

Returning to the case of the young missionary in Kalimantan who questioned communal conversions, we find that in developing a theology of conversion, our Western culture with its emphasis on individualism has tended to emphasize the individual nature of the conversion experience, drawing on Scripture that supports that position (e.g., Acts 8:26–40). However, those who are from a culture where group and communal decision making are emphasized will tend to emphasize the corporate nature of conversion, drawing on Scripture that reports communal conversions (e.g.,

Acts 10:44–48; 16:33; 1 Cor. 1:16). Once again we quote from the *Willowbank Report:*

> Conversion should not be conceived as being invariably and only an individual experience, although that has been the pattern of western expectation for many years. On the contrary, the convenant theme of the Old Testament and the household baptisms of the New should lead us to desire, work for, and expect both family and group conversions. . . . Theologically, we recognize the biblical emphasis on the solidarity of each *ethnos,* i.e., nation or people. Sociologically, we recognize that each society is composed of a variety of subgroups, subcultures, or homogeneous units. It is evident that people receive the gospel most readily when it is presented to them in a manner which is appropriate—and not alien—to their culture, and when they can respond to it with and among their own people. . . . We recognize the validity of the corporate dimension of conversion as part of the total process, as well as the necessity for each member of the group ultimately to share in it personally (1978:22).

It is important that we separate our culture from the gospel. It is only as we separate our culture from the gospel and put it in terms of the other culture that we are able to communicate the gospel. Cultural anthropology gives us the conceptual tools with which to extract the biblical principles from their cultural forms and begin to make them applicable in any culture. As Leighton Ford has said, "Jesus Christ is the captive of no culture and the master of all cultures" ("Hour of Decision," March 9, 1975).

When we communicate our message so that people in another culture understand it, the Holy Spirit can work in their hearts to bring about a conversion experience. As the apostle Paul says, "How, then, can they call on the one they have not believed in? And how can they believe in the one of whom they have not heard?" (Rom. 10:14).

Church Planting

When members of another culture respond to the gospel, these believers should be drawn together into a local assembly. But what should be the pattern for this assembly? What sort of polity should they have? Where should they meet? What should be the meeting schedule? What form should these meetings take? What expressions of worship should be utilized? What should be issues of separation? What form should Christian marriage take? What about polygamy? These and many other questions arise as a new church is initiated. The ethnocentric missionary will naturally want to do things the way they are done at home. But what of the missionary who realizes the need to practice cultural relativism?

Along with theological training, Christian education methods, and Bible knowledge, the well-trained missionary also needs a grasp of cultural anthropology. Cultural anthropology can enable a missionary to understand his or her prospective new culture, to enter the culture with minimum culture shock and maximum adjustment, to insure that the message is being understood, and to plant a biblical, indigenous church and not transplant the church of his or her own culture.

Marvin Mayers, in a paper read at a meeting of the Association of Evangelical Professors of Missions, related the following account:

> As a young teen, I experienced salvation from sin through Jesus Christ. I was mentally, emotionally, and spiritually confused, and I found in Christ, through His Spirit, answers to life's deepest problems. I feel that the Spirit, as an outgrowth of that conversion and through Christian growth and maturity, led me to study social anthropology following one term of missionary service in Central America. . . . I had been educated in college as an historian and in seminary as a theologian. Following that training and preparation, I went to the mission field and encountered problems for which I had no solutions nor preparation to discover solutions. I had theological answers to theological problems, but many of the challenges I faced were not theological ones.
>
> Studying in my various classes in anthropology, in the behavioral sciences, in communication, in social relations, and social structure, I began to see how I could cope with many of the problems I faced on the field. I now had alternative possibilities for dealing with them. I eagerly returned to the field and found that what I had to communicate, namely the gospel of Jesus Christ, was more sound and deeply meaningful than ever and the means I had to communicate this tremendous truth were far more effective than previously (1976).

Missions is the communication of the gospel. The role of cultural anthropology is to insure that the message is communicated in a culturally comprehensible way.

Questions for Discussion

1. Is there such a thing as a "Christian culture"? Explain your answer.
2. Did you suffer any culture shock when you came to your present school? In what ways?
3. Does culture determine whether a given action is right or wrong? Explain.
4. How much of your church's polity, scheduling, programming, and ministry is biblical and how much of it is cultural?
5. What do you see as anthropology's greatest contribution to missions?

Suggested Reading

Engel, J. F., and Norton, H. W. 1975. *What's Gone Wrong With the Harvest?* Professor Engel brings a marketing background to this work while Norton brings one rich in missions experience. Together they develop a fascinating strategy for evangelism based on an understanding of the message and the audience. This work is highly recommended.

Goodenough, W. H. 1963. *Cooperation in Change.* This work is essentially a manual for those who plan to work in underdeveloped countries. Although written for those who will be involved in secular fields, such as economics, agriculture, etc., much of the book may also be applied to missions. While the whole work should be required reading for all missionaries, chapters 17 and 18 are especially relevant to missions.

Luzbetak, L. J. 1963. *The Church and Cultures.* The author, a Roman Catholic scholar, has written an excellent work on the relationship between the church and culture. Although somewhat technical, this work is highly recommended for the serious missionary scholar.

Mayers, M. K. 1987 (2nd ed.) *Christianity Confronts Culture.* In this work Mayers fully develops his strategy of crosscultural ministry. An excellent feature of this work is the case studies Mayers has gleaned from missionaries over the years. Also included are practical exercises and class activities for each chapter. Mayers' book makes a good follow-up to this text.

Nida, E. 1960. *Message and Mission.*

——————. 1968. *Religion Across Cultures.* These two works were written by a linguistic anthropologist who has been active in Bible translation work with the American Bible Society. Both of them are highly recommended to those interested in the anthropological contributions to a translation ministry.

Oberg, K. 1963. "Cultural Shock: Adjustment to New Cultural Environments." *Practical Anthropology*. Groundbreaking article on the concept of culture shock. Good explanation of the problem with practical applications.

Olson, B. 1973. *Bruchko* (formerly *For This Cross I'll Kill You*). An excellent illustration of a culturally sensitive missionary who ministered by working with the culture rather than against it.

Richardson, D. 1974. *Peace Child*. This is an excellent case study by a missionary who received anthropological and linguistic training and used them to understand cultures and reach them for Christ.

Smalley, W. 1967. *Readings in Missionary Anthropology*. A collection of articles from the now defunct missionary journal *Practical Anthropology*. This is an excellent reader on anthropology and missions.

2

Humanity, Culture, and Society

A couple was entertaining a group of friends one evening. At dinner, when the guests had finished eating what they had been served, the wife, who was Bulgarian, offered them a second helping because it is a disgrace for a Bulgarian hostess to allow a guest to go hungry. One of the guests, an Asian student, accepted a second helping. When the Asian student was offered a third helping, he accepted it also, and the Bulgarian hostess hurried into the kitchen to prepare some more food. Halfway through his fourth helping, the Asian student fell to the floor. As he lay on the floor, he thought to himself, *It is better to get sick than to refuse the food, for it is an insult to refuse food when it is offered* (Keesing and Keesing 1971).

When people learn that I was a college professor, they usually ask me what I taught. When I reply, "Anthropology," many get a quizzical look on their face and say, "Oh? That's nice." or "Oh! Are you one of those guys who digs up old bones?" or "What's that?"

The academic disciplines may be divided into two basic groups: the humanities and the sciences. The sciences may be further broken down into the natural sciences and the social sciences. Within the social sciences there are also two divisions, the social studies and the behavioral sciences. The social studies include disciplines such as history, economics, and political science. Although there is some disagreement among scholars as to which disciplines rightly make up the behavioral sciences, most agree that the core of the behavioral sciences is made up of sociology, psychology, and anthropology.

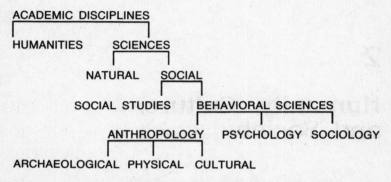

Figure 2-1. THE DIVISION OF THE ACADEMIC DISCIPLINES

So now we know that anthropology is one of the behavioral sciences, but what exactly is anthropology? The word is derived from the Greek *anthropos,* meaning "man"[1] and *logia* meaning the "study of." Literally, anthropology is the study of man (humans). Anthropology is concerned with every aspect of human beings— their origin, their past, their present, and their future. Anthropology studies humans as biological, psychological, and sociological beings. Anthropology is concerned with humans wherever they are found.

How does anthropology differ from sociology and psychology? Sociology is primarily concerned with humans as social beings and their organized social relationships. Psychology primarily deals with people as psychological beings. It is concerned with such areas as personality, attitudes, and behavior. Anthropology has many of the same concerns of both sociology and psychology.

Although all behavioral sciences have human beings as their object of study, one of the major differences between anthropology and the other behavioral sciences is that of approach. Anthropology

---

[1] Man as human, not male.

uses a comparative approach. It studies humans across time and cultures.

The basic premise of anthropology is that there are principles or "laws" that underlie all human behavior. The goal of anthropology is the discovery of these "laws."[2] Anthropology's methodological approach in discovering these universal "laws" is comparative or crosscultural. While sociology might study the effect of urbanization on rural American blacks who migrate to the cities, anthropology would study the effect of urbanization in various cultures on rural racial minorities migrating to urban centers. The anthropologist might compare the rural American black's migration to the cities with that of the rural Latin American Indian or the rural Southeast Asian tribesman.

Anthropology as a Science

Some people question the whole concept of "behavioral science" and do not see anthropology as a science. They point to physics, biology, and other natural sciences with their precise tools of measurement, laboratory experiments, and high degree of predictability. Because the area of study for anthropology is humans in the real world, anthropology does not have the precise tools of measurement that the natural sciences have nor can it engage in laboratory experimentation. However, anthropology qualifies as a science because of its methodology:

1. The procedures are public.
2. The definitions are precise.
3. The data collecting is objective.
4. The findings must be replicable.
5. The approach is systematic and cumulative.
6. The purposes are explanation, understanding, and prediction. (Berelson and Steiner 1964:16–17).

Basically, science is concerned with defining, describing, and predicting. These are also the goals of anthropology. Anthropology is concerned with defining and describing human behavior. However, definition and description are not the end in science but the process; predictability is the end. Even so, anthropology is moving past the definition and description stages into the area of prediction. While the predictions of the natural sciences seem neat and precise, the predictions of anthropology are usually in gross terms.

---

[2]Laws in science differ from laws in the legal sense. Laws in the legal realm are proscriptive. They tell you what to do. Laws in the scientific sense are descriptive. They describe what happens. They don't make it happen. Apples fell before Newton "discovered" the law of gravity.

For example, in polygynous[3] areas of Africa that have had a subsistence economy, anthropologists have been able to predict correctly that the introduction of wage labor reduces the rate of polygyny. However, the anthropologist cannot predict which persons in the society will or will not enter into a polygynous union. Because the anthropologist is dealing with humans and there are so many variables, his or her predictions are usually in gross terms, or in terms of the "average" person. Anthropology is seeking to refine its methodology in order to refine its predictions. However, the real goal in anthropology is not only to be able to predict human behavior but also to understand it.

If we are going to utilize the insights we can gain from the behavioral sciences, it is important that we understand what the behavioral sciences are *not* as well as what they are. This understanding will allow us to utilize these insights with greater confidence. The behavioral sciences are not

1. a new teaching. They are not there to change truth. They enable us to develop a different mind-set, not a different faith.
2. in competition with doctrine or theology. They aid in the development, application, and communication of doctrine and theology.
3. the exclusive domain of scholars. They are being used, at an increasing rate, by evangelical Christian organizations in counseling, as course work in Christian colleges and seminaries, and in the training and preparation of missionary recruits as well as updating the training of experienced missionaries.
4. "behaviorism" or the teachings of B. F. Skinner or J. B. Watson. The theories of men like Skinner and Watson are derived from studies done with animals and deal with determinism. Although some of their work falls under the umbrella of the behavioral sciences, it is not the same thing.
5. a "worldly system" under the control of Satan. Although there are atheistic behavioral scientists, there are also behavioral scientists who utilize the discipline to understand God and His creation more fully.

On the other hand, the behavioral sciences are

1. an academic area of study the same as the humanities or the physical sciences.
2. influencing much of what is being done today in management, education, ministry, and many other areas of life.

---

[3]Polygyny is the form of marriage arrangement involving one male with multiple spouses. Polygamy, polygyny, and polyandry are more fully discussed in chapter 8.

3. the study, through sound research techniques, of human behavior wherever it is found. This study is not designed to supplant God's truth, but may be used to help us better understand it.
4. a tool that can be used to help us better understand and apply God's Word.[4]
5. an approach to social behavior that can help us better understand, relate to, and minister to people in various cultures.

Origin of Humanity

Because anthropology is the study of human beings, a question of great interest to anthropologists is the origin of humanity. Many—but by no means all—anthropologists see human beings as a product of an evolutionary process. Although he did not conceive the idea of evolution, Charles Darwin advanced the concept in his attempt to understand the nuances of change in life forms as he traveled around the world.

Darwin's theory took hold slowly in scientific circles; but when it did, it dominated the scientific scene. Evolution has been seen by many as synonymous with anthropology because of the work done in this area by several prominent anthropologists.

Although Darwin's specific scheme of evolution has long since been replaced by newer schemes, all the schemes hold to the following basic principles:

1. Living things change from generation to generation, producing descendants with new characteristics.
2. The process has continued for so long a period of time that it has produced all the species of life now present or extinct.
3. That all living things, plants, animals, and humans are related to each other and have a common origin.

The theory of evolution is based on several kinds of evidence including (1) variation and change in plant and animal life, (2) fossils, (3) embryology, (4) comparative anatomy, and (5) geographic distribution. One of the major problems in understanding the theory of evolution is distinguishing between the evidence or findings of anthropology and the interpretations of these findings by some anthropologists. For example, when Dr. Leaky discovers a skull in Africa, we cannot argue that the skull does not exist, but we may argue with his interpretation of what that skull represents.

For the person who does not believe in a God capable of

---

[4]This point is explored further in chapter 15.

creating the universe and life, there is only one possible explanation or interpretation for the similarity of life forms: they evolved from a common source. However, for the person who believes in a Creator God, there is an alternate explanation or interpretation: similarity indicates a common creator.

There are reputable anthropologists who hold to a biblical theory of creation. This theory is based on three major convictions:

1. God exists, and He is the Creator, Sustainer, and Ultimate End of all things.
2. The account in Genesis dealing with the creation of the world is a historical fact. God not only made the universe, including the earth, by creative acts, but He also created plants, animals, and humans in such a way that they produce only "after their kind."
3. The reality of sin and of redemption from sin is essential to the Christian faith. However, if humans are in a process of evolving from a lower state, sin tends to become mere imperfection, and the gospel of redemption from sin tends to lose meaning.

Besides those anthropologists who hold either to the theory of evolution or the theory of creation, there is another group of anthropologists who have attempted to synthesize these two theories. They hold to a theory of theistic evolution. They see God as the source of life. He started the evolutionary process and then allowed it to continue to develop by itself. Some theistic evolutionists would apply this theory only to lower forms of life and see mankind as the product of a special creative act of God. Other theistic evolutionists see mankind as the end result of the evolutionary process.[5]

Our approach to the question of the origin of humans is what we call the theory of functional creation. The theory of functional creation is based on the three major convictions of the creationist, but it goes beyond that. The theory of functional creation suggests that the Genesis account is dealing with the creation of three major systems:

1. The natural system consisting of the universe, the earth, plant and animal life—the relationship of people to the environment
2. The social system—the relationship of people with each other
3. The spiritual system—the relationship of people with God

[5] See chapter 7 on biology in Ramm's *Christian View of Science and Scripture* (1954) for an excellent discussion of theistic evolution.

The Genesis account is not primarily designed to tell us when and how these systems were created, but who created them and why.

The theory of functional creation sees all of God's creation as functional or purposeful. It also sees God's creation as orderly with underlying principles or "laws." While the natural sciences seek to discover God's order in the natural realm, the behavioral sciences seek to discover God's order in the realm of human behavior.

Culture and Society

Within anthropology there are several areas of study, including archaeology, physical anthropology, and cultural anthropology.[6] Within each area are many subareas of specialization. This book is primarily concerned with cultural anthropology.

The key concept in the study of anthropology is *culture*. Culture is one of the features that separates humans from the lower animals. Of all God's creatures, only humans are culture bearing. We may define culture as learned and shared attitudes, values, and ways of behaving. Culture also includes the material artifacts created by the members of a cultural group. Sir Edward Tylor, the pioneer British anthropologist, has combined these elements into a classical definition of culture. He says culture is "that complex whole which includes knowledge, belief, art, morals, law, custom, and any other capabilities and habits acquired by man as a member of society" (1871:1).

Culture is composed of culture traits and culture complexes. *Culture traits* are the smallest units of culture, individual acts such as a wave, a smile, or saying "Hi." *Culture complexes* are clusters of related traits seen as a single unit. For example, if I wave, smile, and say "Hi," these three culture traits make up a culture complex that we call a "greeting." Culture traits may be mixed and combined to form any number of culture complexes.

Often smaller social units, called subcultures, are found within larger cultures. A *subculture* is a cluster of behavior patterns related to the general culture and yet at the same time distinguishable from it. The Amish people of Pennsylvania are an illustration of a subculture. In many ways their behavior is similar to that of the general American culture. Their men wear pants and their women wear dresses. They speak, read, and write English. They live in rectangular shaped houses with peaked roofs. They sit on chairs, eat at tables, and sleep on beds. The culture of the Amish people has much more in common with the general American culture than it has with the culture of the Kalapalo Indians of Brazil, but neither

---

[6] Some anthropologists prefer the term *social anthropology*, while others assert that social anthropology is a distinct subfield of anthropology.

the Amish nor the Kalapalo drive automobiles, use electricity, or farm with tractors. However, the Kalapalo Indians speak Kalapalo. They do not read or write. They go naked or wear a G-string. They practrice polygyny. They eat manioc and monkey meat. In other words, Kalapalo culture is not really related to Amish culture.

Counterculture is a nontechnical term. We understand it to mean a person or group whose behavior is counter to that of the general culture. We might say the Hell's Angels are a counterculture. However, anthropologically there is no such thing as a "counterculture." Hell's Angels constitute a culture or, more correctly, a subculture. Members of Hell's Angels are not counter to or against culture. They have learned and shared behavior. Even casual observation reveals the extent to which they conform to their culture. Many of their behavior patterns are related to the general culture. They wear pants, speak English, use American money, sit in chairs, and so on.

Tylor's definition of culture introduces another term: *society*. What is society and how does it differ from culture? Society is a social organization made up of a group of people who share a geographical area and culture. Society and culture are interdependent concepts. One cannot exist apart from the other. However, they are not the same thing. Society refers to people and their social organization, whereas culture refers to their learned and shared way of life. Because by its very definition, culture is learned and shared; it involves more than one person. When we have two or more people interacting with each other, we have the basis for society.

Humans, wherever found on this planet, are both similar and different. The concept of culture helps us see the similarities and understand the differences. Bronislaw Malinowski (1944), the well-known British anthropologist, sees seven basic biological and psychological needs of all human beings. These seven needs are seen as impulses to act. The act is a cultural response leading to biological and psychological satisfaction. This process is known as the *Permanent Vital Sequence*.

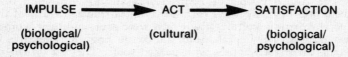

Figure 2-2. MALINOWSKI'S PERMANENT VITAL SEQUENCE. Although Malinowski has used the term *impulse* in describing his scheme, drive or need could also be substituted.

Malinowski's *Permanent Vital Sequence* is a useful conceptual tool for understanding the concept of culture. It is also a very convenient conceptual approach to the analysis of another culture. For the nonanthropologist who wants to begin to understand another culture, Malinowski's scheme can be a good starting point. Because all persons have the same needs, we often assume all persons meet those needs in the same way. Malinowski's approach helps us to be aware that various cultures meet the same needs in different ways. It opens the door for us to begin understanding another culture. This is very important to the task of global evangelism.

Of Malinowski's seven basic needs, the first need is *metabolism*—the need for oxygen, liquid, and food. The metabolism need is met in each society by an organized behavior system for the production, distribution, and consumption of food and liquid. All humans have a biological hunger drive and need to eat to sustain life, but the ways the hunger drive is met vary greatly among societies. People eat many different things to meet their hunger drive. Alaskan Eskimos eat whale meat; the Japanese, raw fish; the French, frog's legs; Australian aborigines, dried root meal; African bushmen of the Kalahari, locusts, ants, lizards, and ostriches; and the Semang of Malaysia, bamboo rats and monkeys.

Humans vary not only in what they eat, but also in when they eat and how often they eat. There are two-meals-a-day cultures such as the Kalinga of northern Luzon in the Philippines, three-meals-a-day cultures such as North American society, and four-meals-a-day cultures such as parts of Scandanavian society. The Semai of Malaya have no set mealtimes but snack all day long.

Humans also vary in how they eat. In North America and Europe, metal utensils are used. In many parts of the Orient, chopsticks are used. In some areas people eat with their fingers. Some cultures use individual eating utensils; and others, communal utensils.

Customs concerning with whom people eat also vary. In North America the immediate family members usually all eat together. Among the Palauans of the South Pacific, men eat separately from women, as in many African societies. Among the Yoruba of Nigeria, mealtime is not only segregated by sex but also by seniority, with the older males eating apart from the younger males.

The ways societies produce and distribute their food and liquid also vary. Food production is dependent on three factors: the environment, the population, and the culture. The Nuer of Africa are pastoralists, most Indonesians are agriculturalists, and the aborigines of Australia are hunters and gatherers. Meeting the metabolism need in most societies involves technology, economics, and social organization. Although the need is biological, meeting it involves several cultural systems.

The second need is *reproduction*. This is the replenishing of society. It includes, but goes beyond, the sex drive. It makes possible the survival of society. It is psychological as well as biological. In every society studied by anthropologists, sex and reproduction are controlled by cultural systems of marriage and kinship. Marriage is a social mechanism used to mark off legitimate sex partners, and kinship is a system for placing and training a person in society.

In the village of Benbarre, Spain, a girl's uncle is responsible for finding her a mate, but his search is limited to males of the same social class. Among the Kalapalo Indians of Brazil, a man may have more than one wife, and a woman may have more than one husband. Although marriage types and customs differ, the function of the family in reproduction remains the same from society to society.

Jose, a Surui Indian of the Brazilian interior, illustrates Malinowski's reproduction principle:

> Farming is a struggle against the continual encroachment of the tropical forest. Lacking complex technology, he can practice only very limited agriculture. Though the forest provides food to hunt and gather, it forces him into a seminomadic existence. His group must remain small lest their demands exceed the forest's supply.
>
> One of Jose's basic needs is a spouse to fill those roles and perform those tasks which nature and Surui culture have defined for the Surui woman. Where will Jose find a wife within the context of this seminomadic band? Through centuries of adaptation to life in the forest, the Surui have provided Jose an answer to this question: the ideal choice for his wife is his own sister's daughter, his niece.
>
> In the harsh tropical forest, a strong brother-sister relationship is very important. If either is without a mate, the other can provide some of the services a spouse would ordinarily supply. She can cook for him; he can hunt for food for her. An unmarried man might even provide food for his sister when she has a husband, thereby helping his brother-in-law in his food quest, which is not necessarily successful on every hunt. When his sister has a daughter, he is a logical choice to be the girl's husband. He is already in the household, and she is able to take on the roles of a wife as her age and experience permit.
>
> Marrying the sister's daughter has some interesting results for the way the Surui classify kinsmen. In particular, there is no term for "aunt." A father's sister is called

"grandmother." Indeed, she *is* a grandmother to her brother's child. Here is how it works:

Figure 1 is a standard diagram showing that two individuals—in this case Jose and Maria—are brother and sister.

Figure 2 indicates that Jose has married Maria's daughter Gloria, and that Jose and Gloria have a son, Roberto.

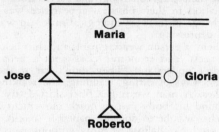

Note that for Roberto, Maria is not only his father's sister, but also his mother's mother—his grandmother. So he refers to her by the Surui term for grandmother; there is no need for a separate term for aunt (Merrifield 1976:8)

The third need is *bodily comforts*. This involves maintaining a range of temperature, humidity, etc., that will allow the physiological processes such as circulation and digestion to continue. Housing and clothing are both used to maintain bodily comfort. However, in most societies they have a dual function. Not only do they function as body protectors, but also as status symbols. A wool coat or a fur coat will keep an American woman warm, but the fur coat is a higher status symbol. Among the Yoruba of Nigeria, status is indicated by beads on the clothing.

Shelter involves technology and economics. While the North American builds a rectangular house, the Dinka of the Sudan in Africa builds a round one. The North American sleeps in a bed, but the Kalapalo Indian of Brazil sleeps in a hammock. Whereas the North American builds his house on a low rock foundation, the Sawi of Irian Jaya and the Semai of Malaya build their house many feet off the ground on poles. All the members of a North American family live in the same house; but the Kapauku Papuans of western

New Guinea have two-part houses, one section for males and one for females.

Culture plays a large role in the way people protect their bodies, as evidenced among the Yagua people of Peru:

> Suppose it is your responsibility to communicate the Gospel to a group of people who dress very differently from the way you do. Does it matter what they wear? Does it matter if they try to adopt your kind of clothing? Paul and Esther Powlison, translators among the Yagua people of Peru, discovered that it does matter.
>
> When two Yagua men began wearing pants, and shirts instead of their traditional Hawaiian-style fiber skirts, the transformation in their physical appearance was startling. But the change in their psychological make-up was nothing less than depressing!
>
> To them, a person wearing pants and shirt belonged to a different social and economic class with a behavior they really didn't understand. They didn't know the socially appropriate ways of sitting, standing, and walking in their new clothes. A man wearing a fiber skirt deftly tucks the fibers around his body in one quick movement as he sits down. What was he to do with pants? In a skirt, he walks through mud or shallow streams without pause, but he cannot do so with pants and remain clean and dry.
>
> Accustomed to a fiber turban that covers the back of his neck, he feels very exposed when wearing the available cloth substitute, a cap. In fear of behavior inappropriate for their newly-adopted clothing, these two Yagua men "froze." Restricting every form of expression—facial, verbal and body movement—they acted like robots.
>
> The Prowlisons saw them later at a Yagua feast. They had reverted to their traditional clothing and were like men resurrected from the dead! Once again they were their jovial selves, moving freely and naturally in that most intimate of environments, their own clothing.
>
> With other Yaguas, women as well as men, the same thing proved true. In cloth clothes, their spirits as well as their bodies were prisoners of a foreign culture in which they did not know how to operate.
>
> The translator must beware of encouraging clothing change along with the communication of the Gospel. By doing so he may psychologically imprison those whom he wishes to liberate spiritually (Merrifield 1976:8).

The fourth need is *safety*, the prevention of bodily injuries by mechanical accident, attacks from animals, or attack from other human beings. The need for safety is met by planning to prevent injury and removal of hazards and organization against attack by animal or man.

In warfare, the types of weapons used, the methods of organization, and the military strategies are all cultural. In Western societies we have highly structured military organizations. There are uniforms, ranks, codes of behavior, regulations, and specific roles and duties. Modern machines of war are employed. There are sophisticated aircraft, missiles, radar, lasers, and nuclear weapons. Computers, maps, intelligence networks, and war games all go into developing military strategy.

The Mossi of Africa are organized for defense by loosely knit kinship groups and fight with bows and arrows. The Palauans of the South Pacific were organized by war clubs. The young men were occupied most of the time with warfare or discussions about it. When engaging in warfare, these clubs acted independently of each other both on the attack and in defense (Barnett 1960).

Competition was great between these clubs in the taking of heads and obtaining other war honors. Although all the clubs were under the authority of the chiefs, once they were given a command they were free to obey it in a way that would bring maximum gain to themselves as well as to the rest of the community.

Most of the fighting involved forcing the payment of money for a crime that had been committed, or as indemnity for injuries or losses, or even in exchange for favors rendered. Although both personal revenge and reputation as a fighter were incentives to fight, money, nevertheless, was always involved in the warfare.

Sometimes the chiefs of two districts secretly conspired against a third. While one district attacked the district conspired against, the other conspiring district offered refuge to the women and children of the attacked district. Afterwards the two conspiring districts divided the money paid for the protection offered the women and children. The money went to the chiefs, not the fighting men, because warfare was considered a patriotic service. The money was used to increase the prestige of the district.

Although various cultures encounter different threats to their safety and use different methods and technologies in meeting these threats, all must develop systems to deal with threats to survive. These systems do not exist apart from the rest of the culture but are an integral part of it. They are usually closely related to the economic system and the value systems as well as other areas of the social system.

The fifth need is *movement*. Activity is necessary to all organisms. Although all humans need activity, types of activity are culturally determined. American boys play baseball, Canadian boys play hockey, Mexican boys play soccer, and Kalapalo Indian boys of Brazil have spear-throwing contests. All human activity appears to be instrumental, that is, directed toward the satisfaction of other needs.

The instrumentality of children's play can be seen in the fact that many learning experiences are attributed to organized sports in our culture. We say it teaches sportsmanship, team play, turn taking, and other values important in our society. F. M. Deng (1972), a Dinka of the Sudan in Africa, explains that like children the world over, Dinka children play a variety of games whose primary purpose is that of entertainment but which are also subtly aimed at developing an awareness of and sensitivity for Dinka values and norms. These values and norms include the importance of cattle, marriage, and distinctive sex roles for men and women.

For example, physical strength and courage are highly valued characteristics for a man. The educational content of the games played by the Dinka children can be understood only in the total context of their culture. The emotional dispositions that are developed in these games prepare the children for the roles they will assume in Dinka culture.

One of the games played by Dinka children is a bathing game played in a river. The children stand in water up to their armpits in a circle. One of the children dives into the water in the middle of the circle. The rest of the children beat on top of the water chanting:

> The diviner of that day
> From where did he come?
> The diviner of Nyandeeng's Mother
> Is that why my mother must die?
> My little buffalo, rest in peace,
> Mankind is passing on.

In its literal meaning, the song does not seem to be saying much. It might be accusing the diviner of bringing death to the child's mother; or, on the other hand, it may be that the diviner is only revealing the source of evil and the inevitable death that will result. The diving under the water as well as the beating on top of the water symbolize death. The interpretation of the game and song are not as important as the effect of the melody, the rhythm, and the mystery of the child under water.

The child is confronted, through the game, with the possibility that his mother might die. The tie between a Dinka child and his or her mother is very strong. Because of this strong tie and dependency, the thought of one's mother dying is a terrifying prospect for a Dinka. The purpose of this shocking game is to prepare the child for the inevitable.

Dinka children also play adult roles even as children in our society do. One of their favorites is playing marriage, or family.

Just as in our culture, the game does not involve any physical relationships but rather deals with the public roles of husbands and wives. The man takes part in public affairs, while the woman does housework and rears the children. These games can be enacted very realistically as they prepare the children for their future roles.

The sixth need is *growth*. Because human beings are dependent in infancy, maturation among humans is slow and gradual, and old age leaves the individual defenseless, the facts about growing up, maturity, and decay impose certain general, but definite, conditions on human cultures. This need is met by the kinship system (chapters 8 and 9) and enculturation (chapter 5).

The Kaguru of East Africa see the creation of a child as a long, complex process (Beidelman 1971). This process must be carefully regulated to insure the security and stability of the new child. This regulation also protects those who are associated with the new child. Pregnancy and birth make the infant's parents and other close kin especially vulnerable to forces that threaten their status and social relationships.

The Kaguru associate menstruation with female fertility and associate the temporary cessation of menstruation with pregnancy. Some Kaguru feel that a couple should have frequent intercourse during the early months of pregnancy in order to "feed" the womb. They also feel that the couple should abstain from intercourse during the final weeks of pregnancy so as not to injure the child.

When a woman has a problem conceiving or retaining a pregnancy, her husband may consult a diviner in order to determine the cause of the problem. The problem is usually diagnosed as disruptive forces associated with the ghosts of ancestors who do not want the unborn to leave the land of the ghosts and go to the land of the living. The diviner will often prescribe medicines for which the husband will pay. Often women under a diviner's care will allow their own hair to grow unusually long, and an infant with an odd topknot indicates that the diviner is caring for this child until it is firmly entrenched in the land of the living.

As Kaguru children approach adulthood, they go through an initiation designed to convert irresponsible, immature youngsters into responsible adults. Until they undergo the initiation, they are not able to exert jural control over others or properly propitiate ghosts. The initiation process involves both physical and moral aspects. The initiate learns the behavior expected in the future. The physical distress experienced during the initiation makes the individual disposed to accept and internalize the values and norms being inculcated during the initiation. Male initiates are circumcised as part of their initiation. Many Kaguru report that their initiation was one of the most important and impressive experiences of their lives. Most exhibit a different tone and style in their behavior following their initiation.

The ritual of marriage differs from the initiation rites for the Kaguru. Marriage involves the creation of new social networks that may create potential problems, which must be dealt with as part of the marriage rite. Kaguru marriage rites emphasize the continuous ties of marriage that will continue beyond the life span of the couple involved.

A death presents two basic problems for the Kaguru. The first is how to get the dead person from the land of the living to the land of the ghosts. Their burial rites involve rituals to speed the dead on their way to the land of ghosts and control them until they arrive.

This account of the life cycle of the Kaguru illustrates the role culture plays in growth.

The seventh need is *health*. That is the maintenance and repair of the biological organism. This need is met by hygiene, which consists of preventive measures and cures.

Medicine and healing involve knowledge and belief about the human body and the causes of disease. In some areas of the world, bloodletting is practiced. It has not been proved to cure diseases, but because it makes the patient feel different and better, bloodletting often leads to recovery.

In Latin America beliefs about curing are tied to a theory of hot and cold medicine that is based more on psychological analysis than temperature per se. If a hot remedy is provided for an illness perceived to be cold, the person does not expect the remedy to work. Beyond such physiological and psychological processes, the healer often uses such basic remedies as aspirin and quinine.

Thus medical action involves a *diagnosis*, the determining of the category of illness from which the individual is suffering, and *therapy*, a plan of action to cure the illness. The therapy or treatment is based on the healer's understanding of the agent and cause of the diagnosed illness: a virus, a parasite, a poison, a curse, or a sorcerer's spell. The healing activities attempt to remove or nullify the influence of whatever or whoever is believed responsible for the illness.

Anthropologist George Spindler and some of his students did field research in southern West Germany in the area of the village of Burgbach. In their report some aspects of *volksheilkunde*, or "folk healing" are discussed, demonstrating that disease is culturally defined and that its detection and cure are also cultural in nature (Spindler 1960).

From interviews with women from various social classes and groups, the following home remedies were cataloged:

Toothache: hold a warm clay-filled sack on the stricken area; bite on cloves; chew hard black bread; use hot compresses; use schnapps-saturated cotton wads; put clove oil on the sore spot; put clove oil on a cotton wad stuffed into the cavity.

Infection and fever: drink a lot of water and other liquids; drink camomile and peppermint teas; drink Lindenblüten tea; wrap the calves of the leg or the entire upper part of the body with compresses soaked in a water-and-vinegar solution; wrap infected areas with compresses of sour milk or pig lard.

Headaches: wrap the head with a compress soaked with water, vinegar, and milk; drink various teas; take a cool foot bath.

Sneezing and coughing: drink honey and cognac mixed together with hot water and lemon; wear a flannel cloth with camphor on the chest; use a vaporizer to which vinegar has been added; inhale camomile-tea steam and drink hot camomile tea; rub oil and fat compresses on the chest; drink onion juice with brown sugar, or drink radish juice with brown sugar; take a steam bath with the addition of camomile tea or eucalyptus oil; drink hot malt wine; drink lemon juice; use a sweat cure.

Insomnia: drink Baldrian tea; eat onions which have been boiled in milk immediately before retiring; drink a mixture of cold milk and honey; place the bed with the feet toward the south and the head toward the north; sleep with the head higher than the feet.

Stomach aches, cramps, and heartburn: drink various cognacs and schnapps; eat zwieback; drink Baldrian and bloodroot teas; drink peppermint tea and put warm cloths on the stomach.

Constipation: eat sour milk or cottage cheese; eat apples and drink apple juice; chew tobacco and swallow the juice; sit in a tub of warm water; use suppositories, particularly in the form of a small splinter of soap; drink honey and water on an empty stomach; eat raw sauerkraut; use any one of a number of medicinal herb teas *(Krauterteen)*.

Burns: use salad oils as a dressing; use butter or codliver oil and bind with muslin; make a paste of vegetable oil and potato meal; cover with the white of a fresh egg; use a compress soaked with one of several teas.

Diarrhea: eat zwieback and drink cold red wine; fast and then drink black teas and zwieback; chew and swallow charcoal;

eat oatmeal; drink hot chocolate cooked with water instead of milk; drink a raw egg mixed with cognac; drink a number of herbs mixed together and steeped, including Kamillenbluten and Anis.

Worms: eat garlic and onions or raw carrots; take honey, use an enema of salt and soap water; drink mineral water with pumpkin or gourd seeds; drink hot milk; use one of several teas recommended for worms (1973:61–62).

It appears that some remedies seem to be physiologically and psychologically effective, but there is no way to measure their effectiveness since most people seem to recover from their ailments with or without the remedies. What we must realize is that health systems are an intricate part of any culture.

We can see from Malinowski's *Permanent Vital Sequence* that although drives are psycho-biological, behavior is cultural. Although the cultural anthropologist does not ignore man's psycho-biological drives, his cultural acts are of primary concern.

In summary, then, anthropology is the study of God's special act of creation: man. Humans have violated the principles of God's spiritual system and broken their relationship with God. In Jesus Christ, God has provided a means of restoring that relationship. Our task, as Christians, is to bring our fellow human beings the message of redemption. Anthropology helps us to understand better both God and people and to play a role in the reconciliation process.

Questions for Discussion

1. What does anthropology have in common with psychology and sociology? How does it differ from them?
2. What is the scope of anthropology as an academic discipline?
3. Of what subculture or subcultures are you a member? How does one of these subcultures differ from the general culture?
4. What are some common culture complexes in the classroom? What combinations of culture traits make up these complexes?
5. Is there a conflict between the Bible and the behavioral sciences? Explain.
6. Describe some ways in which each of Malinowski's seven basic needs are met in your culture.

Suggested Reading

Beals, A. R.; Spindler, G.; and Spindler, L. 1973. *Culture in Process.* 2nd ed. A good, short, clear, and readable introduction to cultural anthropology. This book contains many helpful illustrations.

Buswell, J. O. III. 1975. "Creationist Views on Human Origin." *Christianity Today*. Vol. 19, no. 22: 4–6. An excellent article dealing with the early and late date creation controversy.

Harris, R. L. 1971. *Man—God's Eternal Creation*. A good conservative treatment of creation and Old Testament culture.

Howard, M. C. 1986. *Contemporary Cultural Anthropology*. A well-written introduction to cultural anthropology from a secular perspective.

Hughes, C. C., ed. 1976. *Custom-Made*. 2nd ed. One of many good readers in introductory anthropology. A good range of articles that helps give the reader a "feel" for what anthropology is all about.

Morris, H. M., ed. 1974. *Scientific Creationism*. A helpful treatment of the creationist perspective from a scientific perspective.

Ramm, B. 1954. *The Christian View of Science and Scripture*. The chapters on biology and anthropology give a good discussion of theistic evolution. The whole work is strongly recommended. Its approach is open-minded and even-handed.

3

Fields and Theorists

When Bronislaw Malinowski was born in Cracow, Poland, in 1884, that city was part of the Austrian Empire. In 1908, Malinowski received a Ph.D. in physics and mathematics from the University of Cracow. He was about to embark on a promising career in the physical sciences when he read Sir James Frazer's book *The Golden Bough*. He was so impressed with Frazer's work that he went to England to study anthropology under him.

After four years of anthropological study under the leading British anthropologists of the day, Malinowski set off for Australia to do field work. On his way, World War I broke out. When he arrived in Australia, he was interned, due to his Austrian citizenship. Rather than being idle during his internment, Malinowski persuaded the Australian government to allow him to do field work in their territories. He was so persuasive that the government even provided funds for his work. Malinowski remained in Australia six years and made field trips to Mailu and the Trobriand Islands, where he lived as a native and experienced the culture firsthand. Malinowski was one of the forerunners in establishing the tradition of "participant observer" in anthropological field work.

Anthropologists often find they are caught between two lines of fire: that of the natural scientist who feels anthropology as a behavioral science is not scientific enough, and that of the humanities person who feels there is little validity in the behavioral aspects of the study. The natural scientist would call into question studies done by anthropologists because of the lack of quantitative data. One involved in humanities would claim "facts" derived from the study of people are neither fully correct nor worth the time consumed seeking them or using them.

There is no study of humanity more encompassing than anthropology. Only those not involved in the field, or those failing to have studied the scope of the field, find the discipline limited in studying and understanding humanity. When anthropological researchers enter the field and begin serious study, they discover that humanity's past and present cultures open a vast panorama. Anthropologists gain insight into the past and they also see the present from a new perspective. They not only become aware of the dynamics of other cultures, they also learn significant things about their own culture. They get to know other people, but, more important, they get to know themselves. They also gain a better understanding of God, in whose image humans were created.

Fields of Anthropology

Culture is the integrated system of learned behavior character-istic of the members of a society. *Cultural anthropology* deals with the system as a whole, how the parts fit and function within the whole, and how whole systems relate and compare. *Ethnography,* the descriptive study of human societies, is more concerned with the parts than with the whole; it deals with basic description. Ethnography primarily deals with the patterns themselves and secondarily with how these patterns relate to the whole. *Ethnology* is comparative ethnography. Cultural anthropology becomes more related to the concerns of crosscultural contact and communication.

One way the underlying structure of society is studied is through conceptual models in the discipline now termed *cognitive anthropology* or *studies in cognition,* hence this definition:

Cognitive anthropology constitutes a new theoretical orientation. It focuses on *discovering* how different people organize and use their cultures. This is not so much a search for some generalized unit of behavioral analysis as it is an attempt to understand the *organizing principles underlying* behavior. It is assumed that each people has a unique system for perceiving and organizing material phenomena—things, events, behavior, and emotions. The object of study is not these material phenomena themselves, but the way they are organized in the minds of men. Cultures are not material phenomena; they are cognitive organizations of material phenomena.

In essence, cognitive anthropology seeks to answer two questions: What material phenomena are significant for the people of some culture, and how do they organize these phenomena? (Tyler 1969:3).

Interest in linguistic science and its results grew during the 1950s. In the 1960s a branch of anthropology developed termed *ethnoscience*. This study applied the principles of linguistics to the larger nonverbal culture and resulted in very detailed and systematic studies of kinship systems. The results were gathered primarily through the study of kinship terminology. In time, these and other principles were grouped into an emerging discipline dealing with the way people saw their culture, perceived their universe, and mapped strategies to cope with that universe.

Because language is a vital part of culture and the means by which society maximally expresses itself in detail, language study became significant to the anthropologist. The structures of language developed into a separate discipline within anthropology. Recently anthropologists and linguists brought them together, first in the field of ethnoscience and the broader concerns of language and culture, and later in joining studies of sociolinguistics. The overall outcome of such studies, including grammatical, semantic, and sociolinguistic studies, is the forming of the foundations for recent advances in translation sciences. This area of anthropology is very important to the task of Bible translation.

Individuals within a society are significant in numerous ways. They are society's representatives and thus a characteristic expression of that society. The culture of a society is expressed through them, giving both them and the society its identity. Further, they are the primary source of change within a society, both as innovators and as receptors of change. They can have individual expressions of the culture with their own idiolect of speech while combining and recombining new and old forms into new configurations and patterns. Their reaction both to themselves and their culture is thus a significant concern for the subfields of psycholinguistics and psychological anthropology.

Theoretical concerns are the primary focus of the above disciplines. It took the development of synchronic and structure-function theories in anthropology to lay the foundation for the emerging application of anthropology to social problems.[1] The

---

[1] These theories see society as a structure with the parts as functional. That is, a social structure will exist only as long as it is functional.

broader field of applied anthropology is yielding to more specific concerns of *urban anthropology*, the developments of the industrial and urban influences crossculturally; *educational anthropology*, the comparative study of socialization and enculturation processes; and *medical anthropology*, the application of cultural criteria to the practice of medicine and response to medical, clinical, and educational practices.

The diachronic, or historical dimensions, were always a vital part of anthropological studies largely because of the concerns of the humanities for the past and the factual data of the past. The study of history per se has had two significant areas of study: *ethnohistory*, the cultural history of a people; and *history of anthropology*, the antecedents of theory and practice within the field itself. The history of the culture expressed through artifacts of that culture is *archaeology*. When correlated with the stages of development in culture it is termed *prehistory*. Social, political, religious, and economic concerns are studied as separate subdivisions of the discipline.

In recent years a separate concern for legal and ethical issues within anthropology has developed, particularly with respect to anthropological research. The American Anthropological Association has a standing committee that deals with ethics.

A new area of study, ethnotheology, is being developed. *Ethnotheology* is concerned with de-culturalizing[2] theology, separating theology and culture.[3] Each Christian learns his or her theology within a cultural setting and soon begins to see his or her cultural behavior as "Christian" behavior. Ethnotheology is also concerned with relating the gospel in cultural patterns relevant to the receiving culture.

Philosophy and anthropology have concerns in common. Each society expresses itself uniquely with its own style of living, thinking, and believing. These are significant concerns for the philosopher. But the study of comparative ethical systems makes demands on both. The comparative study of art, or music, or ethnomusicology and other "cultural" expressions has also been increasing.

In addition to cultural and philosophical areas, there has been a longstanding interest in the physical, such as comparative concerns of bone structure, blood types, genetics, and other areas. These are expressed in the discipline of *physical anthropology* and the related

---

[2] The term *de-culturalizing* is widely used in missiological material; nevertheless, we recognize the limitations of the term. Some have argued that de-culturalization is an impossible task and that the coined and positive term *inculturate* is better.

[3] See Charles Kraft, 1973. "Toward a Christian Ethnotheology." In *God, Man and Church Growth*, ed. Alan R. Tippett. Grand Rapids: Eerdmans.

fields of biology, chemistry, and physiology. New and emerging fields have developed in the forms of ethnobotany and ethno-ecology with the increased interest in earth studies.

Increasingly, new concerns are attracting the anthropologist and former concerns are becoming newly reinforced. Research methodology is one of the important aspects of field work within anthropology, especially because of the prominence of field work in anthropological studies. Field work is the functional equivalent of clinical studies within psychology. It is impossible to bring a society into the laboratory; so the anthropologist goes out to the society.

Because it is difficult to bring the field into the laboratory or to take a significant number of students into the field, game theory and simulations have been developing within the areas of anthro-pology and linguistics. Game theory is being used for prediction and modeling interrelationships. These may develop into independ-ent disciplines themselves.

The concerns of crosscultural communication are also coming to the forefront. It is being recognized that all encounters in actuality are crosscultural. One never encounters another person who shares his same integrated system of learned behavior patterns. They must adapt to each other. Adaptation is easier if the crosscultural distinctions are minimal or maximal, and more difficult if there are subtle but deep-seated differences between them. The field of crosscultural communications plays an impor-tant part in missions.

It is important to recognize as crosscultural all encounters that call for the crosscultural question: "Is what I am doing building trust or undermining it?"[4] rather than the monocultural question: "What is my right, duty, and responsibility?" Once the crosscul-tural question is asked, other questions fall into proper place, allowing individuals from two different cultures to be whole persons, maintaining their principles and self-respect. Without this awareness, for example, Christian witness becomes a process of convincing the other person that one's own pattern of behavior is right. This monocultural approach develops a high degree of conformity to the culture of the witness.

In the same way, all ministries are ethnic. While members of the dominant culture do not consider themselves ethnic, they consider those of a different nationality, speech, and lifestyle ethnic. However, all ministries are rooted in cultural practices, no matter how much these cultural practices have been elevated to the level of

---

[4]See Marvin K. Mayers, 1987, *Christianity Confronts Culture*, Zondervan, Grand Rapids. Chapters 1-2.

a biblical absolute. Since all ministries include cultural practices, all are ethnic.

It does not take a discerning person long to recognize cultural practices within a church context. The loudness of speech, the topic under consideration, the development of the topic, the amount of audience participation, and the time of the participation are all components of a worshipful atmosphere for a person. If the person is of the same subcultural expression as the corporate church, he can worship meaningfully. If not, he is distracted. The raised voice saying, "Amen" or increased volume in the service by organ or voice is distracting to one whose background reflects a quieter worship setting.

People have a remarkable dynamic for encountering different peoples. Therefore the potential for an infinite variety of extensions of their lifestyles exists without their having to abandon the principles on which their lives are based or violating biblical absolutes. By way of example, it is possible to learn a second or even a third language and to be able to speak it fluently, without using that language to curse God. In the same way one can adapt completely to another culture without abandoning his or her moral or ethical perspective and biblical lifestyle. This dynamic is vital to missions. The apostle Paul's claim, "I am all things to all people," is the motto of crosscultural ministry.

The goal of anthropology is the total understanding of human beings. It is the study of everything that concerns people. It does not assume total knowledge, for total knowledge cannot be gained by one person or one discipline. There is the need for cooperation between disciplines and the realization that there is a limit to knowledge. The limits of knowledge will be expanded only by transition to the life beyond, when all bounds and limits on knowledge will be removed.

Historical Development of Anthropology

Most people see themselves as normal and others as different. When people have been raised in the context of their own culture, everything they do seems natural and logical to them. When they encounter a new culture, they often see it as strange, inconsistent, illogical, and even bad. The more they move about in a variety of cultures and encounter a variety of lifestyles, the more they become accustomed to differences and the more willing they are to accept them.

Perhaps the earliest scholars who made significant contributions to the discipline that was to emerge in a later century were Herodotus (484–425 B.C.) and Tacitus (ca. A.D. 55–120). Herodotus, credited with being the first to write about and study other cultures, commented on customs of peoples other than the Greeks. His comments, however, were neither systematic nor firsthand. Apparently, they were to stand alone for five hundred years until Tacitus wrote a tract on the origin and locality of the Germans, considered an early ethnography. Few shared the interest of these ancient writers for many centuries. Cultures other than one's own were simply ignored.

A French Jesuit, Joseph-François Lafitau, worked in Sault Saint Louis in the eighteenth century among the Iroquois and the Hurons of western New York. His work was a study of the American Indians, comparing their customs with those of early times. Even as Greece and Rome represented an earlier stage of civilization than eighteenth-century Europe; so too, he reasoned, the cultures of the Hurons and the Iroquois represented an earlier condition of humankind. He expressed three principles that became basic in anthropology. First, contemporary preliterate cultures help us to understand ancient cultures, and vice versa. Second, historic relationships between cultures cannot be assumed but must be demonstrated. Third, non-Western culture must be evaluated from a perspective of cultural relativity rather than ethnocentrically from a Western perspective.

William Robertson, a Presbyterian minister, writing in 1777 in *History of America,* put forth the first systematic presentation of cultural evolution and cultural determinism. He used three stages of evolutionary typology: savagery, barbarism, and civilization. He suggested that similar lifeways in a geographic region can come from parallel development as well as by cultural affinity. He discussed his findings about people under the term *national character,* a concept to be reintroduced by Ruth Benedict and Margaret Mead almost two centuries later.

Between 1860 and 1871 a subtle change occurred when something distinct from other philosophies of history began to come from the pages of new works treating society and human beings. During the Renaissance in Europe there was a growing awareness that others besides Europeans existed in the universe. It was not until the seventeenth and eighteenth centuries, however, that something was done about this awareness.

Political philosophers began developing social theories in an attempt to integrate the strange reports explorers and travelers brought back from their voyages. These reports were full of exotic happenings among peoples of strange and distinctive lifestyles. Such theoretical concerns locked the study of people into the fields of history and philosophy. Exotic facts about strange peoples fit into culturally oriented philosophies of history.

Three men are noteworthy of this period. A Catholic missionary, Fray Bernadine de Sahagun, worked in Mexico between 1529 and 1549 following the destruction of Tenochititlan, the capital of the Aztecs. His original mission was to convert the Indians, but he soon became engrossed in a full-scale effort to record their language and culture.

He began by training young Aztecs of nobility to write their own language, Nahuatl, in Spanish script. Then, with the aid of hieroglyphic paintings done in the ancient Aztec manner, he posed questions of the people and recorded their answers in what is now known as the "Florentine Codex." Subject matter ranged from "The Gods" and "The Ceremonies" to "The Merchants" and "The People."

In 1860 Adolf Bastian's first book appeared, to be followed the next year by Sir Henry Maine's *Ancient Law* and J. J. Bachofen's *Mutterrecht.* In 1864 Fustel de Coulanges's *Ancient City* was released. The next year McLennan's *Primitive Marriage* appeared. Sir Edward B. Tylor's *Primitive Culture* came in 1871. Each of these classic works took the focus from theories of history and philosophy that represented the thought patterns of the theorist's culture and related them to the peoples about whom the theorist was writing. It was this shift, from the theorizing culture to the cultures about whom the theories dealt, that signaled the emergence of a new and developing discipline—anthropology.

By the beginning of the twentieth century, significant anthropological collections had been placed in the major museums of natural history. Journals reporting on these collections and theoretical developments became firmly established. Chairs of anthropology were being established in various noted universities. Anthropological societies were emerging in the United States and England and on the Continent. Systematic field work in ethnography, cultural anthropology, and archaeology were under way. All were necessary foundations for the remarkable achievements in the young discipline during the following century. Anthropology was to come of age and be a major contributor to the understanding of humanity.

Theoretical Development

Classical Evolution

Even though the work of Charles Darwin was not anthropological in scope, his two books, *On the Origin of the Species* written in 1859 and *The Descent of Man* in 1871, had a profound impact on the developments in anthropology.

In the first, Darwin postulated the continuity of all life. He attempted to demonstrate how natural selection working upon inheritable variations resulted in adaptive modifications in life forms, which in turn led through speciation to radiating evolution. In the second, Darwin tried to make it clear that humans are the product of biological evolution just as technology, the arts, and society were the products of cultural evolution.

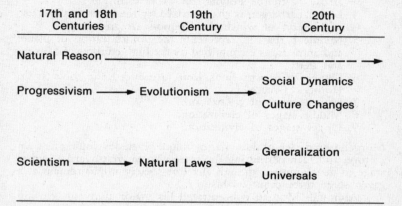

17th and 18th Centuries	19th Century	20th Century

Natural Reason ————————————————— – – – →

Progressivism ——→ Evolutionism ——→ Social Dynamics

Culture Changes

Scientism ——→ Natural Laws ——→ Generalization

Universals

Figure 3-1. CONCEPTUAL DEVELOPMENT OF ANTHROPOLOGY. This diagram shows the development of anthropology along three conceptual lines. The theoretical development of anthropology is progressing toward fuller explanation of the human person as a sociological and biological being. The Christian anthropologist also sees humans as spiritual beings and adds this dimension to his theoretical framework.

Even though Darwin cannot be credited with the concept of cultural evolution, since this was already well developed in the writings of the previous decade, his work certainly reinforced the efforts of the early anthropologists as they propounded their viewpoint. What he did do for anthropology was to establish humans as a subject of study worthy of the natural sciences and to press anthropological studies toward an empirical science.

Lewis Henry Morgan, building on the earlier work of Robertson, took his three stages of evolutionary development of culture and developed them into a nine-point scheme of evolution. He expanded the original three stages by assigning a lower, middle, and upper stage to each. He spelled out his scheme in *Ancient Society* (1877) as summarized below:

1. Lower savagery represents the transitional state from ape to man before fire and speech were used.
2. Middle savagery represents the development of speech, the

control of fire, and hunting and fishing subsistence. Australian aborigines are considered by some anthropologists a contemporary representation of this stage.

3. Higher savagery represents the introduction of the bow and arrow, with the Polynesians as an example.
4. Lower barbarism is characterized by the invention and use of pottery, of which the Iroquois are an example.
5. Middle barbarism represents the domestication of plants and animals, as exemplified by the high cultures of Mexico and Peru.
6. Upper barbarism finds iron introduced for tools as in Homeric Greece.
7. Lower stages of civilization.
8. Middle stages of civilization.
9. Upper stages of civilization.

Morgan found each of these stages unique, each developing its own culture, and each permitting the society to move toward a higher stage of development, though any one society might remain at a given stage throughout its history.

Although Morgan concentrated his major study on kinship and its development through time, E. D. Tylor and J. G. Frazer turned their attention to religion. Tylor asserted that religion moves from the invention of animism and the soul concept to ghost and ancestor worship to nature worship to polytheism to monotheism. Frazer concentrated on the origins of magic and religion. He suggested that man first invented magic and then turned to religious belief when magic failed him.

Frazer attempted to think as he believed primitive man must have thought. He produced a fascinating work entitled *The Golden Bough*. It is noted for its literary style and content, and its theory of magic and religion, although modern scholars no longer hold to the theory. It is a book worth reading, a masterpiece of ethnographic and classical learning.

History

When the German geographer Franz Boas stepped onto the stage of history, anthropology had been dominated for almost three hundred years by a philosophy based on a historical approach to man's culture, an approach that Radcliffe-Brown referred to as "armchair" anthropology. Boas had come to the United States to become professor at Columbia University (1896–1937).

As his nonevolutionary geography approach merged with his field work, he began to formulate a number of methodological approaches that were to become standard field methods for decades to follow.

1. Develop reliable and objective methods of observation and recording.
2. Record the statements of primitive informants in their own language.
3. Utilize the system of phonetic recording. (This set the pattern for intensive linguistic training for anthropology graduate students.)
4. Emphasize the use of vernacular conversation, rather than the memorization of word lists and grammatical rules in language learning.
5. Report ethnographic observations, made in the field, in detail.

Boas taught these principles to such noted anthropologists as Kroeber, Lowie, Sapir, Linton, Benedict, Mead, Spier, Wissler, and others, who have made significant contributions to the field. The combination of theory expressed through his students was to dominate American anthropology for half a century. They were to have significant influence in ethnography, physical anthropology, archaeology, and linguistics. Boas is known as the father of American anthropology.

Perhaps Boas' major contribution lay in a set of premises known as *cultural determinism*. These emphasized the plasticity of humans, their capacity to be what their culture made them be. Although a culture represented the chance historical confluence of multiple influences and borrowings; it nonetheless was a coherent system that shaped and molded the individual born into it. (Boas violently attacked any form of racial, biological, or geographic determinism.) The premises of cultural determinism further emphasized relativism. One had to take each culture as a separate universe of experience, values, and meanings and examine it in its own terms. Finally, Boas emphasized the great diversity and uniqueness of cultures (Keesing and Keesing 1971:382).

Diffusion

The highly specific thinking that revealed itself in phonetic particles as a basis for language study was to be applied to the larger culture in the form of "traits," and the spreading of these traits from one culture to another became known as diffusion.

Clark Wissler proposed a model for a culture area represented as a circle. It has a culture center, which would be expected to have the largest frequency of the typical traits. It also has a culture margin where the traits thin out and interpenetrate with traits of another culture area. One of the numerous classical studies of trait distribution is that by Leslie Spier (1921) on the Plains Indians'

"Sun Dance." Approximately eighty traits of this "complex" are plotted for the tribes practicing it.

An age-area theory developed, suggesting that the older the trait, the wider its distribution. Newer traits would not have had time to be distributed as widely as older traits. Edward Sapir advanced the caution that geographical or social phenomena could slow the distribution of certain traits and skew the results of age-area findings in the field.

The diffusion approach became quite developed in Europe and England. Some highly specialized schemes were set forth by Germans, such as Fritz Graebner and Wilhelm Schmidt, and Britishers, such as G. E. Smith and W. J. Perry. Graebner was one of the main formulators of the culture historical method, or culture complex theory, termed in German *kulturkreislehre*. He sought to trace, historically and geographically, combinations of basic elements, called *kulturkreise*. A single *kulturkreis,* or culture circle, is a cluster of meaningfully associated traits that can be isolated and identified in culture history. The earliest complexes were sought in primitive cultures.

A German Catholic priest and scholar, Father Wilhelm Schmidt, suggested that the modern cultural scene may have resulted from the complex diffusion of elements from nine main early "culture complexes." Three primitive or archaic cultures are represented today among the Pygmies of Africa and Asia, the Arctic primitives, and some Australian aborigines. Three primary culture complexes are represented by advanced or "higher" food gatherers, pastoral nomads, and certain gardening groups with certain matrilineal descent groups. Of the three secondary cultural complexes, all agriculturalists, two practice matrilineal descent and one patrilineal descent. Schmidt is perhaps best known for tracing all religious expression back to a monotheism as expressed in the Bible.

Smith and Perry in England became interested in Egypt. They were impressed by the archaeological findings of Petrie and others. They came to the conclusion, after studying cultural data elsewhere, that the Egyptians must have traded far and wide for gold, pearls, and other valuables and at the same time carried their inventions throughout Asia and even beyond via the Pacific Islands to Middle America.

A heliocentric ("sun centered") school developed from Smith and Perry's studies, suggesting that Egyptian customs, such as the sun cult, kingship, mummification, and megalithic construction, and even earlier elements such as agriculture and the improved working of flint, had been carried widely over the world by these "Children of the Sun." And the name given to this approach was "pan Egyptian," implying that all traits originated in Egypt. There was not independent invention of such traits and trait complexes elsewhere in the world.

Function and Structure

The French sociologists, centering in Emile Durkheim, were to provide a unique course correction in the treatment of culture. Like Boas, Durkheim emphasized the importance of rigorous method and empiricism in building a scientific base for the understanding of culture. However, he himself did not participate in field studies. Perhaps his greatest contribution to the field of anthropology was the concept of the collective conscience. Thus his interest shifted from artifact to the emergent properties of beliefs, sentiments, and symbols when they are shared by a group, and so the conceptual framework of the individual enters into, and takes its meaning from, the shared conceptual framework of the group. The collective conscience has properties that transcend and cannot be explained wholly in terms of the minds of individuals.

Malinowski was the living embodiment of such an approach. (See the anecdote at the beginning of this chapter.) He is typical of anthropological theorists. When we think of a theorist, we usually think of someone locked away in a laboratory or library. While this image may be true in some sciences, it is not true of anthropology. The greatest theorists in anthropology developed their theories about human beings in the field among the people.

Radcliffe-Brown, a British social anthropologist, carried the concept of function into a liaison with the concept of structure. Social structure is a network of social relations, each point in the network relating to each other point and to the whole. Function is the expression of this relationship. This distinction between structure and function became an implicit aspect of almost all British and French social anthropology and American cultural anthropology.

The primary focus of British social anthropology turned to the structure of corporate groups—lineages, clans, work groups, age classes, and territorial organizations—that have an enduring exist-ence within a society. The historically oriented scholar saw Radcliffe-Brown as a-historical in his methodology. Rather, Rad-cliffe-Brown simply put the synchronic first, and the diachronic followed. This is in contradistinction to the historian who puts the diachronic first and in essence never works with the synchronic until the historical perspective becomes clear, thus only as it is diachronic.

French sociology was to produce Claude Levi-Strauss, who also worked in anthropology and linguistics. He proposed a theory of structuralism. It has an abstract mathematical model and shares many characteristics with the transformational grammar approach of linguistic theory. Theoretically conceived images or models of societies are "generated" and then compared to determine what deep-lying rules might exist that govern the actual forms societies take. Whereas British social anthropology tends to be largely inductive, French structuralism tends to be deductive. It emphasizes the general principles that govern the overall organization of societies regardless of the specific forms they may take (see figure 3-2).

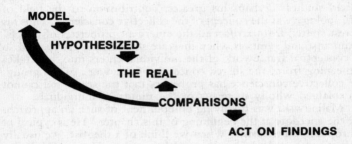

Figure 3-2. One form the structuralism model may take. The researcher makes hypotheses based on his model and tests them. Comparisons are made between the real and actions based on his findings. This comparison feeds back to the model. The model is not static but constantly changing.

Other Approaches

Other approaches noteworthy at this time are the culture and personality or configurational school contributed to by Ruth Benedict with her classical study *Patterns of Culture* (1934), as well as by such people as Margaret Mead, Abram Kardiner, Anthony F. C. Wallace, Ralph Linton, Francis Hsu, and others who founded the approach now called psychological anthropology. This approach has developed concepts such as those of the modal personality, or national character, and cultural patterns in human behavior. Raymond Firth synthesized the approaches of Malinowski and Radcliffe-Brown. This work was refined even further by Walter Goldschmidt, who added statistical analysis for comparative studies.

Robert Redfield was noted for his study of peasantry and his folk-urban continuum, which has been applied in numerous ways.[5]

---

[5] See Harvey Cox, 1965, *The Secular City*.

Missionary Anthropologists

Numerous anthropologists have served the Christian church. Louis Luzbetak is perhaps the most noted Catholic anthropologist, and Eugene Nida the most noted Protestant anthropologist.

Nida has served with Wycliffe Bible Translators and the American Bible Society. He has written extensively in the area of missionary applications of anthropology. Jacob Loewen, a colleague of Nida's in the American Bible Society, has also written extensively in the missionary journal *Practical Anthropology,* as have Robert B. Taylor, William D. Reyburn, William Smalley, James Buswell, Alan Tippett, Paul Hiebert, and Charles Taber. Smalley along with Donald Larson of Bethel College, Charles Kraft of Fuller Theological Seminary, Marvin K. Mayers of Biola University and William Merrifield of Wycliffe have entered anthropology through interest in language and linguistics. Men such as Dean Arnold in new world archaeology and James Buswell and Donald Wilson in physical anthropology are contributing a Christian perspective in the field of anthropology. These men are making significant contributions to Christian missions through application of sound anthropological principles applied to Bible translation and missionary anthropology. Kraft, Mayers, Taber, Hiebert, and Sherwood and Judy Lingenfelter are among those on the leading edge of missionary anthropology today.

Questions for Discussion

1. What implications does anthropological theory have for missions?
2. What areas of anthropology do you feel are most applicable to missions? Why?
3. What do you see as the role of the Christian anthropologist?
4. In studying the history of anthropology, in what areas does a controversy between the teachings of anthropologists and the church legitimately or artificially develop?

Suggested Reading

Beattie, J. 1965. *Understanding an African Kingdom: Bunyoro.* An example of an anthropologist at work. Highly recommended for those who want to get a better idea of what an anthropologist does and how he or she goes about doing it.

Casagrande, J. B. 1960. *In the Company of Man.* The compiler, through a collection of personal memoirs of various anthropologists, attempts to share some of the experience of anthropological field work. This volume allows us to see anthropology as a human science.

Garbarino, M. S. 1977. *Sociocultural Theory in Anthropology: A Short History*. A recent work with a historical overview of sociocultural theory.

Golde, P. 1970. *Women in the Field*. While many occupations and fields have traditionally been closed to women, anthropology has always been wide open. This work is a collection of accounts of the work of twelve female anthropologists.

Hammel, E. A., and Simmons, W. A. 1970. *Man Makes Sense*. A collection of readings dealing with the study of human beings.

Harris, M. 1968. *The Rise of Anthropological Theory*. A fairly complete history of anthropological theory. This is a good place for a person to begin to get a historical overview of the field of anthropology. The author approaches anthropological theory and research from a cultural determinstic perspective.

Hegeman, E., and Kooperman, L. 1974. *Anthropology and Community Action*. A collection of articles dealing with applied anthropology. It is highly recommended for prospective missionaries. The section on problems in cultural communication is especially applicable to missions.

Kluckhohn, C. 1944. *Mirror for Man*. A classic work that looks at anthropology and the anthropologist. It gives the reader a good basic understanding of what anthropology is all about.

Manners, R. A., and Kaplan, D. 1969. *Theory in Anthropology*. A collection of readings covering the major theoretical approaches in cultural anthropology. The section on "Explanations in Social Science" contains some interesting selections.

Mead, M. 1964. *Anthropology, A Human Science*. A collection of articles by one of America's best-known anthropologists. Her chapters on anthropology as a science and on the role of the scientist in society are especially recommended.

4

Enculturation and Acculturation

> The observer is just entering her fifth-grade classroom for the observation period. The teacher says, "Which one of you nice, polite boys would like to take (the observer's) coat and hang it up?" From the waving hands, it would seem that all would like to claim the title. The teacher chooses one child, who takes the observer's coat. The teacher says, "Now, children, who will tell (the observer) what we are doing?" The usual forest of hands appears, and a girl is chosen . . . . The teacher conducted the arithmetic lessons mostly by asking, "Who would like to tell the answer to the next problem?" This question was usually followed by the appearance of a large and agitated forest of hands, with apparently much *competition* to answer (emphasis ours) (Henry 1963:293).

It was snowing and bitterly cold as the man pulled out of his driveway onto the snow-covered street. His mind was on his job as he thought about the departmental meeting that would begin his working day. Suddenly the rear end of his car began to slide to the left on the hard-packed snow. Seemingly without thinking, he turned the steering wheel to the left; with this the rear end began to slide to the right. Immediately he turned the steering wheel to the right. The rear end of the car continued to slide from left to right, and the man continued to steer in the direction of the slide until he had the car under control. Once he had the car under control, he continued on to work at a slower pace and concentrated on his driving. When he arrived at his job he began recounting the harrowing experience to his fellow employees. He said, "Wow, that happened so suddenly I didn't have time to think; I just reacted instinctively."

Instinct is a word we commonly use to speak about certain types of behavior in both animals and humans. As with many terms, *instinct* has both a popular and a scientific use. Behaviorial scientists define *instinct* as a pattern of behavior that is inherited as opposed to learned (Morgan and King 1966). All behavior can be classified as either reflexive, instinctive, or learned. Morgan and King point out:

> When it comes to human beings, with the possible exception of a few behaviors which mature without practice, we cannot say with certainty that there are any instinctive behavior patterns. Man seems to have become so sophisticated in learning to adapt to his world, and in teaching his young how to adapt, that instinctive behavior is not considered to be a prominent human characteristic (1966:41).

They go on to explain that in order to qualify as instinctive behavior, three conditions must be fulfilled:

1. It must be generally characteristic of a species.

2. It must appear full-blown at the first appropriate opportunity without any previous training or practice.

3. It must continue for some time in the absence of the conditions evoking it [a reflex does not]; that is to say, it may be triggered by some stimulus, but it is not controlled by the stimulus (1966:40).

The animal relies on instinct, or "innate fixed action pattern" (Rogers 1965:22). For example, we once had a black walnut tree in our backyard. I had gathered some nuts, planning to process them; but they had already begun to rot. So, I dumped them in the backyard. My attention was caught some time later by a squirrel. He was frantically burying those nuts wherever he could—on the log pile, under the storage shed, in a hollow place in the snow, on a windowsill—because the ground was frozen.

Such a pattern as exhibited by the squirrel is more complex than a muscular reflex since it involves more than muscles. On the other hand, it is not as flexible as purposive behavior since the motor elements run off in a rigid mechanical order. It is not the same as a chain reflex, because it is not motivated in the same way.

Animals appear to have a sign stimulus releaser. For the robin it is the red breast. For the moth and wasp it is a special odor. For the mother hen it is a distress call. In humans, however, reaction is made to any of a large array of stimuli, and the reaction is appropriate to some object or situation of which all these stimuli are signs. The reaction is governed by the situation such as a "child in distress," rather than by any particular stimulus.

Some behavioral scientists say that humans have few instincts, and others say they have none. Without instinct to direct most of their behavior, how do humans function? They have to learn their behavior. Anthropologists call this learning process enculturation. Noam Chomsky (1957) suggests, however, that humans may have innate language ability, something that provides a language readiness, for example:

1. All children in all cultures learn their language at the same time—i.e., between the ages of eighteen months and four years.
2. All children in all cultures learn their language at the same rate.
3. There is no known primitive language—all are adequate for the task of communication.[1]

Thus it is possible for the Christian to say the following:

1. Humans are distinct from animals in that innate fixed action patterns do not dominate.
2. There are certain abilities provided humans which allow them to learn language and culture—though they are not limited to learning a specific language or culture.
3. The enculturation process allows these abilities to be put to use in relation to language and culture.
4. The effective control of such usage lies within the culture itself as well as in supracultural (supernatural) influences upon people within their culture.

Enculturation

The American sociologist Talcott Parsons speaks of the birth of new generations of children as a recurrent barbarian invasion (Brown 1965:193). Human infants do not possess culture at birth. They have no conception of the world, no language, nor a morality.[2] It is in this sense that Parsons uses the word *barbarian* in reference to infants. They are uncultured, unsocialized persons. All an infant needs to live and cope within the cultural context awaiting

---

[1] These observations will be discussed in more detail in chapter 5.
[2] That is, a newborn infant cannot distinguish right from wrong.

him is acquired through the process termed *enculturation* by the anthropologist and *socialization* by the sociologist—the process by which individuals acquire the knowledge, skills, attitudes, and values that enable them to become functioning members of their societies.

Awaiting infants is a society possessing a culture, an ordered way of life. Children possess certain possibilities for processing information and developing desires making it possible for that ordered way of life to influence them. These enduring competencies and standards of judgment, along with attitudes and motives, form the *personality*. The personality, in turn, influences the culture.

Enculturation is "both a conscious and an unconscious conditioning process whereby man, as child and adult, achieves competence in his culture, internalizes his culture and becomes thoroughly enculturated" (Hoebel 1972:40). One internalizes the dreams and expectations, the rules and requirements not just for the larger society seen as a whole, but also for every specific demand within the whole. Society does whatever is necessary to aid any one of its members in learning proper and appropriate behavior for any given social setting and in meeting the demands of any challenge. Enculturation begins before birth and continues until death. Thus children learn respect for the symbols of the nation through reciting the Pledge of Allegiance and singing the national anthem. They learn behavior appropriate to their sex, social class, and peer group. They become aware of their reciprocal rights and privileges as well as responsibilities vis-à-vis other persons (e.g., parents, teachers, friends, store clerks, strangers). The anecdote at the beginning of the chapter illustrates this process.

Some saints and revolutionaries successfully internalize the norms of their society; but they have made a novel system of them, and sometimes novel systems displace established ones. Jesus Christ introduced a new lifeway, and the new proceeded to supplant the old. The American revolution permitted a novel system to progress through time without undue hindrance from the old world. There is no question, however, in the minds of students of history or comparative sociology, that the new in each of these cases was clearly an outgrowth of the old.

The result of the enculturative process is identity: the identity of the person within the group. Society seeks to make each member a fully responsible individual within the whole. While the enculturation process may at times alienate some persons, the intent of society is responsible participation.

God was underscoring this when He presented the Hebrews with the Ten Commandments. He said in effect, "Don't let the system of family, of the economy, of interpersonal relations, and of religion be abused. Let each one work and do his part for the good of the group and each member of the group. I will thus be honored." It is no wonder, therefore, that Jesus and Paul, living in New Testament times, sought to uphold the ideal of one's responsibility within the corporate or group setting. "Render to Caesar" and "obey the government, for God is the one who has put it there" are very specific commands or instructions made to their followers building upon such foundations.

The enculturation process has two major aspects: (1) the informal, which some call "child training" and in some senses precedes and in the other senses runs concurrently with (2) the formal, more commonly termed "education." The former is most likely to be carried out within the context of the family and among friends. The latter is carried out in institutions of learning, sacred or secular.

Child Training

As we have stated, the infant enters a culture that is already formed. Some psychologists suggest that the stresses and strains within the womb begin the shaping of the child's personality. From the moment of birth, however, there is no question as to the socio-personality influences upon the child. The process of increasing awareness, called by some "canalization," is effected in four major stages: (1) the emerging awareness of the child's environment, (2) the differentiation of the child's environment from that of others, (3) the stabilization of the child's understanding of the environment, and (4) increasing control over the child's environment (Bock 1969).

Jean Piaget, a Swiss psychologist, spent much time observing and conducting experiments with children. He concluded that children pass through a series of stages in their development from infancy to adulthood. These stages, with their corresponding ages, are:

1. Sensory motor intelligence (0 to 18 months). During this stage the child at first does not distinguish between itself and its environment. The child is egocentric, and reacts to objects based on their physical characteristics rather than their symbolic meaning.
2. Preoperational intelligence (18 months to 7 years). During this stage the child acquires language, is still egocentric, and deals with objects based on their symbolic meaning.
3. Concrete-operational intelligence (7 years to 11 years). During this stage the child begins to become less egocentric and begins to see things from the other person's perspective; the child develops more complex patterns of thought but they are still based on concrete objects.

4. Formal-operational intelligence (11 years and upward). In this stage the individual begins to adopt adult thought processes including abstract reasoning.

These ages are not absolutes but provide a guide to the maturation of the child. Piaget does feel, however, that the child will go through these stages in order, though the rate of movement will vary from child to child. The child does not cast off the attainments of earlier periods but rather, retains earlier forms of intelligence, integrating them with more advanced forms.

Societies differ in the matter of caring for the young (Bock 1969:56). One means of classification is child care by an individual or group or both. North American parents tend to give individual attention to the child, with the mother primarily responsible for the child's care. However, when both parents work, children are likely to be placed in a childcare center where they are cared for by a small team of professionals. One of the trademarks of the Israeli kibbutzim is that the children are cared for by paraprofessionals, none of whom is necessarily a parent of the child.

Another means of classification of child care is by relative or nonrelative or both. In most societies the child is cared for by the natural parent or a close relative, such as an elder sibling or grandparent if the parent is unable to care for him. However, in cultures or subcultures where wealth or prominence dominate, the child is cared for by a nonrelative such as a tutor, nurse, or maid. The Egyptian princess in the Bible who discovered baby Moses in the river sent Moses' sister to find a wet-nurse and maid. She brought Moses' natural mother. The princess did not expect the girl to secure the natural mother, for anyone could and would have served insofar as she was concerned.

A third type of classification is child care by parents or another relative or both. In Maya-related societies of Central America, as well as in Samoa, the eldest child in the family is given the primary responsibility for the care of the younger children. In Latin societies, this is likely to be the eldest girl. The responsibilities for the baby may start even before the child is weaned. Such care continues until the age of ten to twelve. At that time the father begins to pay more attention to the preparation of the boy for adulthood and the mother brings the girl into the complex workings of the home.

Child care may also be classified by mother or father or both. There are several obvious biological reasons for assigning care of the child to the female parent. Among the Black Caribs of Central America, this is accentuated by the practice of *couvade*. The mother carries on her normal life after the birth of the child and the father symbolically goes to bed. The mother among the Maya cares for the child until he is weaned, as long as two-and-a-half years after birth; and then other members of the family participate, especially the child's grandmother.

Habituation

In habituation, human beings learn those aspects of culture not regarded by the culture as specifically learnable techniques. Babies, being helpless, have their needs fulfilled for them. In the course of the fulfillment of these needs, the way in which the need is fulfilled comes to be almost as important as the fulfillment.

By the time children are able to fulfill some of their own requirements for food and sleep, their habits are well established. These habits may be changed several times during the course of maturation, but even the need to change and the capacity to change are developed into habits. In one sense, the habits are the culture. When the habits of the people change, the culture changes.

Education

Each individual in a given society is provided the means of individual enrichment. No society is without an education program, though few have as extensive and all-encompassing a program as that found in Western nations. The formal education provided in Western nations through a graded school system is provided in other societies through social, religious, political, or economic mechanisms.

The Pocomchi of Central America have a socioreligious organization called the *cofradia*. It provides all members of the society between the ages of twenty and forty with a formal education in keeping with the needs and demands of the society. Each member approaching the age of twenty is elected into one of the eight *cofradias* in the community and serves for a period of two years. After this period of time, he rests at least a year before accepting election into a *cofradia* for another two-year term of service.

When participating in the activities of the *cofradia,* a new member does everything the senior members do. Thereby he or she is trained in all the social processes necessary to maintain the society. By the age of forty the person is fully qualified to handle any problem the society faces and to maintain the smooth functioning of the society as effectively and efficiently as the older leaders. The education given does not meet the standards of our educational system, yet it prepares the new member to function in that society as ours prepares us to function in our society. The training is functionally equivalent to a college degree. A forty-year-old man who enters the top leadership levels of the society is prepared to handle responsibilities as great as those of a corporate executive or high government official in our society.

Extensions of Educations

In every society each member has others with whom special relationships are formed. This person might be part of a nuclear family, an extended family, an age or interest group, or a political or economic team. In societies organized around kinship, this other person is likely a member of the nuclear or extended family. In societies that have economic trading teams, as among some Australian aborigine groups, a close caring relationship develops between trading partners. In societies where there are age-level organizations, as in certain areas of Africa, members of such an organization grow into a deep and abiding relationship with others of the same age level.

In matrilineal societies where the lineage and inheritance are traced through the mother's line rather than the father's, the biological father is a relatively insignificant member of the family team. He is replaced by a sociological father—the mother's brother in most instances. The child's maternal uncle thus functions in the male caring role and is responsible for the well-being and increasingly mature behavior of the child. In societies in which a *joking relationship* permits two members of the society—e g., mother-in-law and son-in-law—to tease and criticize one another, a closeness develops that is impossible within a society where these roles are almost completely separated. These relationships are used to educate the younger members in the ways of the society.

Styles of Education

In most societies where the informal practices of education involve the master-apprentice relationship, a different type of preparation develops than that found in the classroom lecture system. The master teacher is not simply training the apprentice to perform a task, but is also teaching the apprentice to be a teacher some day. Proper master-teacher behavior is passed on along with skills.

In our society, where the teacher-pupil relationship is much more prevalent than the master-apprentice relationship, knowledge and information are of primary importance. The student gains content and task skills but not teaching skills.

In Mayan societies, which use the master-apprentice relationship, missionaries established Bible schools based on a teacher-student relationship. When the students returned to their village after studying at the Bible institute, they presented the same lectures to their own people because the student (apprentice) models the teacher (master). The students even used the illustrations they heard at the Bible institute. However, little of it was relevant to these rural farm people because most of the illustrations were drawn from the missionary teachers' urban industrial background.

In societies where formal education is based on the teacher-pupil relationship, lecture is the primary means of teaching. Personal association between the teacher and student is minimal and usually limited to the classroom. The influence of the teacher on the student is generally limited to the content of the subject matter. Most of the teacher's wisdom, insight, and experience is lost to the student in this educational model. The teacher-student relationship centers around knowledge and information. The process is geared toward the end result, evaluation. Hence the familiar classroom question, "Will that be on the test?" The implication is that if it will not be on the test, it is not important. The concern is with grades and credits, not with becoming a functional member of the society.

In societies where formal education is based on the master-apprentice relationship, modeling of effective behavior is primary. The proper behavior of the skill or trade is communicated along with the proper behavior of the master to the apprentice. There tends to be maximum involvement between the two, since they spend a great deal of time together. This results in greater potential for impact in every area of the life of the apprentice. Evaluation is in terms of life and not just content. The apprentice to a pottery maker does not simply learn to make pottery, but also learns the lifestyle of a pottery maker.

Jesus Christ had a master-apprentice relationship with His disciples. He did not just tell them how to evangelize. He took them with Him. They watched Him in action. Frequently, in the Gospel accounts, we find Jesus pulling the disciples aside to explain what He was doing. The disciples did not just learn a message, they learned a lifestyle. And the tradition was carried on. Paul discipled Timothy and Titus along with others. Barnabas and Peter discipled John Mark. The apostle John discipled Polycarp.

In our society, medical schools use a master-apprentice relationship, the medical students making rounds with physicians. On the other hand, seminaries have traditionally followed an academic model with a teacher-student relationship. However, in recent years many seminaries are requiring a one-year internship in which the master-apprentice relationship can develop.

The Life Cycle

As humans fulfill their biological destiny, they pass through four major stages or "crises" in the life cycle: birth; puberty, or maturity; marriage, or reproduction; and death. Every culture recognizes these major periods in some way, though some are made more prominent than others. Some cultures handle these experiences calmly and quietly; others exhibit much anxiety. In the latter case, the cultural emphasis is on the crisis situation. Within each society, therefore, these rituals or *rites of passage* allow a member to properly and effectively move from one stage of life to the next.

There are prebirth rituals, such as baby showers, which prepare society for the new infant's arrival. The newborn is "baptized" within an eleven-day period in the Philippines and somewhat later in other Catholic- and Protestant-influenced cultures. The shower and baptism or infant dedication are the rituals, or effective means, of transition from unborn state to born state. Some societies take this crisis so seriously that they require the husband to go to bed as replacement for the woman so that no harm will befall her and she will be able to provide sustenance for the baby. The Caribs, Ainus, and Chinese of Marco Polo's time all practiced *couvade*.

It has only been within the last hundred years that humans have had a scientific explanation of conception and the biological and genetic processes. Some primitive people do not understand the connection between the act of sexual intercourse and the resultant pregnancy. Among Australian aborigines, the belief is held that the child is the reincarnation of an ancestral spirit. This belief negates any relation between the sex act and conception, though there is an admission that the woman's body must be opened in some way to permit the entrance of the ancestral spirits.

Failure to connect conception and the act of intercourse is considered by some as naïveté or ignorance. There is an increasing awareness, however, that it may simply be the cultural suppression of physical reality. In such cases the cultural form is designed to support the social system. For example, ancestor worship and totemism are very important themes in Australian life. The continuity of the totemic group is sustained by means of the doctrine of spiritual reincarnation. To focus on the physical paternity would undermine the sacred institution.

The matrilineal Trobrianders believe the male pays no role in conception. To them, the spirit of a dead clan ancestor enters the womb when the woman is wading in the lagoon. It grows and becomes a child. The neighboring Dobu believe semen is coagulated coconut milk which causes the menstrual blood to coagulate and form a fetus. Many peoples of the world note the cessation of the menstrual flow as a sign of pregnancy. Others take note of breast changes, loss of appetite, "morning sickness," or a tendency to laziness on the part of the woman as signs of pregnancy.

Numerous anxieties attend the birth process such as that (1) the child will not develop ideally, (2) the fetus will miscarry, (3) the birth will be difficult, or (4) some evil spirit will adversely affect the fetus and later the newborn child. Special attention is therefore given to those who attend the birth (fathers may or may not be present) and to those who see the child after birth (to the Latin, strangers may convey illness and death by means of the evil eye). What adorns the baby after birth is also important (the Pocomchi tie a string around the wrist of the newborn to protect the child against the evil eye).

Whereas nominally Christian societies use baptism or dedication as indications of the social acceptance of the child, other societies use special presentations and naming ceremonies. Among the Ashanti of Ghana, a child is not considered a human being until eight days after birth. At that time the child is ceremonially named and publicly presented. Should it die before eight days have passed, it would be simply disposed of; for the Ashanti would believe that it was merely the husk of a ghost child whose mother left it to go on a trip and then returned to claim it. Among the Swazi of East Africa, for three months a baby is only a thing. It is not named, and men are not permitted to hold it. If it dies, it cannot be ceremonially mourned.[3]

Thus the question of when life begins is handled differently among the various peoples of the world. Catholic-based cultures hold that life begins at conception. Protestant subcultures differ in when they believe life begins. The stages of development at which people believe life begins range from conception to as late as birth. The medical profession in the United States has accepted a position implying that life begins sometime between the third and fifth fetal months. Therefore, many medical professionals will support abortions up to this time. The Ashanti and Swazi, along with numerous other societies of the world, say life does not begin until some point following birth, perhaps as late as three months later.[4]

Creativity

In the quality and quantity of creative productions there are large variations between cultures and even within the same culture

---

[3] These practices probably developed as psychological defense mechanisms against grief because of the high infant mortality rates in these societies.
[4] We believe life begins at conception.

at different times. Indeed there may be certain characteristics of a culture that encourage or at least make possible greater creative production.

The first of these characteristics is a level of technology and economy that generates sufficient material wealth to make possible the time and opportunity for creative activity. Persons living in a society where every person is involved, full-time, in subsistence activity are less likely to engage in creative activity.

The second characteristic of a creative society is the presence of a communication system that allows for the maximum exchange of ideas and information. Societies that restrict communication also restrict the exchange of ideas and information on which creativity feeds.

The third characteristic suggested is a societal value system that socially and economically rewards creative acts. The fourth characteristic is related to the third. Societies with a climate of acceptance will experience higher levels of creativity than societies that punish creativity economically, socially, or criminally.

The fifth characteristic is opportunities for privacy. Privacy is often necessary for creative production. Although some societies provide or allow for sanctuaries, other societies have no real concept of privacy. Along with privacy, the sixth characteristic is the existence of social mechanisms within the social system that permit or encourage the formation of disciple or peer groups, such as art colonies, professional associations, and other forms of social organization that encourage creativity.

The last characteristic is an educational system that encourages free inquiry and rewards individual research and creativity. Societies with educational systems geared to transmitting what has already been discovered and traditional knowledge are less likely to produce creativity than those societies whose educational system encourages questioning and challenging traditional knowledge and the exploration of new frontiers of knowledge.

Acculturation

Whereas enculturation is the learning of the appropriate behavior of one's own culture, *acculturation* is the learning of the appropriate behavior of one's host culture. One enters, in effect, as a child and is enculturated into the new society through the process of adaptation to that society. To the extent that we do not allow the structures and relationships of our former society to unnecessarily restrict our adaptation, we can become effectively acculturated into the new. Effective acculturation allows us to maintain our principles, and thus our self-respect, and yet cope with all the challenges and opportunities of the new culture

However, we may never become fully recognized as a member of the new culture for a variety of reasons. Anthropologist William Reyburn was known as an outsider simply because of the way he bent over to "haunch" with the Indian men to whom he ministered. But his fluency in the language and his life style permitted him to be accepted into the new society with a minimum of strain.

It is wise at this point to distinguish between what is known as culture shock, the negative emotional response to the mismatching of cues from the new culture with cues from the old, and culture stress, the realization that one will never fully assimilate within the new culture and develop the ability to cope with its various demands. Most people entering a new culture or subculture experience culture shock to some degree. Having passed through it, they imagine they will have no further problems in that area. However, there is likely to be ongoing tension because of the awareness of cultural difference. Such tension leaves no emotional disability, but one simply has a sense of incompleteness in the new culture.

Acculturation and assimilation differ in degree of adaptation to the new culture. Within the context of acculturation, people adapt to the degree they can effectively function within the context of the new culture. They assume they will leave the new culture at some time and return home. They are fully accepted and respected members of the new culture, yet in essence have a dual identity.

Assimilation is the more extreme process. It comes from the realization that one will never return to the society of origin. So one takes on the entire lifeway of the new. The process is more thorough, all-encompassing, and likely lengthier. Someone visiting from outside the culture could not tell if one had been born there or not. First-generation immigrants may achieve a high degree of adaptation. Second-generation people most likely reach a high degree of assimilation. (Some anthropologists do not distinguish between acculturation and assimilation. They speak of this difference in intensity of response in some other way.)

Once people become aware of the principles underlying the acculturative response, they increasingly recognize that all encounters are crosscultural in effect. No one has the identical, sociocultural background of another. Even twins always wheeled together in a tandem walker have distinct experiences. One will look more to the street and the other more to the yards being passed. Even this subtle difference will produce distinct cultural backgrounds.

Marriage brings together representatives of two separate subcultures. School brings together representatives of different local neighborhoods. Church draws people from a variety of religious experience. Such differences brought to awareness by social or geographical mobility cause little problem within the corporate body as long as an agreement is made to ignore them. But they become very significant, even to the point of disruption, if an issue is made of them. For example, musical background for prayer in a church service is no problem until someone whose background did not incorporate this practice challenges it as being distracting.

As the foundation for enculturation is positive reinforcement, the foundation for the acculturative process is the functional equivalent.[5] Direct equivalence focuses on form of expression and produces this response. "It looks the same, therefore it must be the same." Functional equivalence, on the other hand, focuses on meaning or significance and produces this response: "It may not look the same, but it does the same thing—what is intended."

For the Maya of north central Guatemala, the fox speaks with a falsetto whereas the wildcat is sly, crafty, and rapacious. Therefore Herod, referred to in Luke 13:32, cannot be described as a fox but as a wildcat. A fox would give a false impression—not to the outsider, for he can make the adjustment of equivalence, but to the insider. They have no other knowledge than what the idea or concept communicates to them in their culture.

A key principle in adapting to another culture is the question of trust: "Is what I am doing, thinking, or saying building or undermining trust?" The question of rights, privileges, and status considerations must follow from such a question in the crosscultural context even though they might be primary within the context of one's own culture. If trust is not built within the context of interpersonal and intergroup relationships in the crosscultural encounter, there will always be a challenge to rights, privileges, and status considerations. This will produce tension and alienation that will adversely affect all that is done individually and corporately (Mayers 1987 [2nd ed.]).

Every society has a way of protecting each "inborn" and "adoptive" member from the risk of violating norms and losing self-respect. This device is the cultural cue that is the society's provision for correct behavior and behavior response. In fact, it is the cue that the child learns through the enculturative process.

The sum total of all cues learned is the culture itself. Outsiders simply need to tune into the correct cue for their purpose, and they can do whatever they have to do. A teetotaler in a drinking community simply needs to learn the cue for "I don't drink, but you may." Then she can maintain her own self-respect, allow the

---

[5] A functional equivalent is something in one culture that performs the same function as a different thing in another culture. The two things are equivalent in meaning rather than form.

other to maintain his self-respect, and still leave the channels of communication open for further contact and mutual influence.

Many Christians in the early days of television refused to have a television set in the house. But they slowly adapted to the new subculture. They found they could control their viewing and make effective use of television as they had the radio, which their parents had initially reacted to adversely. In *Future Shock* Alvin Toffler alerts us to many ways we are challenged to adapt. We realize the adaptive process is going on because we are able to handle today what we assumed yesterday was too much for us.

The blockage of adaptation and assimilation comes from an attitude of mind termed *ethnocentrism*. In its positive expression ethnocentrism allows one to be satisfied and complete as a person within the context of one's own culture. In its negative effect it subtly communicates the superiority of one's own culture over all others. The end result of ethnocentrism is the reinforcement of one's own life style, the inability or unwillingness to change, and the subtle demand that others must change to become like oneself to be fully accepted.

Such a closed attitude to change, which is taking place all about us, results in a phenomenon called drift. Society changes in inconsistent ways rather than consistent; it changes by whim rather than by design. Its members must take what comes rather than being able to plan for that which will aid them.

Cautiously guarding against a change by adherence to form and expression rather than meaning and by concern for the reinforcement of one's own culture to the exclusion of the other, usually has the opposite effect from that which was intended. Instead of reinforcement of the good desired within one's own context, evil forces are let loose. Instead of respect comes loss of respect. Instead of reinforcement of principle there is abandonment. Instead of growth, there is immaturity. Instead of truth, there is falsehood.

The end of adaptation and assimilation is bilingualism and biculturalism. Bilingualism refers to one's fluency within the crosscultural context. One is able to speak two or more languages fluently and is recognized as an adequate, correct speaker of both. Biculturalism refers to one's ability to cope with all the demands of verbal and nonverbal behavior so effectively that he or she is recognized as a member of a culture, rather than an outsider.

After all, what is our mission in life—to make our culture known, to make our hang-ups the hang-ups of others, to force others to change their lifestyles, to create great gaps in communication, or to introduce men and women to the Lord Jesus Christ and allow Him through His Spirit to do His work in their lives as He wills?[6]

Questions for Discussion

1. In the opening anecdote two levels of education were taking place. What are they? Explain them.
2. Do human beings have any instinctive behavior? Can you think of any?
3. What acculturation took place in your life style when you came to this school?
4. What role does acculturation play in missions?
5. Is it desirable for a missionary to become totally assimilated in the culture in which he or she is ministering? Why?

Suggested Reading

Barnow, V. 1963. *Culture and Personality*. A good introduction to the field of psychological anthropology. It contains an excellent section on methods used in culture and personality.

Benedict, R. 1934. *Patterns of Culture*. A classic in the field of psychological anthropology. Benedict compares three cultures and their effect on the personalities of their members. She demonstrates how personality is formed as the individual adopts the culture's value system.

Chapple, E. D. 1970. *Culture and Biological Man*. This work deals with the relationship between heredity, biology, and culture in the formation of personality. It contains an interesting section on the biological basis of emotional behavior.

Clausen, J. A. 1968. *Socialization and Society*. A collection of readings dealing with the socialization process. Although most of the articles deal with childhood socialization, there is an article on adult socialization. It also contains an article on the moral development in childhood.

Henry, J. 1963. *Culture Against Man*. A very well written, easy-to-read critique of American culture and its values. It deals with overt and covert socialization. It demonstrates the power of culture over the individual.

Levine, R. A. 1973. *Culture, Behavior and Personality*. An introductory-level text dealing with the relationship between culture, behavior, and personality. A good place to begin extra reading in this field.

Levine, R. A., and Campbell, D. T. 1972. *Ethnocentrism: Theories of Conflict and Group Behavior*. The work was written by an

---

[6] The concept of biblical absolutism and cultural relativity will be further developed in chapter 14.

anthropologist and social psychologist team. It is somewhat technical, but it is recommended for the serious student who wants a deeper understanding of ethnocentrism.

Lingenfelter, S., and Mayers, M. 1986. *Ministering Crossculturally*. This work deals with the process of acculturation and adapting to a new culture. Basic values and how they influence behavior in various cultures are discussed.

Rogers, E., and Shoemaker, F. 1971. *Communication of Innovations: A Cross-cultural Approach*. A well-written introduction to the field of crosscultural communication of innovations. Concepts are well illustrated with case studies. This work should be read by all prospective missionaries.

5

Verbal and Nonverbal Communication

A popular American politician traveled to a Latin American country several years ago. When he arrived at the airport of the host country, he emerged from the aircraft waving and greeting the assembled crowd, which included dignitaries and reporters from the local press. Someone asked the American politician how his flight had been. In response he flashed the common "O.K.!" gesture as the news cameras busily clicked away. Leaving the airport, the visiting politician went for a short visit with local government officials. Next he went to the major university in the area to deliver an address. He was accompanied to the university by his official government translator, a military man in full uniform. The American politician's speech dealt with the United States' desire to help their Latin American neighbors by way of economic aid that would help develop their economies and better the economic conditions of the poor.

The entire trip was a disaster. Why? Because, while the American politician's communication on the verbal level was satisfactory, he communicated, nonverbally, an entirely different message.

When asked how his flight had been the American had flashed the common "O.K." gesture. This act had been photographed by the news media and was printed on the front page of the local newspaper. The same gesture that means "O.K." in North America is a very obscene gesture in that part of Latin America.

The university where the American politician chose to deliver his policy address had just been the site of violent demonstrations against that government's policies. The government saw this choice of a site for his address as indicating sympathy for the students and their position. However, the students saw the American politician as a friend of the local government who was invading their university with a military translator. The presence of the military translator convinced the students that the American politician supported the policies of the local government.

The American politician had communicated two messages: one verbally and one nonverbally. Which one do you think came through the clearest? (McCrosky 1972:109–10).

What is the first thing you notice about people when you first meet them? Their clothing? Their faces? Their grooming? Whatever it is, it is probably not their language. Even so, although language may not be the most prominent characteristic of a person, it is certainly one of the most revealing. Until verbal communication is established, knowledge of other people is limited and one-sided. Language opens up their other side—their thoughts, their interests, their view of life—in effect, themselves.

Language is spoken. Language is heard. The oral, audible form of language is its most obvious form. It consists of audible symbols expressed by the speaker. Our responses to these symbols vary according to our understanding of and familiarity with the specific language. Communication also occurs in a nonverbal, inaudible context. Certain body movements correspond with audible speech messages. In some cases, the associated body movement may replace speech altogether. A raised eyebrow may indicate "yes" or a hand movement may signal "good-by."

Language may also be in written form—no longer audible. Various alphabets, such as hieroglyphics, pictoral, or phonetic orthographics have been used throughout history. Not every society has a written form of its spoken language. However, every language has the potential of being written, and every speaker of that language is a potential writer of it.

Language communicates what members of a society need to know. It is a major tool of the social group, effecting loyalties based on past, present, or future events and relationships. Language can also disrupt society. It can destroy relationships and loyalties. James' description of the tongue as a fire is apt, for he says, "Consider what a great forest is set on fire by a small spark" (3:5).

This leads us to define language as verbal, systematic, and symbolic communication. Language is always verbal. Spoken language is the basis for all other forms of language: written language, sign language, and gestures. The written symbols stand for sounds.

The study of the sounds of language is called *phonology*. While humans are capable of an infinite variety of sounds, each language is made up of a limited number of sounds. One of the first steps in analyzing a language is to determine the basic sounds it uses. Some languages use more sounds than others. In the English language there are forty-five distinct sounds, while fewer than twenty are used in most Polynesian languages. The distinct sounds are called *phonemes*. For example, in English we distinguish between [r][1] and [l] as in the words *rake* and *lake*. However, some languages do not distinguish between [r] and [l], which are acoustically similar. Speakers of such languages have trouble with these sounds when they are learning English.

Language is not only spoken, it is also systematic. All language is structured. This structure is called *grammar*. There are two levels of grammar—morphology and syntax. *Morphology* is the organization of the basic sounds of a language, phonemes, into meaningful units. These meaningful units are called *morphemes*. A morpheme may be a word or simply a prefix or suffix. *Syntax* is the way a language combines words to make a sentence. For example, both English and Spanish use the same word order to make a statement: subject, verb, object. However, in English, modifiers (adjectives and adverbs) precede the word they modify, in Spanish they follow. In English we say, "the big house." In Spanish it is *"la casa grande"* (the house big). *Discourse* is the process of structuring phrases, clauses, and statements into meaningful units called *discourses*.

By five years of age the native speaker of any language has mastered its grammar. The child cannot tell you that the action word is a verb and the person doing the action is a noun. But the child knows what order the words follow to make a statement and what order they follow in asking a question. We all know the grammar of our native language even if we cannot explain the rules. For example, as English speakers, we know that to say something is "more big" is wrong and so is "comfortabler." While we know when to add *er* to a word and when to use *more,* most people do not know the rule. In English a general rule is that when we use a word with fewer than three syllables we add *er,* when it has three syllables or more we use *more.*

Besides being verbal and systematic, language is also sym-

---

[1]Brackets are used around a letter to indicate basic sounds.

bolic. We use symbols to stand for classes of things. These symbols are arbitrary and not directly related to the class of objects they represent. For example, there is nothing about a four-legged, furry animal that suggests "dog" or *"perro"* or *"chien."* These are sounds that the English, Spanish, and French have agreed to call that particular beast in their culture. Symbols are abstract; that is, we can talk about a dog that is not present or one that has never existed. We can manipulate the symbol. Language is possible because man is capable of symbolic activity.

While language is verbal, systematic, and symbolic, its function is communication. Basically, language is communication. It is a vehicle used to transport what is in one person's mind to another person's mind. It is a vehicle for abstract concepts.

The Phenomenon of Language

Language serves as a bridge between biological and cultural aspects of life. Malinowski dealt with seven biological bases for human life: metabolism, bodily comforts, safety, growth, reproduction, movement, and health (see chapter 2). Human beings, responding to these biological needs, form and perpetuate social structures and institutions designed to fill these needs.

Language serves the social group by providing a vital avenue of communication among the members establishing and perpetuating such institutions. Communication is far more than simply language usage. It involves the sum total of message sent within the social context: organizational messages, positional and relational messages, and verbal and language source messages. By linking the past with the present, communication assures the group that needs are being met, or it indicates that some reorganization of society is necessary.

Speech begins in the brain. The capacity and complexity of the human brain permits language learning and the ability to produce speech. While only humans have the unique design of lips, teeth, palate, tongue, and larynx to produce speech, some researchers have thought that some primates may have the capacity to learn language. These researchers have developed sign languages that they have attempted to teach to chimpanzees. These experiments have met with limited success. Chimpanzees have acquired "vocabularies" of up to 240 words and have used two-word combinations. However, in the same amount of time a human child acquires a vocabulary of over 5,000 words and uses complex sentences. Recent reviews of some of the research with chimpanzees indicates that they did not produce the two-word combinations on their own but were only responding to the unconscious prompting of the researchers (Terrance, 1979). It is apparent that only humans have a capacity for language.

Evolutionists have tried to explain language as a development from simple to more complex forms or, according to Otto Jespersen, from complex to more simple and thus more efficient expression. Perhaps their major pitfall was that they distinguished between "primitive" languages and "true" languages. Primitive languages did not qualify as fully developed languages. "True" languages were basically the European languages.

In reality, all known languages are capable of fully expressing any idea or concept necessary to its speakers. All languages are grammatically able to express any abstract concept. While some languages have a larger technical vocabulary because their speakers are industrialized, the languages of less industrialized people are fully able to incorporate technical vocabulary when they are exposed to it. The English language of the seventeenth century did not have any vocabulary relating to computers, airplanes, automobiles, or space travel. However, anyone reading the King James Bible would not call seventeenth-century English "primitive" language. When technology was developed, the English language developed the vocabulary to express it within its grammar. The languages of preindustrialized peoples are capable of the same development. All languages have the capacity to express the same things. There is no known "primitive" language.

In reality, all known languages are adequate expressions of the cultures in which they function. All languages have a regularity of structure, a potential to express abstract concepts, and characteristics generally associated with "true" languages. It *is* significant to consider that some languages are more advanced than, but not superior to, others in the areas of technological and philosophical expression. The less advanced languages can be termed "local," and the more advanced, "world" languages. Even though all languages have the resources to express the same things, languages directly associated with industrial and urban growth have developed additional vocabulary and syntactic flexibility.

Early attempts to explain language in a more scientific way worked with the supposed transition of language from some unsystematic form of communication to language proper. Linguists dealt with the nature of the situation in which this transition took place. Edward Sapir deals with the transition of language from the expressive to the referential function. That is, language begins as a spontaneous reaction to reality; then it develops into a highly specific symbolic system representing reality.

The well-known linguist Noam Chomsky feels that primitive languages have never existed. Language, wherever it is found, is full-blown and adequate for its usage by the social group.

Language Acquisition

All human societies use language. The means by which the members of these societies acquire their language is of great interest to anthropologists and linguists, and the following observations help in understanding this process (Chomsky 1965).

First, there is no evidence that there are any primitive languages. All known languages have a full-blown grammatical structure and are capable of expanding to incorporate any new technology or concepts that enter their respective societies. Not only are there no known primitive languages now, but also there is no evidence that primitive languages ever existed.

Second, children in every society begin learning their society's language at about the same age. American, Mexican, Chinese, and Saudi children all begin acquiring their language at about eighteen to twenty-four months of age. There is no known society where language acquisition begins earlier or later.

Finally, children in all societies learn their language at the same rate. The Chinese child learns Chinese at the same rate as the American child learns English and the Mexican child learns Spanish. Children in all societies have usually mastered the grammatical structure of their language by the age of five.

Based on these three observations, Chomsky has concluded that there is a readiness factor involved in language acquisition. He postulates that people have an innate language ability.

Evolutionists have a problem with Chomsky's scheme because he sees no evidence for the evolution of language. In fact, Chomsky's observations point to the sudden appearance of full-blown language. This, of course, is in harmony with the creationist position.

Language in Culture

Language changes through time. This prompts the study of historical and comparative linguistics. Language also varies from location to location, calling for a study of dialectology. The result of such language change and variation is *dialect*—when a smaller group has language varieties not common to the majority of speakers of the language, and *idiolect*—when a person has developed his own peculiar usage of the language.

Dialects of languages can vary in pronunciation. For example, Central American speakers of Spanish pronounce *c,* when it appears before *e* and *i,* and *z* as the English *c* in *city,* whereas in most of Spain c and z are pronounced like the English *th* in *thin.* Variation may also develop in the grammar when structures are changed by addition, replacement, or subtraction of grammatical units.

Dialects may also vary in vocabulary. Those variations serve as reference points in dialect geographies. Certain social dialects of English include the term "pancake." Others call the same thing "flapjack," and still others, "griddlecake." The reality is the same. Dialects have simply developed different terms.

Distinct sociocultural groups will also assign differing qualities to objects, animals, or people. In the United States the dog is considered "man's best friend," whereas in the Hebrew culture of the Old Testament the dog was a despised animal.

It becomes necessary, therefore, to shift from a concept of language as an expression of a culture, to one of communication through the use of language. Language is the servant of the culture that gave it birth. There is no sacredness of language apart from the large context of meaning established within a culture. Therefore, students in more traditional foreign-language courses are often unable to speak that language when they enter the normal cultural setting of the language. The students have learned the language in relation to their own sociocultural values and perspectives, not those of the people who speak the language as their mother tongue. Fluency is hindered by previously learned incorrect habits. Relearning of language skills takes a long time. Some never break the bad habits, and so never gain fluency.

Language is learned behavior and is therefore part of culture. Adaptation to one's cultural setting begins even before birth. Time schedules, for example, are cultural. The fetus is subject to its mother's time schedule before birth. After birth, feeding, sleeping, and other activities are some of the baby's first lived experiences. Each culture has its own time schedule. People in some cultures rise early; people in others retire late. The power of this routine is felt only when one leaves his or her own culture or subculture and moves into another that has a clashing routine. One's schedule may be so internalized that forced change of schedule, or clash with another schedule, is emotionally disturbing and disrupting.

Cultures vary in the values, qualities, or characteristics they assign to things, animals, or humans. Cultures, or sociocultural groups, also divide the entire universe in their particular pattern. Assignment of characteristics and categories is made to fit that pattern. Each society has its own division of the color spectrum. There are languages with only three vowels, and others with as many as twelve or fifteen vowels. In the same way, some societies have a reduced inventory of colors and others have an expanded inventory. North American women can usually recognize and name more colors than their husbands can. Women working with fabrics can usually distinguish and name more colors than can the average female. But any North American, male or female, probably recognizes far more colors than does the Mayan Indian of Central America. To the Mayans the color spectrum is divided into five parts plus a sixth quality of "no color." Their language reflects this division of the color spectrum, assigning only six words to colors. Introduction of a color shade not recognized as one of these six calls for the creation of a new term, the borrowing from a language having more color categories, or the modification of the color word with such concepts as very light or dark, or some reduplication of the stem word to indicate intensity of color.

Sapir and Whorf claim humans are enslaved to their own cultural process of dividing the universe into categories. Thought patterns are based on language. Linguistic categories are not the result of a process of thinking. Rather, the thought is dependent on already existing, arbitrary linguistic categories.

Their hypothesis can be demonstrated by the way various languages divide the color spectrum (Brown 1965). All humans who have normal vision see the same range of color. They all differentiate the same wave lengths of light. If language or linguistic categories were the result of thinking, we would expect the color spectrum to be divided into the same color bands in all languages. However, this is not true. In English the color spectrum is divided into seven basic categories: *red, orange, yellow, green, blue, violet,* and *purple.* In Shona, a language of Zimbabwe, the color spectrum is divided into three basic categories: *cips uka* (reds and purples at the two ends), *citema* (blues running into greens), and *cicena* (greens and yellows). In Bassa, a language of Liberia, the color spectrum is in two basic categories: *hui* (the blue-green end of the spectrum) and *zĩza* (the red-orange end of the spectrum). The Zuni Indians of New Mexico see yellows and oranges as a basic category, and the Taos Indians, also of New Mexico, see blues and greens as a basic category. In Madagascar the speaker of Malagasy distinguishes over one hundred basic categories of color (Nida 1952). (See figure 5-1.)

Ethnoscience

Ethnoscience is the branch of anthropology concerned with the cultural aspects of cognitive structure.[2] It is concerned with the effect of culture and language on the cognitive processes; that is, How does language affect how we think about and look at things? The Hanunoo have names for ninety-two varieties of rice, whereas the English speaker would label them all rice. The Hanunoo sees ninety-two different things while the American sees one. The Eskimo has six names for snow, all of which we would call snow. We distinguish between a Ford Escort, a Ford Mustang, a Chevrolet Nova, a Plymouth Duster, and many more makes and

---

[2] Some anthropologists prefer the term "cognitive anthropology" or "studies in cognition."

models, while the Hanunoo and the Eskimo call them cars. Roger Brown concludes:

ENGLISH

purple	blue	green	yellow	orange	red

SHONA

cips uka	citema	cicena	cips uka

BASSA

hui	zīza

Figure 5-1. Lexical mappings of the color spectrum in three languages (Brown 1965:316).

     The findings of ethnoscience and comparative semantics suggest that it is a rare thing to find a word in one language that is exactly equivalent in reference to a word in an unrelated language. If each lexicon is regarded as a template imposed on a common reality, these templates do not match up. On the level of grammar, differences of meaning between languages are more striking and probably of greater significance. Benjamin Whorf (1956) has described some fascinating differences and has argued that they result in unlike modes of thought.

     If reality were such as directly to impose itself on the child's mind, one would expect it to have imposed itself in the same form on the languages of the world. The ubiquity of linguistic nonequivalence suggests that reality can be variously construed and, therefore, that the child's manipulations and observations are not alone likely to yield the stock of conceptions that prevail in his society. . . . For any concept that is cultural rather than natural the problem set by the need to master its linguistic expression is sufficient to cause the concept to be learned (1965:317).

One's identity is manifested and defined partly by how he responds to language within the sociocultural context. Identity is expressed in three primary ways: by the language one speaks, by the degree to which one uses speech or silence, and by the use of nonverbal behavioral cues.

The language or dialect a people speak identifies them with a geographic region. If we cannot identify a person's dialect, we can at least tell if the person is native to the area. A native speaker of English can usually recognize the various American dialects—from New England, the New York area, the Southeast, the Southwest, or the Midwest. We also identify people by the language they speak; e.g., we say that a person is "Spanish-speaking."

North American society is a verbal culture. We find silence uncomfortable. It is difficult for the average North American to spend more than a few minutes with someone without words being spoken. Although we use nonverbal communication, we feel the need to use also verbal communication. To us, the message has not been fully communicated until it has been verbalized.

In North America a subordinate is expected to respond to a superior when being corrected. The subordinate must verbally respond indicating the instructions were understood. However, in the Philippines a subordinate is expected to remain quiet while being corrected. Any verbal response would indicate disrespect for the superior. Rather, a nonverbal response is called for and is understood.

In some cultures language is taken more seriously than in others. This is an international sore spot in encounters between East and West. For the most part, Asians take language more seriously than North Americans. They tend to react negatively to our apparently flippant use of language.

Nonverbal Communication

Nonverbal communication refers to the process whereby a message is sent and received through any one of the senses without the use of language. Such messages may be intentional or unintentional, conscious or unconscious. A preacher may gesture during a sermon with well-thought-out movements designed to emphasize the points he is making. On the other hand, the same man may gesture in private conversation and not even be aware of it. The fact is we are always sending out nonverbal messages whether we realize it or not.

Patterns of nonverbal behavior are culturally defined. Yes or no messages are conveyed by the nodding or shaking of one's head. These patterns are part of the arbitrary selection of symbols of the culture. They must be learned, along with language and other aspects of the structure of society, by new members entering the culture.

Learning these nonverbal clues can present problems. The same symbol may transmit opposite messages in two different cultures, or two opposite signals may mean the same thing in the two cultures. The hand motion with fingers extended down from the palm and moved in rhythm toward the speaker signifies "good-by" to someone from the United States but means "come here" to most Latin Americans. Yet, the Latin American symbol for "good-by" is almost identical to the American symbol meaning "come here." Obviously, this can be confusing and frustrating. When members of one culture visit or live within another culture, they must master these signals until they perceive them according to the intent of the other person.

Nonverbal communication is expressed and perceived through all of the senses—hearing, touch, smell, sight, and taste—and also through body temperature, body movement, and time and space. For example, people who perspire intensely when they are nervous are communicating that message with their "wet" clothes as though they had verbalized their nervousness. That the two messages, verbal and nonverbal, may not coincide is a fascinating study in the field of social psychology. The person who perspires heavily but claims he or she is not nervous may be either consciously trying to deceive others or unaware of his or her motives in denying nervousness.

A young Mayan Indian man, viewing an elephant for the first time in a zoo, stood comfortably by the fence until the elephant approached him. By an unconscious movement, he gradually backed away from the fence until the elephant turned away. Then the young man moved gradually toward the fence once again. He was totally unaware of his actions. His description of the encounter was effusive, but he never mentioned any "fear" of the giant beast.

Kinesic communication involves muscle or body movement. Specific messages are transmitted by hand waves, eye contact, facial expressions, head nods, and other movements. In an interpretive dance the movements of the entire body are high in message content. In fact, in certain Southeast Asian nations the interpretive dance is the primary nonverbal means of communicating to a group. The Thai easily read the symbolic message of the formal dance without its being verbalized.

Sometimes kinesic symbols cause much frustration in cross-cultural encounters. North American eye contact is far too intense for Filipinos, who tend to break eye contact early. They break eye contact (1) to show subordination to authority; (2) to differentiate roles—e.g., man and woman or adult and child; and (3) to indicate that staring is not proper behavior. North Americans, while not staring, encourage eye contact to show they are respectable and trustworthy. A Filipino woman in a North American class, resisting the culturally determined eye contact of the professor, cried out, "You make me feel naked!" In other words, she was saying, "You stare at me as if you want to see right through me."

Cultural factors govern body movement—determining what moves, when it moves, where it moves—and restrictions on movement. Hips may move in sports or dancing but not in a church service. A child may move the body freely in gym but not in the classroom. A North American woman who grows up in Latin America may return home with more body movement as part of her flirtation pattern and find she is classified as "loose" among her peers. A Latin woman tends to move more of her body when men are present than does an American woman, although neither communicates loose morals within her own culture. When the North American woman moves into the Latin American culture, she may be seen as "cold." Conversely, when the Latin American woman moves to North America, she may be considered "loose."

Proxemic communication implies relationships of space, duration, distance, territory, and the perception of these on the part of the participant.

Standing patterns have been classified by Edward T. Hall (1969) as intimate, personal, and public. North American intimate space extends two feet from the person; Latin American intimate space extends only a foot or so. This intimate-personal space border defines the space within which one feels uncomfortable in a personal, but nonintimate, conversation. Thus, Latins feel quite comfortable conversing just a foot away from the face of another person. When they move that close to a North American, however, they are invading that person's intimate space. Such an invasion causes the American to react defensively with visible muscle tension, skin discoloration, and even the body movement of "retreat."

Living rooms are often arranged in keeping with the personal space relationships of a culture. People may sit close to each other more comfortably when they sit side by side than when they sit face to face. The Mayan equivalent of a living room is designed for standing or sitting only in the extremities on a log by the walls. A North American living room is arranged so that no one is farther than ten feet from another. If the room is larger than this, a conversation area will be arranged with the seats closer than the perimeter of the room would indicate.

Public distance includes that space in which a person feels comfortable in a public area or gathering. The definition of this space will vary according to the situation. For example, when people are on an elevator, they will invade one another's intimate space; but reduced body movement compensates for this intrusion. The outer limit of public space is the maximum distance one feels he can maintain and still feel a part of the gathering. This usually means being within the sound of the activity, closer with a public address and farther away at a musical performance.

Seating patterns are arranged with a purpose. Frequently the pattern includes a focal point, the performer or speaker, with the audience arranged in rows or in a semicircle facing the focal point. In theater in the round, the audience surrounds the stage; but the focus is still on the actors. Involvement theater in the sixties attempted to bring everyone into the performance itself. This was resisted, however, by many in North American society because of public space preferences.

Competition versus cooperation is also signaled by seating patterns. When classroom desks are separated, competition is signaled. No one can copy the work of another. The seminar room, with people seated side by side 'around a table, signals cooperation because each one sees and shares in the work of another.

Walking patterns are also part of public space involving schedule, direction, and distance. Certain Hebrew laws were devised according to the distance one could walk from his property in a day. A limit was placed on Sabbath journeys, and the distance was called, logically, "a Sabbath day's walk." Hebrew people soon learned to carry some of their property with them and lay it at the end of one "Sabbath day's walk"; so they could then walk an additional distance from that property.

The schedule of walking patterns concerns the time of day one may be seen in public in a given society. Among the Pocomchi in Guatemala, men can be seen sweeping the house and walking before 6:00 A.M. but never after that hour. Likewise, no one would be on legitimate business after 9:00 P.M. In the Philippines, Saturday night is a very late night. People stroll in the parks until 2:00 A.M. on Sunday.

The following selection from Helen Keller illustrates the frustrating and exhilarating process by which one discovers a correlation between nonverbal and verbal experiences. For most of us, this process occurs gradually, when we are too young to appreciate it. Helen Keller was old enough at the time to remember the experience later. We go through a similar process, although on a much smaller scale, when we become fluent in a second language.

The morning after my teacher came she led me into her room and gave me a doll. The little blind children at the Perkins Institution had sent it and Laura Bridgman had dressed it; but I did not know this until afterward.

When I had played with it a little while, Miss Sullivan slowly spelled into my hand the word "d-o-l-l." I was at once interested in this finger play and tried to imitate it.

When I finally succeeded in making the letters correctly I was
flushed with childish pleasure and pride. Running downstairs
to my mother I held up my hands and made the letters for
doll. I did not know that I was spelling a word or even that
words existed; I was simply making my fingers go in
monkey-like imitation. In the days that followed I learned to
spell in this uncomprehending way a great many words,
among them pin, hat, cup and a few verbs like sit, stand and
walk. But my teacher had been with me several weeks before
I understood that everything has a name.

One day, while I was playing with my new doll, Miss
Sullivan put my big rag doll into my lap also, spelled
"d-o-l-l" and tried to make me understand that "d-o-l-l"
applied to both. Earlier in the day we had had a tussle over
the words "m-u-g" and "w-a-t-e-r." Miss Sullivan had tried
to impress it upon me that "m-u-g" is *mug* and "w-a-t-e-r"
is *water,* but I persisted in confounding the two. In despair
she had dropped the subject for the time only to renew it at
the first opportunity. I became impatient at her repeated
attempts and, seizing the new doll, I dashed it upon the
floor. . . .

We walked down the path to the well-house, attracted
by the fragrance of the honeysuckle with which it was
covered. Someone was drawing water and my teacher placed
my hand under the spout. As the cool stream gushed over
one hand she spelled into the other the word water, first
slowly, then rapidly. I stood still, my whole attention fixed
upon the motions of her fingers. Suddenly I felt a misty
consciousness as of something forgotten—a thrill of returning thought; and somehow the mystery of language was
revealed to me. I knew then that "w-a-t-e-r" meant the
wonderful cool something that was flowing over my hand.
That living word awakened my soul, gave it light, hope,
joy, set it free! There were barriers still, it is true, but barriers
that could in time be swept away.

I left the well-house eager to learn. Everything had a
name, and each name gave birth to a new thought. As we
returned to the house every object which I touched seemed
to quiver with life. That was because I saw everything with
the strange, new sight that had come to me. On entering the
door I remembered the doll I had broken. I felt my way to
the hearth and picked up the pieces. I tried vainly to put
them together. Then my eyes filled with tears; for I realized
what I had done, and for the first time I felt repentance and
sorrow.

I learned a great many new words that day. I do not
remember what they all were; but I do know that mother,
father, sister, teacher were among them—words that were

to make the world blossom for me, "like Aaron's rod, with flowers." It would have been difficult to find a happier child than I was a I lay in my crib at the close of that eventful day and lived over the joys it had brought me, and for the first time longed for a new day to come. . . .

I had now the key to all language, and I was eager to learn to use it. Children who hear acquire language without any particular effort; the words that fall from others' lips they catch on the wing, as it were, delightedly, while the little deaf child must trap them by a slow and often painful process. But whatever the process, the result is wonderful. Gradually from naming an object we advance step by step until we have traversed the vast distance between our first stammered syllable and the sweep of thought in a line of Shakespeare.

At first, when my teacher told me about a new thing I asked very few questions. My ideas were vague, and my vocabulary was inadequate; but as my knowledge of things grew, and I learned more and more words, my field of inquiry broadened, and I would return again and again to the same subject, eager for further information. Sometimes a new word revived an image that some earlier experience had engraved on my brain.

I remember the morning that I first asked the meaning of the word, "love." This was before I knew many words. I had found a few early violets in the garden and brought them to my teacher. She tried to kiss me; but at that time I did not like to have anyone kiss me except my mother. Miss Sullivan put her arm gently around me and spelled into my hand, "I love Helen."

"What is love?" I asked.

She drew me closer to her and said, "It is here," pointing to my heart, whose beats I was conscious of for the first time. Her words puzzled me very much because I did not then understand anything unless I touched it.

I smelt the violets in her hand and asked, half in words, half in signs, a question which meant, "Is love the sweetness of flowers?"

"No," said my teacher.

Again I thought. The warm sun was shining on us.

"Is this not love?" I asked, pointing in the direction from which the heat came. "Is this not love?"

It seemed to me that there would be nothing more beautiful than the sun, whose warmth makes all things grow. But Miss Sullivan shook her head, and I was greatly puzzled and disappointed. I thought it strange that my teacher could not show me love.

A day or two afterward I was stringing beads of different sizes in symmetrical groups—two large beads, three small ones, and so on. I had made many mistakes, and Miss Sullivan had pointed them out again and again with gentle patience. Finally I noticed a very obvious error in the sequence and for an instant I concentrated my attention on the lesson and tried to think how I should have arranged the beads. Miss Sullivan touched my forehead and spelled with decided emphasis, "Think."

In a flash I knew that the word was the name of a process that was going on in my head. This was my first conscious perception of an abstract idea (Laird and Gorrell 1971:55–57).

Verbal and nonverbal behavior are what social interaction is all about. These skills are learned within the context of one's society. They are expressed as normal behavior within the settings defined by that society. Only through adequate grasp of the language and nonverbal aspects of the culture can communication be carried out.

Translation

Christians believe the Bible is the inspired Word of God. We believe it is God's revelation to man. It is God's message of salvation. We believe it is important to make God's Word available to everyone in his or her language. The job of putting the Bible into the language of other people is the task of the Bible translator. Bible translation is a major part of the missionary enterprise. Ethnoscience and linguistics can be invaluable tools in translation work.

At first glance it may seem to some that translation involves little more than learning another language and then substituting words from the new language into the text. Such people feel that although translating might mean changing some word orders to fit the new grammar, it is basically a mechanical process. Eugene Nida, a Bible translator with the American Bible Society, gives us some illustrations of the hazards of mechanical translation:

The translator must constantly ask himself, "What does this expression mean in the native language?" Without such attention to the actual meaning of a rendering, he may find himself saying things which he does not intend to say. For example, in a recent investigation of three translations made into Indian languages of Latin America, it was found that the literal rendering of Acts 9:1 was interpreted in one case as meaning that Saul's spirit had died. In the second instance, the native speaker said that it meant that Saul's ghost was going out to frighten the disciples. In the third case, the informant, who had actually been one of the native translators, said that the passage meant that Saul was afraid to die. We as English speakers have become so used to the idiom "breathing out threatenings and slaughter against" (AV) that we assume naïvely this can be translated directly into any language and the meaning will be obvious. But this is not the case.

In one of the Bantu languages the translators rendered literally Rom. 14:7 "For none of us liveth to himself and none dieth to himself." The translation seemed completely acceptable, but a more careful examination of this translation in the light of native religious beliefs revealed that the translation was quite unusable. In its literal form this verse would have constituted a direct confirmation of the native belief that people do not live or die because of their own power, but because of the presence or lack of black magic employed by others. That is to say, they contend that no man "dies to himself," but rather his death is caused by the forces of evil let loose against him by an enemy. If one is to translate Rom. 14:7 adequately into the particular Bantu language, one must say "we are not alone in our living and we are not alone in our dying." This does not represent the literal wording of the Bible, but it does represent the closest equivalent in meaning, while the literal rendering would give an entirely wrong impression. . . .

A literal rendering of "blessing I will bless thee" (Heb. 6:14) in one of the languages of Central Africa actually meant "if I bless, I will be blessed." This literal rendering of a specialized Semitic idiom completely misses the mark. The Biblical expression does not mean reciprocity of blessing but the abundance and assurance of the act. The closest native parallel is "I will bless you and bless you."

A related problem is found in the translation of "grace for grace" (John 1:16). In one Indian language of Latin America the literal rendering of this idiom actually means "favor in exchange for a favor," but with the definite denotation that God only grants a favor in exchange for a favor granted to him by people. This is actually a denial of grace. . . .

The literal rendering of "walk not after the flesh" (Rom. 8:4) actually means in one translation "do not walk like butchered meat." The word used to translate "flesh" means only "butchered meat." A different word is used to identify human flesh. Furthermore, even the use of the term for human flesh would be inappropriate and rather meaningless. It would have been better in this instance to translate "body." However, the idiom "walking like the body" has no metaphorical meaning as it might have in English.

Accordingly, the rendering must be changed to "do not do what the body does." This is the native equivalent and fully understandable (1947:1–3).

These illustrations show the importance of understanding what the language means to the speaker. Translators need to see the world through the sociolinguistic eyes of the speakers of the language into which they are translating God's Word. Some may object to some of the departures from the literal renderings suggested by Nida in the above illustrations. They may say we should teach the people the right meaning of the language. Nida, anticipating this objection, says:

> Certain missionaries object to any such departure from the literal rendering of a passage, insisting that by proper teaching they can instruct people as to the right meaning and at the same time deny native practices. Such assumptions are largely wishful thinking. People can and will understand material only in terms of the cultural situation in which such words are used by them. A great deal of explanation is necessary to correct false meanings (witness the constant difficulty of explaining some word problems in the King James Version, e.g., "prevent" 1 Thess. 4:15, and "let" 2 Thess. 2:7). In most cases no amount of explanation can change a wrong meaning into a right one (1947:2).

Nida feels that it is very important that the translator avoid the pitfalls of both literal translation and paraphrase translation (1969). In an effort to avoid the built-in problems of both literalism and paraphrase, Nida has come up with a translation approach he calls "dynamic equivalence." Dynamic equivalence is a rendering of a passage so that the same or an equivalent effect is produced in the heart and mind of the reader in the second language as was produced in the heart and mind of the reader in the original language, as the following explains:

> The ultimate test of a translation must be based on three major factors: (1) the correctness with which the receptors understand the message of the original (that is to say, its "faithfulness to the original") as determined by the extent to which people really comprehend the meaning, (2) the ease of comprehension, and (3) the involvement a person experiences as the result of the adequacy of the form of translation. Perhaps no better compliment could come to a translator than to have someone say, "I never knew before that God spoke my language" (1969:173).

The dynamic-equivalence approach has much promise and solves many of the problems inherent in literalism and paraphrase.

However, Nida's approach does have problems of its own, the major one being how one determines what effect the original produced in the hearts and minds of the original readers. Also, Hebrew and Greek are not "holy" languages. One of the major problems is that most words have more than one meaning, and although context often indicates which meaning is meant, this is by no means always so. The dynamic-equivalence approach does present problems, but it seems to us to have more potential than either word-for-word translations or paraphrases.

Dr. Mayers, addressing the Association of Evangelical Professors of Missions, spoke of his experience with the translation process of dynamic equivalence:

> I stumbled over this principle early in the process of translation for a Maya-related people of Central America. I was translating in the book of Luke, chapter 13, where Herod is referred to as a "fox." In Pocomchi the word for fox is *bahlam,* but upon using the word, I received a very strange reaction. Enquiring further, I discovered that a fox to the Pocomchi is not seen as sly and crafty—that is what the wildcat is. Rather, the fox talks in a falsetto voice. Once I had clarified the point utilizing the word for wildcat, their reaction to the entire chapter revealed to me that they had grasped the truth intended in the passage. Had I continued with the word "fox" they would have learned falsehood.

The job of the Bible translator is to bring God's Word to people in their own language. A good grasp of anthropological principles, vast linguistic skills, and enormous Bible knowledge does not insure a good translation. The Holy Spirit is the author of the Bible. The translator must turn to Him for wisdom. The translator is an instrument through which the Holy Spirit may work. However, the translator should also be a prepared instrument, working in harmony with God's creation, which includes different languages and cultures.

Questions for Discussion

1. Is abstract thought possible apart from language? Explain. What about Helen Keller's experience?
2. In what ways does language influence thought? How might this affect the communication of the gospel?
3. When a person has learned the vocabulary, grammar, and pronunciation of another language, has he or she learned that language? Explain.
4. What does the arrangement of the room in which this class meets tell you about the assumed communications patterns?

5. What implications does the concept stated by Roger Brown on page 95 have for translation work? Relate this to what Eugene Nida says on pages 102–4.

Suggested Reading

Birdwhistell, R. L. 1970. *Kinesics and Context.* The author views communication as taking place in several channels such as verbal, movement, and smell. This work is concerned with the channel of body movement. The first part of this book is less technical and can serve as a good introduction to the study of kinesics.

Hall, E. T. 1969. *The Hidden Dimension.* The author examines man's use of space, public and private. He deals with the relationship between space and culture. He points out how we use space in communication.

Harms, L. S. 1973. *Intercultural Communication.* An introductory text dealing with the relationship between culture and communication. This work makes good use of case studies. It also includes a section on student projects.

Hymes, D. 1974. *Foundations in Sociolinguistics.* A good introduction to the field of sociolinguistics. The section on linguistics as a science should be of interest to those who are considering a career of linguistics.

————. 1971. *Language in Culture and Society.* A collection of articles dealing with language, culture, and society. It contains an excellent section on the relationship between language and worldview. It also has a good section on the relationship of language to social structure.

Nida, E. A. 1947. *A Translator's Commentary on Selected Passages;* 1961. *Bible Translation;* 1952. *God's Word in Man's Language;* 1969. *Toward a Science of Translation.* These works by an experienced linguist and translator are well worth reading by anyone who is contemplating becoming involved in translation work.

Samover, L., and Porter, R. 1972. *Intercultural Communications: A Reader.* A good collection of articles on intercultural communication. The articles deal with practical problems. The book also contains a useful section on intercultural communication research.

Sitaram, K. S., and Cofdell, R. T. 1976. *Foundations of Intercultural Communication.* An excellent introductory text on intercultural communication. The strength of this work lies in its extensive use of apt illustrations and clear style.

Tyler, S. A. 1969. *Cognitive Anthropology.* A collection of articles dealing with and defining the field of cognitive anthropology. It contains a good section on the relationship between language and culture.

6

Economy and Technology

A tractor moves up and down a field in southern Illinois, turning over the soil in precise rows. In northeastern Iowa a combine moves efficiently through a field ready for harvest. The same farmer is operating both of these machines in addition to several dozen more in fields throughout the Midwest. How is this possible? The machines are all being operated by remote control by the farmer in a three-piece business suit sitting at a computer console in a large office building in the Chicago loop. Impossible? Science fiction? No, this technology is already on the drawing board (Cohen 1968).

What effect will this technology have on our economy, on our social structure, on the economies and social structures of other societies? How will primitive societies be affected by modern technology?

Economics

Economic anthropology is the study of primitive and peasant economies wherever they exist in the world. The study in its broadest form encompasses economic and technological systems.

Economic systems involve the ways people, time, and materials are organized to produce, distribute (and redistribute), and consume goods and services. Such goods and services include the following:

1. Food for physical sustenance along with goods and services for religious, defense, and justice purposes; rites of passage; and other aspects of social and community life.
2. Natural resources such as land, water, and minerals; human cooperation involved in the division of labor; and technology.
3. Market places, foreign trade, monetary objects, devices for measuring and record keeping.

Technological systems are those parts of culture that enable man to produce objective changes in his physical and biological environment. This part of the larger system of society consists of learned categories and plans for action manifested in the tools, techniques, and skills employed by the members of society.

Levels of Subsistence Technologies

All humans share the same basic needs for the maintenance of life. These needs include food, shelter, protection, and health. Since all human societies share these needs, each society must develop social patterns and organizations to exploit its environment to meet these needs. The economic institution is made up of the standard and routine behaviors and social organizations in a society used for the production, distribution, and consumption of goods and services. Like other basic social institutions, the economic institution is integrated into the whole social fabric of the society. It is influenced by many noneconomic factors such as societal values, traditions, and customs (Babbie, 1977:249–50; Gordon and Harvey, 1978:84; Perrucci et al., 1977:160).

We may categorize economics by five basic subsistence technologies. From least to most advanced, these are (1) hunting and gathering, (2) animal husbandry, (3) horticulture, (4) agriculture, and (5) industrialism (Otterbein, 1977:40–42). The more advanced technologies will often incorporate elements of less advanced technologies. For example, industrialized societies usually utilize agriculture and animal husbandry.

Hunting and gathering, which includes fishing, is a technology that exploits its environment without controlling or changing it. Native game in the area is hunted, but there is no attempt to control the game or to introduce new species. The vegetation, including fruits, that grows naturally in the environment is gathered, but there is no attempt to cultivate the vegetation or to introduce new varieties.

Animal husbandry involves the breeding and raising of animals.

Animals are domesticated and maintained to provide food, skins, and transportation. This level of technology allows humans to have the animals at hand as opposed to having to go out and hunt for them.

Horticulture is a farming technology that involves raising crops with the use of hand tools such as digging sticks or hoes. This technology involves clearing a field of grass, brush, and trees. The ground is then broken up with a digging stick or a hoe. Crops usually consist of grains such as corn, wheat, and millet, or roots such as manioc, yams, and potatoes. The field is weeded as the crops grow, and when the crops are mature, they are harvested. These fields usually decline in fertility in two or three years. They are then allowed to return to their natural vegetation, and new fields are cleared. In societies where these first three subsistence technologies are practiced, the whole population is generally involved in food production.

Agriculture is a farming technology that utilizes the plow and either draft animals or tractors. Agriculture also involves more intense cultivation. Farmers use fertilizers—either animal refuse or chemicals—and rotate crops. With intensive cultivation, the same fields can be used permanently and plantings yield larger harvests per acre. Agriculture is usually such an efficient means of producing food that a significant part of the population is freed from food production to engage in manufacturing and trade. Agriculture makes possible the transition to *industrialism*. The freeing of a major segment of the population from food production leads to five major social changes related to the emergence of industrialism: (1) increased occupational specialization—instead of each family providing all of its needs, it specializes and overproduces in a few areas; (2) a market for the exchange of goods and the development of a barter economy; (3) the emergence of political leadership and a governmental structure; (4) a management of labor and an alloca-tion of resources; and (5) different rewards for different tasks, leading to a status system and stratification.

While the above five factors figured in the development of industrialism, three additional factors were responsible for the continued growth of industrialism. The first of these was the development of money. By using tokens of fixed value, economies could advance from barter economies to cash economies. With the development of a cash economy, wage labor was possible. Instead of one person making the whole shoe so as to have something to barter or trade, several shoemakers could work for one industrial-ist, one making heels, one making soles, one making bodies, and another assembling the shoes. The owner of the business could sell the shoes for cash and pay wages that the workers could use to purchase their necessities.

The second factor responsible for the growth of industrialism was the development of the alphabet. When people became able to read and write, further industrial development was possible. Messages did not have to be carried personally but could be written and delivered by another. This facilitated increased trade and enabled governments to operate more efficiently. The development of writing and reading also led to the development of postal services.

Even with the development of money and the alphabet, the growth of industrialism would still have been limited if it had not been for the third factor, mechanical technology. As mechanical technology advanced, more efficient farming implements were developed, allowing each farmer to produce more food and freeing more workers from the land. The latter migrated to the cities and entered the wage labor market. As mechanical technology increased, the need for wage laborers increased. New factories began to open, and the need for skilled artisans such as blacksmiths decreased, while the need for laborers increased.

However, the real growth in industrialism took place during the industrial revolution. Although not all historians agree on the beginning and ending dates of the industrial revolution, 1760 to 1918 would be accepted by most. With the invention and development of steam for industrial use, factories began to spring up in urban areas where there was a ready supply of laborers (Hawley, 1971:63–86).

Anthropologists do much of their research among hunters and gatherers, pastoralists (those who practice animal husbandry), and horticulturalists, whereas sociologists are primarily concerned with examining contemporary industrialized societies.[1] Some of the areas that anthropologists are interested in include the division of labor, specialization, unionization, labor-management relations, economic systems, and manifest and latent functions of organizations and associations.

Primitive Economies

Primitive economies are those in which the main transactions involving land, labor, tools, and produce are socially obligatory gift giving. These societies are nonmarket and noncommercial societies in which the major part of resources and produce are transacted in nonmarket contexts. The Tiv of Africa and the Trobriand of the Pacific fall into this category.

One of the most interesting systems of reciprocal gift exchange is that of the Trobriand Islands. Shells are exchanged in a

---

[1] Anthropology is becoming increasingly involved in studying industrialized societies. For example, urban anthropology is a growing field of study.

pattern specified to include the various islands. As these shells are exchanged, various food and other produce are traded from island to island. The complete system, which is explained in further detail later in this chapter, illustrates one system in which a market economy is necessary.

In Tiv society, a market economy and a gift reciprocity economy exist side by side. The gift exchange is a long standing relationship

> between persons or groups in a more or less permanent relationship. The gift may be a factor designed to strengthen the relationship, or even to create it. There are several Tiv words for "gift," the examination of which would require another chapter the length of this one. For our purposes, it is primary that any of these "gift" words implies a relationship between two parties concerned which is of a permanence and warmth not known in a "market" and hence—though "gifts" should be reciprocal over a long period of time—it is bad form overtly to count and compute and haggle over gifts (Bohannan in LeClair and Schneider 1968, 300).

In Philippine society, a pattern of gift reciprocity operates in cementing social relations, though the economy is sustained by market and commercial activity.

Primitive economies are considered small-scaled from three points of view. First, in contrast to the economies of Europe and America, most resources, goods, and service transactions take place within a small geographical area and within a community of persons numbered in the hundreds of thousands. Second, in many cases, one or two staple items commonly produced within the small framework of the village, tribe, or lineage comprise the bulk of the total produce. Finally, in terms of quantity, a relatively small number of goods and services are produced in contrast to the thousands produced in modern industrial societies.

The simple level of technology and geographical or cultural isolation are important factors that mutually reinforce the size, structure, and performance of primitive economies. Consequently the people involved are limited in their production activities by physical resources and thus depend primarily on human cooperation for production processes as well as in times of catastrophies. This human ingredient in primitive economies calls for close association of the economic structures with the social structures of kin relations and social statuses. The economy is rooted in community relationships and not separated into economically defined associations.

Because of the small size of primitive economies and the close ties with the social organization, the individual person tends to be in sharp focus, and he or she, not the system, is the central figure. Tools, for example, are either made by the user himself, purchased from a specialist craftsman, or acquired directly from a construction group specifically organized for the task. Such services are remunerated primarily by the host providing food, or food and specialties, not readily available to the workers.

Peasant Economies

Peasant economies are generally subsocieties of a larger stratified society that is either preindustrial or partly industrialized. They may be characterized by all or some of the following traits: rural residence, familial agriculture on self-owned land holdings or other simple rural occupations that provide a modest or subsistence livelihood; the family as the centrally important social unit; low social status; economic interdependence in varying degrees with urban centers; attachment to the local community and tradition; and finally the tendency to limit production to goods that can be directly utilized by the producers. Commercial transactions for resources and produce are quantitatively important; so cash transactions, the pricing of land and tools, and wage labor are common.

The peasant societies generally have a visible marketplace where people transact their exchange. In a modern pluralistic society such as the United States, the market may have a central location—e.g., Wall Street—yet have various extensions so that one participating in the whole may never encounter more than one or two of its parts. Further, a pattern of distribution of goods may make a central market unnecessary, as for milk and bread delivery or the door-to-door selling of Avon products.

There are at least two sets of characteristics that help distinguish between primitive and precapitalistic peasant economies (Dalton 1973:469). Most people depend for the bulk of their livelihood on production for market sale. Cash sales transactions are frequent and quantitatively important. Frequently, resource markets are present. These include significant quantities of labor, land, tools, and equipment available for purchase, rent, or hire at money price.

The relative importance of markets for resources and products and cash transactions is the principle feature delineating precapitalistic and primitive economies. This feature gives peasant economies their crude resemblance to the least productive or more advanced farming sectors and justifies Tax's appropriate phrase "penny capitalism" (Tax 1963). But in all other ways relating to productive activities, peasant economies, especially traditional peasantries, more closely resemble the primitive than they do the modern. They are characterized by a simple technology and a narrow range of output. A few staples comprise the bulk of output with unusual reliance on physical resource endowment because of the absence of applied science and the technology of extensive fabrication. The result is often poverty and material insecurity.

In precapitalistic peasant economies, the rudiments of capitalist economy are present and important, but they are incomplete and underdeveloped compared to the market organization in a modern national economy. By incomplete, we mean that within a given peasant community petty land may be frequently purchased or rented but labor is not hired out, or vice versa. In many households subsistence production may still be quantitatively important. The term *underdeveloped* implies the absence of facilitative institutions and social capital—banks, insurance companies, and stock markets plus the lack of hard technologies—electricity, paved roads, and educational facilities beyond the elementary school. In peasant communities the extent of economic, cultural, and technological integration with the province and nation is markedly less than it is in the hinterland communities of developed nations.

The spectrum of peasantries is wide and contains varying mixtures of primitive and modern institutions. At one end are those in medieval Europe and present-day Latin America. They are peasant in religion, language, and political subordination yet have primitive economies due to the lack of market dependence and cash transactions. There are also cases of peasant economy with a primitive culture, as in the early transition period of African groups. They enlarged their cash earning production while retaining their tribal organization and culture (Dalton 1964).

Grimes and Hinton (1969) describe a Mexican Indian society with primary characteristics of a primitive economy set within what would otherwise call for a peasant group. They mention some of the values that shape Huichol attitudes toward economic activity as expressed in the concept of "life," propitiation of the gods as a necessary part of economic activity, kindred solidarity, communal and private property, and a uniform standard of living:

1. A certain linguistic form connotes desire for life, health, and good fortune.
2. Propitiation of the gods by sacrifices has economic motivations.
3. Kin are expected to work together cooperatively when a labor force larger than that available in a household is required.
4. Most land, except orchard areas, is communally owned.
5. The Huichol standard of living is connected with religious ideas of not arousing the envy of the gods by doing too well.

Labor is the dominant factor in the Huichol economy. There

are sufficient free resources available to maintain the community at its present standard of living, and the capital factor is almost insignificant. Natural resources involve local timber, vegetation, waterways, and more or less fertile lands. Slash and burn agriculture is practiced, and livestock is maintained on agriculturally marginal lands. All of the natural resources are in scarce supply as the population continues to increase. Little or nothing is being done to replenish dwindling supplies. Domesticated animals are kept partly for food, partly for ceremonial use, and partly for prestige. Sometimes chickens, turkeys, and ducks are kept for their eggs as well as their meat. Hunting and fishing supplement the food supply. All animals and fish may be used in ceremonial practices.

The Huichol make services available to one another in the form of cooperative labor and in ritual and governmental capacities. Chanters, hired privately, perform at ceremonial occasions. The Catholic priest provides ceremonies and baptisms and makes jobs available in his boarding school. Governmental services involve resolution of disputes and representation before state and national governments. The community requires labor services for building and maintenance of communal property.

In the Huichol economy, the bulk of the produce is claimed by the producers. The immediate household has first claim, but it is one's duty to feed relatives who may be present at mealtime. Ceremonial requirements are part of an individual's claim on the product. Government claims different amounts of the produce from different people. There are set funds connected with some of the offices designed to be passed from incumbent to successor. It is possible that these constitute a working capital that the official who controls it must relinquish by any means within his power. Most material items are attributed a money value, so transactions are usually discussed in terms of money. This does not mean, however, that money is basic to Huichol economy. Most items, produced for personal consumption, still may be sold when there is surplus.

Crosscultural contacts for economic purposes allow for acculturation. There is an exchange of material items as well as extension of social contacts with the outside. The Huichol people have generally favorable relations with outside employers and local Catholic priests and nuns. Generally, those who have been educated outside the area and have been in boarding school and those who have been in military service are reticent to accept new things as valid within the Huichol setting. Although Huichol economic values have been subjected to pressure to change, there has been little evidence of change.

The analytical distinctions for primitive and peasant economies, taken from Dalton's table of conceptual categories and relevant questions in economic anthropology, are summarized as follows:

1. Organization
   a. Size of economy; natural resource endowment.
   b. Transactional modes (reciprocity, redistribution, market-exchange; dominant-integrative modes distinguished from petty modes).
   c. Production processes: (1) allocation of resources (land acquisition, use, and transfer of tools and equipment); (2) work organization; (3) disposition of produce; (4) specialist services and their remuneration.
   d. Organization and role(s) of external trade (reciprocal gift trade, politically administered trade, market trade).
   e. Organization and role(s) of internal markets and market-places (marketless economies, petty marketplaces, small-scale market-integrated economies. Resource markets and produce markets).
   f. Organization of money and money uses (distinctions between general-purpose and special-purpose monies, between commercial and noncommercial uses of money; relation of money uses to transactional modes).
   g. Operational devices: record-keeping, accounting, and measurement devices (quipu strings, pebble counts); devices of culture contact (silent trade, border markets, ports of trade).
   h. Prestige economy contrasted with subsistence economy (transactional spheres and conversions, bride-wealth, ceremonial transfers, valuables and treasure items as special-purpose monies).
   i. The relation of economic to social organization (the place of economy in society): social control of resource allocation, work organization, and product disposition; social guarantee of livelihood through resource allocation and the provision of emergency subsistence.

2. Performance
   a. Number of goods and specialist services produced or acquired.
   b. Level of output, fluctuations in output, frequency or extent of famine (emergency devices in death caused by famine: use of trade partners for emergency gifts, use of less-preferred foods, emergency conversions, e.g., sale of treasures and people for food).
   c. Distribution of real income: equal or unequal?

    d. Distribution of subsistence goods contrasted with distribution of prestige goods (spheres of exchange, conversion between spheres).
    e. Growth in total product (1973:466).

Trade Patterns

The earliest trade patterns were established on the basis of social relationships as illustrated by the following examples.

In the Yir Yiront group of Australia, quarried stone for axes was traded north in exchange for fish bones for spear tips that were traded south. All along the route trading partners were established for life. They met at set times during the year and traded their bones and stone. Generally, festivals brought them together. Closer to the quarries more stone was traded for fewer fish bones. Closer to the water more fish bones were traded for less stone. These trading partners were the backbone of the socioeconomic organization of the Yir Yiront.

Another type of trade pattern practiced by the Trobrianders, who had trading partners on neighboring islands, was the exchanging of white shell armbands called *mwali* and long necklaces of red shells called *soulava* (Malinowski 1922). Exchange was intertribal and interisland. Soulava was always traded in clockwise direction. Mwali went counterclockwise. These armbands and necklaces met each other and were constantly being exchanged. This exchange network was called the Kula Ring since the articles, the armbands and bracelets, are known as *kula*. The movement of the kula around the Kula Rings was controlled by a set of traditional rules and customs. Some of the exchanges were accompanied by public ceremonies and elaborate magical rituals.

It was a relatively small number of men in each village and on each island that actually took part in the *kula* exchanges. No man in the Kula Ring ever kept any of the articles for an extended period of time. The articles were exchanged regularly and were kept in circulation.

While on the surface the exchange of *kula* articles was the major purpose of the Kula Ring, further investigation revealed a number of important secondary activities also taking place. The trading and bartering of everyday items that were essential to life also took place during the Kula exchange.

These secondary activities were economic trading activities incidental to the main exchange. However, the trading would likely not have been done were it not for the Trobriand equivalent of the British "crown jewels." The shells were worthless in themselves; but because they had value in exchange and use, the production of the islands was distributed in more even and equitable patterns than would likely have been done otherwise.

Another form of trade is the potlatch as practiced by the Kwakiutl Indians of northwestern Canada. This is a major scheme for the redistribution of surplus goods. Individuals and families inherit their statuses and honorific titles through their family and clan lineage. However, their statuses and titles have to be validated by holding a feast at which all their wealth is shown off. The host and his kinsmen demonstrate their status by giving away their wealth to their guest from another lineage or clan. The more they give away, the more their prestige is increased.

Granted, the potlatch is a rather inefficient means of distribution of goods. It is intended mainly as a means of assignment of honorific titles. However, it provides goods to those in need, even though much of the excess is lost in the practice of traders gorging themselves with food or the burning of objects, such as blankets. It is quite possible that when the potlatch was instituted, it was an efficient means of distributing goods from the wealthy to the poor. Excesses came later through abuse of the basic system. It is understandable that the people have complained about a national Canadian program of income tax, since the potlatch is an "oppressive" tax already assigned the people by their own social organization.

Market distribution is another trade pattern. This is illustrated by the Maya of Guatemala. Goods are produced in mountain fields and carried to town on market day to be sold for money (pennies) and then carried to the home of the purchaser. Retail marketing of foods and objects in small quantities is the responsibility of the women. Marketing of larger items, such as furniture, or larger quantities of a product, such as lime, is the prerogative of the men. The market is thus divided functionally into two parts: the women seated in the main area and the men standing in one end of the marketplace with their furniture and clothing or grains and lime. Local merchants maintain stalls on the perimeter of the marketplace.

Redistributive exchange is the basis of product exchange for advanced civilizations and the urban community. We can see this in the area market of Central America. Goods purchased in one market are frequently sold in another, and thus a class of middlemen has developed. Such a market is economic in function, whereas the rural market is social. Many markets are both, as middlemen will be in any large market buying and selling in quantity. As one moves toward the capital city, however, the balance changes until the city market is primarily an area market, the produce sold being gathered in local markets or raised for the express purpose of making money.

We can also see redistributive exchange in the income tax of North America. The tax is a primary means of redistribution of funds and thus of benefits to be derived from the funds. The more well-to-do pay the living expenses of the poor and subsidize various government functions. Solomon had such an extensive taxation system that it finally caused his kingdom to split into two parts. In the United States, tax revision is constantly being made to divide the tax burden more fairly. Yet, the tax burden increases continually. Besides distributing the wealth, taxation makes it possible for members of the society who might otherwise be unemployed to be given work; thus the government is the largest single employer in the United States.

Traditional Latin American social obligation calls for the extended family and the patron or "boss" to carry out most of the functions otherwise fulfilled by the tax program in the States. Again, it is understandable that Latins resist a national income tax.

Technology

Technology is the sum total of all the social customs by which people manipulate entities and substances of all kinds. Technology permits people to adapt to their nonhuman environment; it is the manipulation of the environment for cultural ends. "If language is the human attribute that makes culture possible, technology is the characteristic of culture that makes it advantageous to man" (Goldschmidt 1971:86).

There are four features about humans that have allowed them to develop a complex technology. The first is bipedal locomotion. They walk on two legs, leaving their arms free for other activity. The second is an opposing thumb. Humans are able to grip and manipulate items. The third is stereoscopic vision. They can estimate distances and focus on close and distant objects at the same time. The fourth, and most important, is language. Language enables them to think conceptually and communicate abstract ideas. Language also makes the accumulation of technology possible.

Technology is developed within what might be called the ecological setting, or ecosystem as Taylor calls it (1972:199). Techniques for manipulating and modifying the natural habitat and for making and using tools, houses, clothing, and other artifacts are linked to one another, to nontechnical customs, and to extracultural features of the ecosystem. Whether it is a Tikopean roof construct- ed to withstand the strong winds that sweep across the islands or the woodworking craft of the Tonga connected with religious expression, social and economic organization link together to permit personal expression within the total context of environ- ment.

Artifacts are any portion of the material environment deliber- ately used or modified for use by humans. They are the end result of the technological system. People make use of their environment and the objects in their environment to order, control, and manipulate their universe. Artifacts may be physical objects such as arrowheads, pots, or cars. Artifacts may be tools, techniques, or skills.

Tools are devices for transforming, transmitting, or storing energy. They are artifacts used to supplement or augment a person's ability to act upon the physical world. Tools may be *primary* in that they are used directly, such as a simple spear for fishing. Or they may be *secondary*, used to fabricate other tools: a knife may be used to shape a harpoon shaft. Tools can also be *simple*, a sharpened stick used as a spear, or *complex*, a bone point attached to a stick.

On a different level from these arbitrary distinctions are the *folk taxonomies*. These are the ways members of the society itself classify their tools. These classifications are closely related to the ways the tools are used. Associated with each category of a folk taxonomy is a plan of action in connection with the items classified together. A familiar example is the Spanish term "machete." This labels a particular category of tools that have several traditional uses, as for cutting sugar cane or clearing paths through thick undergrowth (Bock 1969:223).

Based on *technological function,* the way a given tool acts on matter or energy or both, there may be four basic tool types, although most tools are a combination of several basic types. The types are (1) containers, (2) media, (3) selectors, and (4) converters (Bock 1969).

Containers are tools used to store matter or energy over time while preserving its contents against loss or contamination. Since no container is perfect, there is always some deterioration of the contents over a period of time. But different containers can be evaluated as more or less suitable for various purposes. Tools that function primarily as containers include baskets, pottery, jars, wooden boxes, test-tubes, and bank vaults. When a container is evaluated in terms of what it can keep out, it may be termed a shield.

Media are tools used to transmit matter or energy through space while preserving their essential qualities. Pipe lines, irrigation ditches, copper wires, and railroad tracks are among media that people have devised for the transmission of matter or energy. When a medium is combined with a suitable container, the result is a *vehicle,* a tool used to transmit stored objects, energy, or information through space with minimal change over time. Carts, canoes, and space capsules are vehicles.

Arrangements of media designed to transmit or modify the application of power, force, or motion are referred to as *mechanisms*.

The wheel, lever, and pulley are among the two dozen or so simple machines that fall into this category. In general, mechanisms consist of several parts (media) arranged so that they transmit forces to one another in a predetermined manner. Thus, a rope used to pull a heavy object is simply a medium; but used in conjunction with a wheel in a pulley, it becomes part of a mechanism.

Selectors are tools used to discriminate among several inputs. Used in conjunction with a medium, a selector becomes a filter rejecting or absorbing certain inputs and passing others. A filter may lose its selective action in two ways. If it rejects all inputs, it acts as a shield. If it passes all inputs, it is simply a medium. When a filter is combined with a mechanism that alters its selective action, the result is a *valve,* a device that passes different kinds or quantities of input at different times. From this point of view, a *switch* is simply a valve with a finite number of positions. The ideal valve is one that acts as a shield when closed and allows free flow through its medium when opened. A selector combined with a container is a *trap,* a device that selects certain inputs and then stores its contents without loss or decay. Automobile oil filters are traps familiar to our culture. They allow oil to pass while trapping, or selecting out, harmful particles.

A *converter* is a tool that changes one kind or form of matter or energy into another. The ideal converter could change anything into anything else. For thousands of years the only converter of energy known to man was fire. The most important converters used today are engines and generators. An engine converts various forms of energy into mechanical motion by harnessing an energy source to a mechanism. A generator reverses this, converting mechanical into electrical energy for transmission via media or for storage in containers.

Techniques

A *technique* is a set of categories and plans used to achieve a given end. If I wish to go fishing, I need a line, hook, bait, and body of water. However, I could sit all day and catch nothing if I had no skill in fishing. A *skill* is the acquired ability to apply a given technique effectively and readily. One either knows or does not know a technique; but the skill of persons who share the same technical knowledge varies greatly.

The techniques and skills necessary for the survival of a human society must be shared and applied by specific categories of persons. Techniques are usually attributes of social roles. As such, they are expected to be manifested in culturally defined situations. The technological ability of a population also sets limits on its size and forms of social structure that the society may manifest (Bock

1969:217). The American Technological system is artificial in that it is the accumulation of a wealth of shared techniques and skill developments founded in the past.

The study of primitive technological systems provides a valuable perspective from which we can better appreciate our advantages as well as our debt to the past. The primitive was called upon to adapt to difficult and hazardous environmental conditions.

The Arunta have a technology simpler than that of many other societies. They do not weave baskets or cloth and do not make pottery. They wear virtually no clothing, in spite of some suffering from the cold. Their dwellings are simple brush shelters. Most of their artifacts are of stone, wood, and fur cordage. A few are of bone and hide. They modify stones for rough tools, which they abandon after use.

While most of their tools are disposable, a few permanent tools are made by flaking. They select a slightly tapered lump of stone about eight inches long, six inches in diameter, and relatively flat at the larger end. Holding the tapered end to the ground, the technician delivers a series of sharp blows to the flat end with a small piece of quartzite. The first blows, placed near the edge, knock off two flakes, which leave two flat surfaces that intersect one another along the stone's length. Additional blows detach a large flake with three or four surfaces. This serves as the working part of a knife, spear, or pick. Numerous attempts may have to be made before a proper tool is formed because of the varying quality of raw materials. These blades are four to five inches in length and may have additional chips removed, leaving a serrated edge.

Central Eskimo groups, such as the Netsilik, have developed various techniques and skills related to skin usage because of the availability of skins from the animals that inhabit their environment and the hunting skills they have developed (Asen Baliki 1970). Animal skins are highly useful in such intensely cold climates.

Caribou skin is used extensively for clothing because of its lightness, warm fur, and softness. The wearer is kept warm yet is free to move, in spite of numerous layers of clothing. Sealskin is tougher than caribou and more water resistant. It is more frequently used for kayaks than for clothing but does appear in pants, coats, some kinds of mittens, tents, shaman's masks and belts, and water containers.

The men skin the caribou; then the women, who do most of the skin work, spread the hides on the ground to dry. When especially soft skins are desired, the skins are slept in for a night to warm them. This process also stretches the skins, softening them further. The skin is then moistened and stretched out in the cold to freeze. Finally the women remove the subcutaneous tissue with a sharp scraper, and the men complete the process with an energetic scraping. The result is a soft, warm item of clothing.

The Nootka, like many other Indians of British Columbia, produce a wide variety of highly crafted items, mainly of red cedar (Philip Drucker 1965). Cedar logs are split into planks by wedges with different degrees of taper to control the direction of the cut. The planks are used in the large houses at the winter village sites near river mouths. House posts and roof timbers are often carved. They also craft wooden containers. A storage box is made of a single piece of wood. They also make dishes, spoons, ladles, bowls, trays, cradles, urinals, canteens, trinket boxes, masks, quivers, war clubs, shaman's wands, whistles, and totem poles.

Perhaps the most noteworthy item of the Nootka is the canoe made from cedar log halves. The hull is hollowed by small fires, the craftsman using wet moss to control the spread of the fire. The men complete the hollowing with axes. If a more seaworthy craft is desired, the beam is filled with water brought to a boil with hot stones. When the wood is soft, the hull is spread by driving in crosspieces and the water and stones are allowed to cool. Then, additional prow and stern pieces may be added to increase its seaworthiness. The joining is done with such skill that it is difficult to detect. The hull is sanded with dogfish skin or scouring rushes.

Cedar bark is used extensively. The women wear front aprons of cedar bark shreds held together across the top by several courses of twined fabric. The top of the body is covered by a cape and often a cedar robe. Men wear robes of yellow cedar bark and red bark hats when it rains. Newborn infants are dried with shredded cedar bark, their cradles are padded with it, and their heads are flattened by it. The body of a deceased Nootka is rolled in an old cedar bark mat for burial.

The Pocomchi of Guatemala utilize the back strap loom for weaving. The warp threads—the base threads stretched parallel to one another on the loom frame—are soaked in water used for making the tortilla, the bread replacement of the Pocomchi. These threads are stretched on the loom and divided into two sets of alternate threads. These are raised and lowered relative to one another to permit insertion of woof threads between them in one movement. A rod, called a heddle, is attached by short threads to every second warp strand. This makes it possible to raise one set of threads so that a shuttle, a small instrument containing the woof thread on a bobbin, can easily be passed between the two sets of warp threads. A second heddle is attached to the other half of the warp threads in the same way. Reversing the positions of the two sets of threads secures the previously inserted woof thread in place and makes it possible to pass the shuttle in the opposite direction. After a woof thread has been inserted, it may be packed tightly against the previous one by means of a batten, a bar across the width of the loom.

If the design is complex, there may be several shuttles, one for each color of yarn. With a back strap, tension is controlled by the weaver's body. The loom is thus positioned between two rods, the upper one attached to some immovable object and the lower one to a strap or belt stretched around the weaver's body. Forward and backward movements control the loom.

Social Influences

There is probably no aspect of economic life not influenced in some way by social, political, and religious aspects of life. The following are examples of this.

1. Production for the sake of social honor: Potlatch.
2. Economic well-being for political advance: Philippines.
3. Production wages for the sake of social and religious pursuits: United States.
4. Economic well-being for continuation of family and its place in society: Latin America.
5. Economic production to maintain one's standing among nations: Western nations and Russia; and to gain one's standing: the underdeveloped nations such as Zaire and the less technologically developed nations such as India and China.
6. Economic trade to bring people to festivals: Australia.

There is constant intrusion of other aspects of life into the economic life. Among the Maya-related Quiche in Guatemala, the emerging industrial complex constantly struggles against the encroachment of the old and its practices. The festival cycle calls for so many religious-oriented holidays that industry is often stopped. In the Maya-related Pocomchi area, crafts and industries other than farming are constantly competing for the time of their employees. A worker works only enough time in a given work period to make his basic living. He then retires to his farm. He associates his well-being with the land; he never wants to be far from it and unable to see it produce.

World views also enter into the practice of economic life. The Latin American views the land as the source of products that can be sold to produce income. The Maya of Central America see the land as a source of production. It is far more important to them that the land produce than that they be able to utilize the return from the produce. Thus the Indian is somewhat a "slave"—not to the boss, but to the land. The first concern in moving is "How will the land I am leaving be cared for?"

In understanding the economic structure as part of the total life-way of the Mayan Indian people, the following principles must be considered:

1. *Multicrop harvest.* In reality there is sufficient food in the Mayan area because of the varying altitudes and accompanying climates permitting a multicrop harvest. However, because corn and beans are the major staples, a short supply of these may result in "famine."

2. *Penny capitalism.* The penny is the primary monetary piece used in trading. The Indian economy is run on the basis of the penny. The Indians always have a penny for a purchase but seldom a dollar. Their perspective expands and contracts on the basis of what a penny will buy. There is minimum stress on luxury buying. It is enough that necessities are met.

3. *Rural market.* The market system regulates the movement of people within the ethnic group area. The market schedule dominates the time schedule of the people. It is the single most important activity of the Indians; so all other activities must wait until the market experience is fulfilled. It is primarily a social event. Indians on their way to market refuse to sell any or all of their produce until they get to the market. Otherwise, they would have no "reason" to go.

4. *Fiesta and the church.* The festival schedule provides the spending stimulus for the people. The major town festival is the high point of the spending year, much as is Christmas in North America. The festival makes spending legitimate, including the purchase of seldom eaten foods and new clothes, and the engaging in certain appropriate activities such as drinking and dancing.

5. *Work cooperation.* Few services call for monetary reward. Most work is done on a cooperative basis. Primary cooperation comes from family, secondary cooperation from friendship groups named *confradias* or brotherhoods, and tertiary cooperation from the community level supervised by people of Spanish background who speak that language.

6. *Specialization.* The Indian is primarily a farmer. Some, however, go into different lines of work and specialize—usually breaking their ties with both the Indian community and the land. They may become salesmen, carrying produce purchased in local markets to area markets.

7. *The patron-client relationship.* This is the key to economic production in Central America. Latins are oriented to the gain from products of the land; Indians are oriented to the

land. Thus both groups want to see it produce. This creates a balanced relationship for the good of the economy, though at times the Indian becomes an oppressed minority.

Technology, Economics, and Missions

The technology and economic system of a society is an integral part of the culture, as we have attempted to demonstrate. There are at least three reasons why an understanding of the technical and economic systems of a society are important to a person ministering in that society.

First, an understanding of the technology and economic system of a society helps us better understand that society and its people. A person could not really understand our society or the lives of our people without an understanding of such things as hourly wages, salaries, checking accounts, credit cards, income tax, and mortgages. An elementary knowledge of our banking and financial systems is basic to survival in our society. In the same way, we need to learn the technical and economic systems operating in the societies in which we wish to minister.

Second, an understanding of the technology and economic systems of a society helps us present the gospel in ways relevant to the hearers. In His teaching, Jesus drew heavily on the technology and economic system for illustrations. He spoke of farming and business in the parable of the vine grower (Matt. 20:1–16). He referred to the tax system, investing, sheepherding, and even house construction (Luke 20:20–25; 19:11–27; 15:4–7; 6:47–49).

Third, an understanding of the technology and economic systems of a society can aid in church planting. Where will you build a church? How? With what materials? Of what design? How will the tithe be determined in a barter economy? What will you do in a society where Sunday is market day? These and many other situations face the missionary as he or she enters another culture. An understanding of the technology and economic system of that society will be a real asset.

We tend to think of the technological and economic aspects of society as secular, but we must remember that God created vegetation and animal life and instructed the first man in utilizing these things (Gen. 2 and 3). God also instructed him to use the earth, not abuse it. The Christian has a responsibility to understand technology and economic systems in order to minister more effectively.

Questions for Discussion

1. What are the four characteristics about human beings that allow them to develop a complex technology? How do these four characteristics interact?
2. Can a person believe in the evolution of cultural technology without believing in the evolution of human beings? Explain.
3. What is the relationship between technology, economics, and culture?
4. How much Western technology should a missionary introduce when ministering among a people with a primitive culture? Why?

Suggested Reading

Bohannan, P., and Bohannan, L. 1968. *Tiv Economy*. A case study in economic anthropology taken from a tribal society in Africa.

Chayanov, A. V. 1966. *The Theory of Peasant Economy*. This work deals with peasant economies. It is recommended for those planning to work in peasant societies or those who have a scholarly interest in this area.

Dalton, G. 1967. *Tribal and Peasant Economies*. A collection of readings. It has a good introductory section followed by readings concerned with major culture areas.

Forde, C. D. 1963. *Habitat, Economy, and Society*. A good basic introduction to various forms of economic systems.

Hill, P. 1970. *Studies in Rural Capitalism in West Africa*. A study of a type of economic system found among various rural societies in Africa.

Malinowski, B. 1961. *Argonauts of the Western Pacific*. In this classic work, Malinowski describes the Kula Ring, a pattern of intervillage trading among the natives of the Trobriand Islands.

Sahlins, M. D. 1960. *Political Power and the Economy in Primitive Society;* 1972. *Stone-Age Economics*. A two-volume work dealing with the economic systems of less developed societies.

Tax, S. 1953. *Penny Capitalism*. A case study dealing with a Guatemalan Indian economy.

7

Role, Status, and Stratification

A man and his son were out for a drive when they were involved in a serious accident. The father was killed and the son was seriously injured. The boy was taken to the nearest hospital and rushed into the operating room. When the surgeon entered the room and saw the boy, the surgeon exclaimed, "I can't operate; that's my son!"

Wait a minute! I thought the boy's father was in the car with him and killed. He was, the surgeon was the boy's mother.

In the United States, when someone speaks of a surgeon, we immediately think of a man. Surgeon is generally a male role in our culture. However, in Europe many women are doctors, dentists, and barbers.

Indeed every person performs many roles in a society. In the opening anecdote the woman filled three roles: surgeon, mother, and wife. The roles people perform are associated with sex, age, education, and many other factors. Roles are also associated with statuses.

A *status* is a position or place in a social system and its attendant rights and duties. Status defines a place in a social system in relation to other places or statuses. Often a status has a value attached to it. In North American society, for example, a lawyer has a higher status than a janitor has.

Usually status is public, that is, there are symbols that signify the status. These symbols include titles and objects that indicate the status. Probably one of the clearest illustrations of titles and objects indicating status is in the U.S. Army. Soldiers have titles such as private, sergeant, captain, and general. Along with these titles are insignias that indicate the soldier's rank or status.

Although the status symbols of the military are very obvious and clear, the status symbols in other areas of society are understood by the culturally initiated. In North American society a gold band on the left ring finger of a person indicates marital status. A minister is called "Reverend" and may wear a clerical collar. A judge is called "Your Honor" and wears a robe. In many occupations statuses are indicated by unique uniforms such as those of policemen, firemen, nurses, pilots and others. Uniforms play an important function when the status of a person—for example, a policeman—needs to be quickly identified.

However, North American society is not the only society that utilizes status symbols. Among the Sudanese West Africans, the hair is parted into patterns of diamonds and squares indicating a person's social affiliations. Among the indigenous peoples of New Guinea, only political leaders wear hats. They are called "hatmen." Scarring the face is a status symbol among the Zaire Bantus. A male is not considered a man until his face has been scarred. Age groups are differentiated among the Tiv by patterns of facial scars. Among the Asari of the western highlands of New Guinea, the status of a woman's husband can be determined by the necklace she wears.

It is important for a person who works in another culture to be aware of the status symbols of that society. The symbols will guide one in knowing the place various individuals have in their society.

Role is the behavior, attitudes, and values associated with a particular status. Every status has a role, but the two are not the same thing. Role is a blueprint for the behavior associated with a status. Role behavior is usually predictable and others anticipate it. An instructor anticipates that students will come to an appointed room at an appointed time. Students anticipate that an instructor will come to the class at that time and conduct the class. When instructors and students behave as anticipated, the class can take place. When we go to a medical doctor, we anticipate that he will treat our illness. When we go to a barber, we anticipate that he will give us a haircut. No society could function if the behavior of its members was not predictable, at least to some extent.

Certainly "the functioning of societies depends upon the presence of patterns for reciprocal behavior between individuals"

(Linton 1936:113). In order to function properly in a new culture people need to know, not only the symbols of a status, but also the pattern of behavior or role that goes with it.

For example, a missionary nurse trained in the United States has learned his or her role in relation to physicians and patients. Also the nurse has learned that the role of a nurse has certain medical limitations. When the nurse begins to work in another culture he or she may find the role expectations are quite different. The nurse may be expected to perform procedures that would not be permitted in the United States. Or the nurse may find that he or she must relate to physicians in more or less formal ways.

Sociologist Robert K. Merton (1957) has put forth the concept of role-set. By role-set Merton means an array of roles that accrue to a particular status. For example, a medical doctor has one role or behavior pattern with patients, another with nurses, and still another with other doctors. Each of these relationships calls for a different behavior.

Statuses and roles are the major building blocks of social structure. If society is thought of as a network of relationships, then statuses are the connecting points, and roles are the connectors. It is through reciprocal behavior or roles that one status is related to another. A customer expects to be sold an item by a shopkeeper and the shopkeeper expects to be paid by the customer.

A status and its accompanying role exist apart from the individual that possesses them. That is, the doctor and patient relationship is more or less the same, regardless of who the doctor and patient are.

As an illustration of this concept, consider the instructions given new soldiers concerning saluting officers: "You are saluting the uniform (status) and not the man (individual)." One of the rights of an officer (status) is to be saluted (duty) by enlisted men (status). This does not mean that statuses exist apart from individuals, but a status has its rights and duties and its role regardless of the individual who fills that status.

Types of Status

Anthropologists distinguish between two types of statuses—ascribed and achieved (Linton 1936).

Ascribed Status

An *ascribed status* is one that a society assigns to an individual, usually on the basis of characteristics of birth such as sex, age, race or ethnic group, and social class. An individual usually is born into or inherits his or her ascribed statuses and has little or no chance of

changing them. However, ascribed statuses may facilitate enculturation for positions in the division of labor.

Some ascribed statuses are based on sex. All societies divide
statuses into male and female roles. Although biology limits certain
roles to women, such as giving birth and nursing infants, and
others to men, such as fathering children, it is society that assigns
most roles to one sex or the other. What may be a male role in one
society may be a female role in another.

Blanket weaving is a male role in Hopi society but a female
role in Navaho society. While hunting and fishing are predominately male roles in most societies, agricultural work is a female role in
almost as many societies as those in which it is a male role. In some
societies farming is practiced by both sexes. The presidency of the
United States is traditionally a male role. In some churches only a
male can become an ordained minister.

In many societies political offices are ascribed, and a specific
offspring of the present officeholder holds exclusive right to
succession. In England, the eldest son of the reigning monarch,
called the crown prince, has the exclusive right of succession to the
throne of England. The monarchy of England is inherited (ascribed), not earned or achieved.

Age is ascribed because it is based on time of birth. Some
statuses are ascribed on the basis of age. Among the Nuer of Africa,
age is an important status consideration. In that society every
individual is categorized or stratified in terms of an age-set system.
Every male is junior to, equal to, or senior to all other males in the
society. A male's behavior or role toward another male is based on
his age relationship or status relationship with him. He acts
superior toward a younger male, informal with an equal male, and
shows deference to an older male. Women are also plugged into the
system by age, but it is based on their relationship to a male. A
woman is someone's daughter, wife, or mother.

Birth order, as well as age, is ascribed. In some societies birth
order determines inheritance rights. *Primogeniture* refers to a system
of inheritance in which the family's wealth and position pass to the
first-born son. The Hebrews of the Old Testament practiced
primogeniture. The oldest son inherited the birthright, a double
portion, and a special blessing. Primogeniture is practiced among
many primitive and traditional societies today.

Besides age and sex, social class also determines status. A
social class system that allows no vertical mobility is called a *caste
system*. A person born into a caste society finds himself ascribed a
status by the chance of birth. India is a classic example of a caste
society. Indian society has four castes, from highest to lowest:
Brahmans, Kshatriya, Vaisyas, and Sudra. Those not belonging to
one of these casts are considered "outcastes." Each of the four

castes is composed of many subcastes called *jati*. An Indian's birth determines his or her place in the social system and is unchangeable throughout that person's life.

Race and ethnic groups are also status determiners. In the United States many black people have an inferior social standing that is reflected in their occupational and economic status. Although the American constitution and laws guarantee racial equality, America has not achieved racial equality. In both Canada and Mexico the native Americans are discriminated against and given a lower status. Apartheid in the Union of South Africa has created a racial caste system there.

Racism is a sin and must be seen as such by all Christians.[1] This is especially important for those planning to minister in another culture. The Bible teaches that all people are part of God's creation and have a common origin (Gen. 1:27–28). The Bible also teaches that God is not a respecter of persons and accepts all people equally (Acts 10:34; James 2:8–10). One of the real contributions of anthropology has been the demonstration that many differences in human behavior are cultural, not biological. A person who wants to truly minister to another, must be able to accept the other as an equal.

Achieved Status

While ascribed status is assigned to a person, achieved status is obtained through choice and achievement. In American society many statuses are achieved. Political offices are achieved through election rather than ascribed by birth as among the Mossi of Africa. Occupations are achieved through education, training, ability, and choice rather than being ascribed as they are in traditional Indian caste society.

Some statuses are both ascribed and achieved. Only a woman (ascribed) can become a mother, but not all woman become mothers (achieved). Likewise, only a man (ascribed) can become a husband, but not all men are husbands (achieved). In the State of Illinois only persons over sixteen years of age (ascribed) can become licensed drivers, but not all persons over sixteen are licensed drivers (achieved). Although statuses such as those mentioned above may be conceived as both ascribed and achieved, for practical purposes they are considered achieved statuses.

Vertical Status

Although a status is a place or position in a social network, that place or position usually has a rank or value attached to it. The

---

[1]Racism is the assumption of one's own racial superiority and the arrogance and behavior patterns that accompany that assumption.

hierarchical ordering of statuses is called *vertical status*. This can be seen in the Indian caste society and the military rank system, as well as in our own general society. We see a vertical difference between a janitor and a lawyer.

In societies where there is vertical mobility, that is, where individuals are able to move up and down the hierarchy of statuses, people usually seek to move up. The means and modes of upward mobility are provided by the culture.

There are three major avenues of upward mobility in traditional Latin society. The primary avenue is marriage. In Latin society status is carried by extended families as much as by individuals. If a person can marry into a family of higher status, he or she has the potential to move up in status to the family's level. The second avenue is education. An educated person has a better chance of getting a higher status job and moving in higher status circles than an uneducated person has. Wealth is the third avenue of upward mobility. However, wealth without a family name or education is the least desirable avenue of moving upward because it is more difficult for a person with wealth alone to be accepted by the upper-status families.

Movement up or down the status hierarchy is referred to as *social mobility*. In a caste system, there is very little mobility, either vertical or horizontal. In a society such as the United States there is more opportunity for social mobility, as the following cases of upward mobility illustrate:

> In 1976 James Kong and his wife arrived in America from Korea. Each of them worked two jobs, saving every penny possible. They eventually bought the small tailor shop where Mrs. Kong had worked as a seamstress.
>
> The Kongs are now the owners of five dry-cleaning stores and a wholesale plant. Their businesses gross over a million dollars a year.
>
> In 1962, Joe Nkash came to New York from Israel at age 19. He had only about 25 dollars. He spent his first nights in New York sleeping in subway stations. He started doing menial labor in the garment district.
>
> He went on to found Jordache Enterprises. His annual salary is over a million dollars a year. (*U.S. New and World Report,* April 12, 1982:50)

A person may also move downward in the status hierarchy, for example:

> For twenty years Mr. Weaver worked as a truck driver and mechanic in Oklahoma. In 1982 he was laid off from his job, which had paid $16,000 annually. Less than a year later his unemployment benefits ran out. When he could not

make the mortgage payments, he lost his house. He and his pregnant wife lived in their car for four months. They moved into a camper without utilities just before the birth of their child. (*The Wall Street Journal,* March 7, 1983:1).

Horizontal Status

Horizontal status refers to statuses on the same level or of the same rank. Horizontal mobility is usually easier to accomplish than vertical mobility. It is easier for a machine operator to change companies than for him to move up to the position of foreman. Much of the mobility in American society is horizontal rather than vertical. When a minister changes churches, this is usually a horizontal move.

Role Conflicts

Role has been defined as the behavior that accompanies a status. When there is a conflict within a role or between roles, it is referred to as *role conflict*. Role conflict may result from conflicts within a single role, as the expectations of others for a pastor, for example, as the following humorous description illustrates:

> He is young yet has many years of experience. He has a sense of humor while being serious minded. He regularly calls on the members of the church yet is always in the office. He enjoys working with the young people and never neglects the older folks. He dresses fashionably yet is modest in appearance. He preaches against sin but never offends anyone. His sermons are profound yet entertaining. He deals thoroughly with issues in his messages yet never preaches more than twenty minutes. (Source unknown.)

Besides conflicts within a role, there may also be conflicts between some of the roles a person may have. A man may be a husband, a father, a son, a teacher, a friend, and have many other statuses at the same time. Many times the change of one status brings the role of the new status into conflict with the role of one of the other old statuses. For example, two men may be friends and co-workers. If one of them is promoted to the position of foreman, his role as foreman may come into conflict with his role as friend when he has to supervise his former co-worker.

Role conflict can also result from a change in the social structure. An example of this type of conflict can be found among the Soga of Uganda, Africa. The Soga are a patrilineal people, that is, inheritance is only through the father's line, including inheritance of political offices. The lineage from which the rulers came were considered royal lineages and others were considered commoner lineages.

When the British colonized Uganda, they initially worked through the existing political system. However, as time went by and the British began to consolidate their holdings, they began to develop their own administrative organization. When they needed an administrator, they chose the person they felt was best qualified, regardless of his lineage. When a person of commoner lineage was assigned to an administrative position, he faced a role conflict between his new status as an administrator and his status as a commoner. This also created role conflict for the rest of the people who were accustomed to being led only by members of royal lineages.

This example illustrates the problems that may arise when an outsider tampers with an existing social structure without first understanding the structure. What the British thought to be a more efficient system was actually less efficient and created new problems. In most cases, the best way to work in another society is to work with the system, not against it.

Two ways of resolving role conflicts are (1) changing one or more of the statuses with which whole roles are in conflict and (2) changing the role behavior that goes with one or more of the statuses. In the illustration of the friends and co-workers, when one was promoted to being foreman over the other, the role conflict resulting from the promotion could have been handled in either of two ways. The foreman could have discontinued his friendship with his former co-worker and started new friendships among his fellow foreman, or he could have changed some aspects of his role as a foreman and of his role as friend to make them more compatible.

Three additional processes for handling role conflict are *rationalization, compartmentalization,* and *adjudication* (Horton and Hunt 1972). The first two are subconscious processes. If they become conscious, they will cease to function. It is the very fact that they are subconscious that makes them functional.

Rationalization is a psychological defense process in which an individual recasts a difficult situation into one that is acceptable. The student turned down by a certain graduate school rationalizes by telling himself the school really did not have anything to offer him. People rationalize racism by seeing members of other races as less than human or genetically inferior.

Compartmentalization is the process of boxing off one's roles from each other and accepting the obligations and responsibilities of each role separately. This is how a Mafia chieftan at the office can coldly order a person murdered and be a sweet, compassionate, loving husband and father at home. It is also how a Christian businessman can sing in the choir on Sunday and be involved in shady business practices on Monday.

While rationalization and compartmentalization are subconscious processes, *adjudication* is a conscious process involving delegating decisions that will lead to role conflict for a third party. This relieves the individual of responsibility and guilt. If a Christian businessman has not successfully compartmentalized his role as a Christian from his role as a businessman, he may let his partner, his superior, or his subordinate carry out the shady business deal.

Christian: Status and Role

When a person becomes a Christian, he or she acquires a new status with its rights and duties and a role or expected behavior. Christianity is an achieved status rather than an ascribed one. That is, one is not born a Christian. Having Christian parents does not make one a Christian. A person chooses to be a Christian and achieves that status by an act of faith in Jesus Christ.

Christian status is also vertical. In India most Christian converts come from the low castes and outcastes. Christianity is a relatively low status in India. However, in Japan many converts have come from the upper class and from among the more educated. In Japan, Christianity is a relatively high status.

Christianity as a status also has a role. Although the role of a Christian has similarities across cultures, it also has differences. For example, many Christians from the northern United States see the use of tobacco as un-Christian behavior. To some Christians from the southern United States, this is not an issue. In the United States, the use of alcoholic beverages is considered un-Christian by most fundamentalist Christians. However, in Europe, the use of alcoholic beverages is generally not an issue among evangelical Christians, at least among those not influenced by American missionaries.

In all cultures Christians often find that their Christian status brings them into role conflict with one of their other statuses. These conflicts can be overcome by changing some statuses or by modifying role behavior.

Stratification

In most social systems, statuses are distributed on a vertical scale. *Stratification* refers to this hierarchy of statuses. Stratification is a hierarchy of inequality. This differentiation may be based on descent, wealth, skill, physical appearance, race, and many other attributes or a combination of attributes.

A *social class* is made up of those people on the social scale who see themselves as equal and are seen as equal by others on the scale. This equality is usually relative rather than absolute. Social class may be based on any factor or combination of factors a society sees as determining social class. In American society, social class is based on several factors. Three of the major factors are wealth, power, and prestige, which are interrelated. Each tends to reinforce the others.

The operation of stratification and social class can be illustrated by the farming community of Alcalá de la Sierra in the mountains of southern Spain. There are about four hundred families in Alcalá. In this community, farm plots vary in size from a couple of acres to thousands of acres. Social class is primarily based on land owner-ship. About twenty families own two-thirds of the farmland in Alcalá. Much of the land is farmed by tenant farmers.

The lowest class in Alcalá is that of the propertyless beggars. Just above them are the landless domestic help and farm laborers, and next are the tenant farmers. Though these farmers do not own the land, they can work it as their own, giving a percentage of the harvest to the owner. Above the tenant farmers are the small landowners.

The middle class of Alcalá consists of farmers with moderate-size land holdings, as well as shopkeepers, government officials, and professionals, such as teachers. The upper class is composed of those with extensive land holdings. Land is so important for reckoning status and social class in Alcalá that those who have made their wealth in manufacturing or some other enterprise use the money to buy land.

The lower and middle classes of Alcalá are almost completely locked into their positions. The middle class guards its position against the lower class, while the upper class guards its position against the middle class. The members of the upper class reap profits from their extensive land holdings, allowing them to buy still more land. They are also the only ones who can afford to send their children away to school. In addition, they hold the major political offices. They allow their children to marry only within their class. The male and female members of the upper class are addressed as *Don* and *Doña,* terms of respect reserved for superiors.

The stratification systems of different societies vary along a continuum from a classless society, such as that of the Pocomchi Indians of Guatemala, to a society where each extended family is a separate stratum, such as traditional Latin American society (see figure 7-1).

The Pocomchi Indians see each other as equals and members of the same class. No one sees himself or herself as of higher or lower status than anyone else or as being richer or poorer than anyone else. They do not see themselves as having varying degrees of influence. Some people have larger homes and some have smaller; some farm more land, some less. However, this does not become the basis for social distinctions and is not associated with authority or privilege. The Pocomchi can be considered a classless society. Attempts by researchers to get them to rank the members of their society have ended in failure. They can see the differences in rank among the Latins in the larger society, but see no such distinctions among themselves.

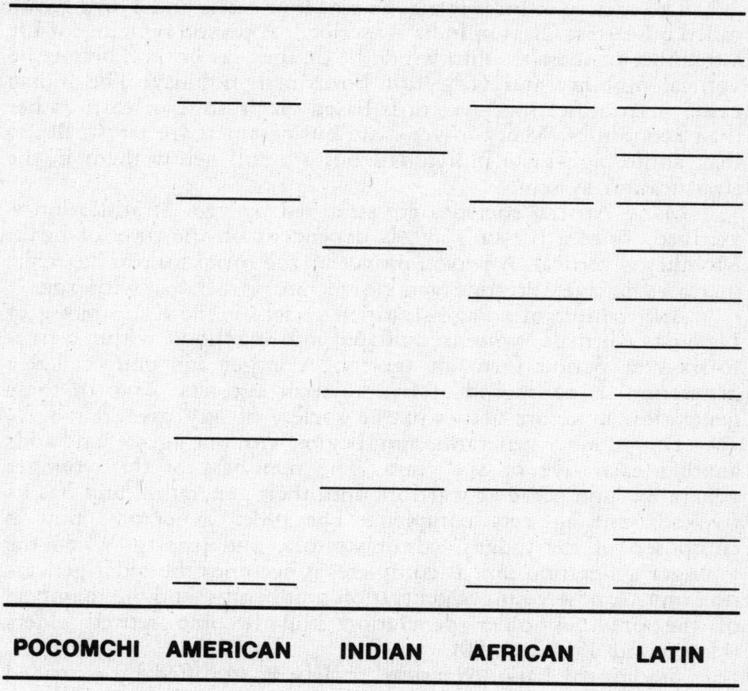

POCOMCHI   AMERICAN   INDIAN   AFRICAN   LATIN

Figure 7-1. CLASS DIVISIONS IN FIVE SOCIETIES. The Pocomchi are a classless society. American society is divided into three classes with each class subdivided into upper and lower. Indian society has four castes plus outcastes, making five distinct classes. African society is divided by age groups, while traditional Latin society is stratified by extended families.

American society is basically a three-class society: lower,

middle, and upper, with each class divided into two subclasses, upper and lower.[2] Although American society is advertised as a society with achieved status and vertical social mobility, in reality it is essentially an ascribed-class and horizontally mobile society. "Most people die as members of the same class into which they were born" (Hammond 1971:209). Although most American young people can and do enter an occupation different from that of their parents, it is usually in the same social class. The American stratification system tends to be dominated by economics.

The society in India is made up of four castes and a fifth group called outcastes. Class in India is ascribed. A person remains for life a member of the class into which he or she was born. There is no vertical mobility and very little horizontal mobility. The Indian caste, or stratification, system is based on prestige or caste rather than economics. Many lower-caste businessmen are far wealthier than some high-caste individuals but are still below them in the stratification system.

Many African societies are stratified by age. Stratification is ascribed, since a person's age is dependent on the time of birth. Mobility is vertical. A person moves up the social scale as he or she increases in age. Prestige and power are associated with age.

An example of an age-stratified society is the Karimojong of Uganda. All males who are initiated into manhood within a five-to-six-year period form an age-set. A larger age unit, called a generation, is composed of five adjacent age-sets. Two of these generation units are active in the society at any given time.

The younger generation unit begins with one age-set and adds another each five or six years. The members of this younger generation unit serve as warriors until their generation unit has its five adjacent age-sets complete. The older generation unit is composed of the judges, administrators, and priests. When the younger generation unit is complete, it becomes the older generation unit. A new younger generation unit begins, and the members of the previous older generation unit become retired elders (Hammond 1971:189–90).

Traditional Latin American society is stratified by extended family. Each family sees itself as being above or below every other family. Many sociologists and anthropologists have tried to understand Latin society in terms of the American three-class system. In the large urban areas, this approach has some validity; but in traditional Latin society, class analysis breaks down. To fully understand the operation of traditional Latin society, the analyst must approach it by seeing each extended family as an individual stratum. Strata are ascribed by birth and may be achieved by

---

[2]The middle class, however, is divided into upper, middle, and lower.

marriage, education, and wealth. As in American society, vertical mobility is possible but usually not probable, and at best, it is slow.

Stratification of the Church in American Society

Just as societies are stratified, so are their social institutions. Religion, as a social institution represented by the institutional church, is stratified in America along class lines. This holds for the Roman Catholic Church, major Protestant denominations, and cults (see figure 7-2).

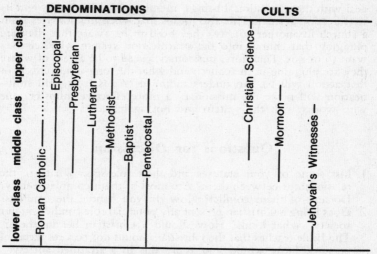

Figure 7-2. RELIGIOUS STRATIFICATION IN AMERICA

In America, though the Roman Catholic church spans the entire society, its strength is in the middle and lower classes. Among the Protestant denominations, the Episcopalian church is the church of the upper class, the Presbyterian church is next, and the Pentecostal church is basically of the lower class. Among the cults, Christian Science is the cult of the upper class, Mormonism of the middle, and Jehovah's Witnesses the lower.

Obviously, all religious groups draw from all classes. What is being referred to is the majority of their memberships. Professor T. Edwin Boling points out:

> Although religious organizations are not homogeneous with regard to social class, their members tend to be drawn

predominately from a single social class, providing a consistent pattern of religious socialization within denominations and subcultures (1975:74).

This stratification of religious groups is culturally logical. People tend to associate with others of their social class in most activities, including religious activities.

Although we recognize that God is no respecter of persons and that there are only two classes of people according to Scripture, saved and unsaved, we must also recognize that people are part of their culture. If we are to minister to people effectively, we have to deal with them as cultural beings, members of their society and its stratification system. This also means that when missionaries plant a church in another society, they need to be aware that they are plugging that church into the stratification system whether they want to or not. Therefore, missionaries need to be aware of where they are plugging in the church and what the long-range effects of that action will be. An understanding of status, role, and stratification will make the missionary a more effective minister, one who works with the system and not against it.

Questions for Discussion

1. List some of your statuses and their role-sets. What are the relationships between them? Are most of them complementary? Do any of them conflict? How do you handle the conflicts?
2. Does being a Christian present any potential role conflicts in our society? What kinds? How should a Christian handle them?
3. The Bible teaches that the Christian should not be a respecter of persons. How would you apply this in a stratified society?
4. How might becoming a Christian affect the status of the member of another culture?
5. Think of some ways in which being aware of the concepts of status and role might help a missionary adjust to a new culture.

Suggested Reading

Bendix, R., and Lipset, M. 1966. *Class, Status, and Power*. A major collection of readings dealing with class, status, and power. These readings on the theories of class structure are highly recommended.

Bottomore, T. B. 1966. *Classes in Modern Society*. A good introduction to the field of class and social structure. This is a short, easy-to-read volume.

Linton, R. 1936. *The Study of Man*. An early introductory anthropology text. The chapter on status and role is a classic. Most work in the area of status and role builds on the foundation laid by Linton.

Mayer, K., and Buckley, W. 1970. *Class and Society*. This work deals with stratification, class, and power. It contains a good section on the major types of stratification systems in complex societies. Also deals with social mobility.

Mead, M. 1950. *Male and Female*. A classic work by the well-known anthropologist. This book deals with sex roles in several cultures. The last part of the book deals with sex roles in America. Even though this work is over twenty-five years old and woefully out of date, many of the principles and insights are still applicable today.

Sahlins, M. 1958. *Social Stratification in Polynesia*. Describes the interrelationship between kinship and stratification in these societies. The first chapter is a good introduction to social stratification in kin-based societies.

8

Marriage and Family

A young man from India came to a midwestern Christian college for his graduate work. He brought his new bride with him. The Indian wife became acquainted with the wife of an American student. They often got together to talk.

One day they discussed how they met their husbands. The girl from India explained that her parents had selected the young man for her to marry. Because she came from a Christian family, her parents first checked to see if he was a Christian. Then they checked his family, his education, and other important matters. When the parents were satisfied, he was presented to her for her approval. A week after they met, they were married.

How awful, thought the American wife. She explained that she dated several fellows until she found the one she wanted to marry. How awful, thought the girl from India. She asked, "Do you mean you had to try out several different men and then make the choice yourself? In India our parents make the choice; so we know it is the right one."

While there are diverse schemes for forming marriages, the family unit is found in all societies. Specifically, the unit is composed of the husband, his wife, and their immature children. After sampling 250 societies, George Murdock (1949) concluded

143

that no matter what type of family unit existed in a given society, every society recognized a husband, a wife, and their immature children as a distinct social unit.

Why is the family a universal social institution? The answer is found in the biological make-up of humans and in their societal living pattern.

Biological Basis for the Family

Most animals become sexual creatures during limited periods of time when the female is in the state of *estrus,* or "heat." The female animal is not excited by external stimuli, such as the advances of an attractive male, but rather by the activity of her hormonal system. Most female mammals have an *estrous* cycle marked by the beginning of the estrus period. It is only during the short estrus period that the female is able to conceive. During this period, the female animal's hormonal system stimulates the female to seek sexual activity. Most animals participate in sexual activity only during the female animal's estrus period.

As opposed to the lower forms of animals, the human female is not limited to specific periods of sexual receptivity but can engage in sexual activity at any time. While the lower forms of animals are internally stimulated by their hormonal systems, the human female is externally stimulated. Whereas among lower forms of animals sex is primarily a physical act, among humans it is often psychological as well as physical. The sex act is usually associated with emotional states.

Because human sex needs are more or less continuous, and usually associated with emotional states, humans need more or less permanent sex partners. Marriage is the social mechanism used by human societies to designate or recognize legitimate sex partners. Although this mechanism varies from culture to culture, it is present in some form in all cultures.

Sex is more than a biological and psychological drive. It is God's gift of life and love. In keeping with the functional view of creation, God ordained sex to serve two functions. The first is to propagate the race (Gen. 1:27–28).

Although sex serves a reproductive function in all of the animal kingdom, it serves a second function among humans. It reinforces the relationship between a man and a woman (Gen. 2:24; Prov. 5:18–19; Eph. 5:22–31). Sex is two people's sharing of each other, a physical intimacy that expresses the spiritual intimacy between them. Sex is God-ordained. It is not just for reproduction but also for expression of love between a husband and wife. Sex is a beautiful thing. Only the misuse of sex is ugly and sordid.

Another biological basis for the family is the long maturation period of the human infant. This encourages the continuation of the sexual partnership that conceived the baby.

Young monkeys are born with well-developed bones and muscles. They can fend for themselves and gather their own food as soon as they are weaned, a month or two after birth. The human baby is totally helpless without the nurture and protection of its parents or other adult humans. The human child has the longest maturation period of any animals. The child is dependent on adults at least until sexual maturity (puberty) and until the child has acquired a minimal number of social and technical skills.

Sociological Basis for the Family

Humans are more than biological creatures. They are also social, culture-bearing creatures. Human children not only have a long period of biological dependence on their parents, they also depend on their parents to teach them what they need to know to survive in their culture. The process by which children acquire culture so that it becomes a part of them is called *enculturation*.

Since humans appear to have few instincts, they must learn most of their behavior. In all cultures a large part of this teaching job falls to the family. Even in Western, industrialized countries with extensive school systems, a child's most important learning still takes place in the family setting. It is in the family setting that a child learns to walk, talk, and interact with other humans.

A second sociological function of the family involves status and role. Where does a newborn child fit into the societal network? The family gives its children status, plugging them into the societal network. All of a newborn's statuses are ascribed. As children grow and become active participants in their society, more and more of their statuses become achieved. However, they will always carry many of their earlier ascribed statuses.

Malinowski (1955) has developed the concept known as the *principle of legitimacy,* which states that all cultures have rules of legitimacy under which a child, ideally, is to be born. Or, to say it another way, all cultures have a class of births labeled illegitimate.

Sociologically, according to Malinowski, the purpose of marriage is not to legitimize sex but to legitimize parenthood. In all societies—including matrilineal societies, where the mother's brother seems to play such an important role—both the mother and the father have a role in the enculturation process, though it may vary from culture to culture.

William J. Goode (1961) cites a Caribbean society that, on the surface, seems to refute Malinowski's principle. There about half the births are illegitimate. However, the norms of legitimacy still exist and marriage is the ideal. (The fact that half the births are called illegitimate demonstrates there is a principle of legitimacy functioning.) Also, a legitimate child enjoys a higher status and has social advantages over the illegitimate child.

In all societies the family also prepares the child for his or her social roles. The earliest training is usually in the area of sex roles. The child is taught sex-appropriate behavior, given sex-appropriate toys, and pointed to sex-appropriate adult models. The child is also reacted to and interacted with according to his or her sex. In North American culture if a girl gets into a fight, "she isn't very ladylike." However, if a boy fights, the response is "Boys will be boys."

Besides its biological care for the child, the family provides the child with a place in society and teaches him or her how to get along in that society. It is easy to see why the family is so critical to the maintenance of society.

Social Mechanisms for the Maintenance of the Family

The need for sex partners to stay together and raise their offspring is so important to the existence of human society that the family is found in all societies. Because the family is the key to the maintenance of the society, all societies have developed mechanisms to encourage the maintenance of the family.

Among the Karimojong of East Africa, the social mechanism for maintaining the family is the *bride price*. If a young man wants to marry a girl, he must pay a bride price to her father. If a man's wife leaves him, the bride price must be returned. Often the bride price has been consumed, since it is usually paid in livestock. Therefore the father of the wife will make her return to her husband because he cannot repay the bride price. Usually a man will not leave a woman for whom he has paid dearly.

Another means of paying for a bride is by working for the bride's parents. This is called *bride service*. Among the Kekchi of the highlands of Guatemala the groom is expected to work for his in-laws for several years to pay for his bride. In the Old Testament we find that Jacob worked seven years for his wife Leah and seven years for his wife Rachel (Gen. 29:18–30).

Among the West Africans a similar social mechanism is used. But in this case, the bride's father pays the groom a dowry. Again, if the marriage is dissolved, the dowry must be returned. Both of these social mechanisms are economic in nature.

In addition to economic mechanisms, legal mechanisms, such as the strict divorce laws in Russia, are used to maintain families. After the Communist revolution and takeover, the new Communist leaders, thinking that rules pertaining to sex and fidelity were only part of a Christian ethic, encouraged premarital sex and enacted laws that made obtaining a divorce as easy as getting married. As they began to see their society disintegrate, they realized the rules for family maintenance were sociologically sound. Today it is quite difficult to get a divorce in Russia and promiscuity is officially discouraged.

In addition to the use of economics and law, religion is also utilized as a social mechanism for the maintenance of the family. This is illustrated by the strict rules of the Roman Catholic Church against divorce. A person's salvation is used to maintain the family, since divorce is classified as a mortal sin.

Whatever form these social mechanisms take, their purpose is the same: to maintain the family and ultimately the society.

Marriage

What is marriage? Marriage is sometimes easier to describe than define. One biblical picture of marriage is found in Genesis 24:67: "Then Isaac brought her into his mother Sarah's tent, and took Rebekah, and she became his wife" (KJV). My wife and I stood before an ordained minister in a church in Maryland and repeated some ritualistic expressions, after which he declared us husband and wife. Marriage is a social institution, that is, a pattern of norms and customs that define and control the relationship between a man and a woman and the relationship between them and the rest of society.

Potential Mates

Whom may a person marry? Not all those of the opposite sex of one's same age are potential marriage partners. There are two general sociological rules used in defining potential mates. The first is known as *endogamy*. In an endogamous society a person selects a mate from within a culturally defined group of which both are members. Endogamy was practiced among the Hebrews of the Old Testament. Abraham sent a servant back to Haran to obtain a wife from among his own family for his son Isaac. Among the Arabs today a form of endogamy, known as *parallel cousin marriage*, is practiced. A man has the first right to the daughter of his father's brother. This is the ideal marriage. She may not marry anyone else, unless the son of her father's brother marries another or releases her.

The second general sociological rule in defining potential mates is *exogamy*. This requires that potential mates come from different groups as defined by the culture. *Simple exogamy* is the prohibition of marrying a genetically related kinsman. *Restricted exogamy* prohibits marriage to certain genetically related kinsmen but prescribes marriage to other genetically related persons, not considered kinsmen by the culture, as ideal. One of the most common forms of restricted exogamy is *cross-cousin marriage*, the marriage of a man to the daughter of his mother's brother.

Restricted exogamy is a functional mechanism, used primarily to reinforce alliances. This is used especially to tie together groups that may already be tied together genetically but that are not seen as tied together by the culture. In many of the societies where cross-cousin marriage is practiced, the male's genetic role in reproduction is not understood, although it is realized that sexual intercourse is necessary for conception. These societies may not recognize the genetic ties that are obvious to medically informed Westerners.

Incest Taboo

All societies observe a special aspect of exogamy known as the *incest taboo*.[1] The incest taboo is the prohibition of mating with or marrying a close kinsman. Although the cultural definition of a close kinsman differs from culture to culture, the incest taboo always includes the prohibition of marriage between brother and sister and between parent and child.

Three exceptions to the brother–sister incest taboo are found in history. Brother–sister marriage was practiced among the royal families of Egypt, Hawaii, and the Incas. However, in these cases it applied only to the royal families, not to the rest of society. In each case the royal family was considered divine, thus unable to mate with mere mortals. To sustain the royal line, they had to engage in sibling marriage.

Anthropologists have speculated on the origin of the incest taboo, especially since it appears to be a universal phenomenon. Two early anthropologists, Lewis Henry Morgan (1877) and Edward Westermarck (1894), theorized that early man became aware of genetic deterioration resulting from close inbreeding. To preserve the race, early man placed a strong prohibition on close inbreeding. Although this view is still popularly believed today, the fact is that inbreeding does not necessarily produce physical deterioration.

> Inbreeding does no more than intensify the phenotypic traits that the inbreeding population possessed at the outset. Recessive traits have a better chance of obtaining somatic realization where inbreeding is marked. If undesirable recessives are in the stock, they may well come to fore, and deterioration may then result. Nevertheless, it is equally true that inbreeding intensifies the influence of dominant traits. A stock with desirable dominants becomes stronger. The end result may be good or bad; it all depends on the distribution

---

[1] *Taboo* is a Polynesian word used by anthropologists to mean religiously inspired prohibitions against some form of behavior.

of traits with respect to dominance and desirability (Hoebel 1972:398–99)

Westermarck (1894) also postulated another theory to explain the incest taboo. He said people are so repulsed by the idea of having sexual relations with a close family member that they have initiated this rule. However, this is dismissed by anthropologists who answer, if it is so repulsive, why do you need a rule against it? Rules are created only to keep people from doing what they would do if there were no rule.

Malinowski (1927) sees the incest taboo as a functional mechanism for the maintaining of the family. We saw earlier the importance of the family to the maintenance of society. He maintains that sexual relations between any family members, except the mother and father, would disrupt the family with rivalry and jealousy. Malinowski was greatly influenced by Freud's concept of the Oedipus complex and saw the incest taboo as a mechanism for eliminating sexual rivalry in the family.

Talcott Parsons (1954) also sees the incest taboo as functional, though different from that hypothesized by Malinowski. While Malinowski sees the incest taboo as a mechanism for maintaining the family, Parsons sees the incest taboo as a mechanism for education of the young and getting them to leave the home. Parsons claims all of a young person's needs are met in the home: nourishment, shelter, protection, companionship, and affection. Parsons sees the incest taboo as denying maturing young people satisfaction, in the home, of their new and strong need for sex. Since the young people cannot have that need met in the home, they are forced to learn the skills necessary to leave the home and to find a mate.

First Edward Tylor (1871) and later Leslie White (1949) suggested that the incest taboo came into being as a mechanism to promote alliances between groups. Tylor said there was "the simple practical alternative between marrying-out and being killed-out" (1888:267). By marrying-out, people would have a larger family and a wider circle to call on for support, help, and defense. White suggests that those groups that initiated an incest taboo survived and those that did not died off; thus the incest taboo developed as a survival mechanism.

The Bible sets forth the incest taboo in Leviticus 18:6–16. It is written from the male point of view and forbids a man to have sexual relations with his mother, his father's wife (not his mother), his sister (full or half), his granddaughter by either his son or daughter, his aunts on both sides (by blood and marriage), his daughter-in-law, or his sister-in-law. The wording in this passage indicates that when a person has sexual relations with one of these forbidden partners, the offense is against the forbidden partner's rightful partner.

For example, verse 16 says, "You shall not have intercourse with your brother's wife; she belongs to your brother" (Amplified Bible). The biblical incest taboo seems to be functional in nature. It is concerned with avoiding jealousy and maintaining family relations. The Bible seems to see incest as a source of jealousy and disruption in the family. This, of course, makes sense, since God's commands are not arbitrary but for our good.

Levirate Marriage

Levirate marriage is a mechanism for continuing the family. Under this system, if a woman's husband dies and leaves her childless, she must marry her brother-in-law (levir in Latin), her husband's brother, to continue the family. This type of marriage is usually found in patrilineal societies in order to continue the male line.[2] Levirate marriage was practiced among the Hebrews. It was commanded in Deuteronomy 25:5: "If brothers are living together and one of them dies without a son, his widow must not marry outside the family. Her husband's brother shall take her and marry her and fulfill the duty of a brother-in-law to her." Apparently levirate marriage was still practiced in Jesus' day, as the Sadducees asked Jesus about it in Matthew 22:23–33.

Sororate Marriage

Sororate marriage is another mechanism for the continuation of the family. Under this system, if a man's wife dies without bearing children, he must marry her sister to continue the family. This type of marriage is common among matrilineal societies. It is practiced among most North American tribes with the exception of the people of the Pueblo area (Hoebel 1972:409). Sororate marriage should not be confused with sororal polygyny, which will be discussed later in this chapter.

Obtaining a Mate

The method of obtaining a mate that is widely practiced in the United States is commonly called "courtship." Under this system, a person finds his or her own spouse, usually by a process known as dating. Although parents are usually consulted about the choice of a spouse, they rarely make the choice. However, in many parts of the world, the person to be married is usually consulted about the choice but rarely makes the choice. That is left to the parents or some other designated adult. In some societies a middleman is used

[2] A patrilineal society is a society where descent is traced through the father. This is explained in greater detail in chapter 9.

to arrange marriages. In India the *gor,* a type of marriage broker, bargains for the families of the bride and groom. Each family wants to give as little as possible and gain as much as possible in terms of rank and wealth. The parents, of course, are also concerned that the marriage will be good for their child.

Elopement

Elopement is not found only in America, where marriage is based on romance, but is practiced in almost every society in the world. It is a mechanism for marrying a desirable mate when it would otherwise be against the marriage rules of that society. Among the Kurnai of Australia, the marriage rules make it almost impossible for a young man to take a wife. The old men dominate the society and have first choice of the young women. A young man and woman often elope to marry. After they have their first child, they may return to their village, where they receive a ceremonial "beating" and are accepted as legitimately married.

Wife-Capture

We have all seen the cartoons of the cave man dragging a clubbed woman back to his cave to be his mate. Although we are amused by these cartoons, *wife-capture* is practiced among some societies today. Among some of the aborigines of Australia and the Bahima of Africa, the wife-capture is ceremonial. All those involved know what will take place and act out their part in the ceremonial wife-capture.

Anthropologists speculate that while wife-capture has now become a marriage ritual, it may at one time have been practiced for real. The plains Indians of the United States practiced wife-capture, taking wives both from other tribes and from white men who invaded their land. Women have often been considered legitimate prizes of war. In the Old Testament when the Israelites fought the Midianites, all the virgin women were considered the spoils of war along with the livestock and precious metal captured (Num. 31:35).

The Bible also records an incident of wife-capture in the Book of Judges, chapters 19–21. A Levite from Ephraim traveled to Bethlehem to bring his concubine back home. Traveling back to Ephraim with his concubine, he decided to spend the night in Gibeah of Benjamin. Several men of Gibeah gang-raped and killed his concubine. Then the other tribes of Israel assembled to punish the men of Gibeah. When the Benjaminites refused to give up the men responsible for the rape and murder of the concubine, the other tribes of Israel went to war with Benjamin. Only six hundred men of Benjamin survived the ensuing battles. Later the rest of the tribes of Israel suffered remorse over their almost total destruction of Benjamin and desired to see the tribe restored. However, the other Israelites all vowed not to give their daughters to the Benjaminites as wives. The Israelites were able to obtain four hundred women for the men of Benjamin from Jabesh-gilead but two hundred more were needed. The men of Benjamin were advised to hide outside the city of Shiloh because the inhabitants of Shiloh were about to celebrate a feast and the young women would be dancing outside the city. When the women danced outside the city, each of the two hundred men who had not received a wife from Jabesh-gilead captured one of the young women of Shiloh as a wife.

Dissolution of Marriage

"If a man marries a woman who becomes displeasing to him . . . he writes her a certificate of divorce, gives it to her and sends her from his house. . . ." (Deut. 24:1).

While the ideal in nearly every society is a lifelong partnership between a man and woman, most societies realize this is not always possible and have a mechanism for dissolving a bad marriage. Of the 271 tribes surveyed by Hobhouse, Wheeler, and Ginsberg, only four percent forbade divorce (1965). Even in the Roman Catholic Church, where divorce is forbidden, there is a mechanism for dissolving marriages. A marriage may be annulled, a mechanism that pretends the marriage never really took place (at least legally).

Types of Family Systems

The two main types of family systems are monogamy and polygamy. *Monogamy* refers to a family in which each person has only one mate, that is, the marriage unit consists of a husband and wife. *Polygamy* refers to a family where there are multiple mates.

Polygamy takes several forms. *Polygyny* refers to the marriage of a man to more than one wife.[3] *Sororal polygyny* refers to the marriage of a man to a woman and her sisters. The Old Testament patriarch Jacob practiced sororal polygyny when he married Leah and her sister Rachael. Under the Law of Moses sororal polygyny was forbidden for the Hebrews (Lev. 18:18).

Polyandry refers to the marriage of a female to more than one husband. Polyandry is a rare marriage arrangement practiced in parts of Tibet, Nepal, Sri Lanka, and India. Incidents of polyandry have also been reported among the Kalapalo Indians of Brazil (Basso 1973). The type of polyandry generally practiced is *fraternal polyandry*. In fraternal polyandry all brothers in a family share one wife. The Pahari of Jaunsar Bawar in northern India practice

[3]The issue of polygyny and Christianity is dealt with in chapter 14.

fraternal polyandry. The oldest brother usually arranges the wedding. All the brothers share sexual access to the wife, and any children call the brothers father, regardless of biological paternity.

Group Marriage

This refers to a household in which several men and women have legal sexual access to one another. The Nayar of India may practice such a form of group marriage (Gough 1971:365–77). *Serial polygamy* is a tongue-in-cheek term sometimes used to refer to the practice of having several mates, one at a time. Serial polygamy is often practiced in the United States.

Bases for Polygamy

The most common form of polygamy is polygyny. In fact, polygyny is the most common form of marriage in the world. About half the world's societies practice polygyny as the preferred form of marriage, another third permit polygyny, and only a little over an eighth practice monogamy exclusively (Murdock 1949).

While most Westerners view polygyny as a sexual arrangement, the basis for polygyny is not usually sexual. Among the Kaka of Eastern Cameroon in Africa, the basis of polygyny is economic. Children are a source of wealth among the Kaka. Daughters bring in the bride price, and sons are a source of labor for herding and farming. Obviously, the more wives a man has, the more children he is likely to have. The first wife of a Kaka man will often urge him to take a second wife. Like any American wife, she wants to get ahead, move up the social ladder, and have life easier, as the following account illustrates:

> A Kaka tribeswoman, the mother of three children, sat on a low stool with a mortar between her bare legs. . . . Her left hand shot into the mortar to stir around the manioc meal. . . . A child sat silently in the dirt beside her. . . . Soon the child arose and tried to move in toward a lank breast that was bobbing back and forth. . . . The woman stopped, took the child and put it to her breast, wiped the sweat from her forehead, and turning to her husband said, "If you had two wives, I could go to my mother's tomorrow." Her husband lay stretched out on a mat, appearing to pay no attention to his wife. The woman continued in a louder voice: "Look across the courtyard at Abele. She sits and plays with her children while Kana cooks tonight." Turning toward her husband she picked up a stick and pointed it at him and with an angry scowl on her face she called out, "Poor man, poor man, who respects a poor man?" (Reyburn 1959:1)

Polygyny can also have a political basis. Alliances between rulers are often sealed through marriage, in that a ruler or his son marries the daughter of another ruler. A ruler making several alliances may have several wives. This was practiced in Old Testament times. In 1 Kings 3:1 we read, "Solomon made an alliance with Pharaoh king of Egypt and married his daughter. He brought her to the City of David." This form of political alliance is still practiced among many African tribes. Sudanese chiefs acquire many wives through the making of political alliances. Marriage alliances are used not only by chiefs but also by regular families to make alliances with other families for the achievement of some mutual end.

Living Arrangements

Families are typed by their living arrangements as well as by their marriage arrangements. There are two ways of looking at living arrangements. The first is to see who lives with whom, and the second is to see where they live.

The *nuclear family* refers to the husband, wife, and their immature children as a unit. When the nuclear family lives apart from the extended family, its residence is termed neolocal. *Neolocal* means that the spouses are living by themselves in a new location as opposed to living with either set of parents or other relatives.

The *extended family* refers to a living arrangement by which two or more related, nuclear families share a household. This arrangement may be vertical, with the household including grand-parents, parents, and grandchildren. It may also be horizontal, including married siblings, cousins, and other married relatives of the same age-set. The extended family may extend either vertically or horizontally, or it may extend both vertically and horizontally at the same time.

The extended family is illustrated by the compound group, the domestic unit of production among the Tiv of Nigeria. As described by the Keesings, the compound consists of an open central area surrounded by huts and granaries arranged in a circle or oval. The compound group is headed by the senior man, the oldest male in the group, who functions as the group's leader. He usually has several wives, each of whom generally has a separate hut in the compound. Also included in the group compound are the head man's minor children and unmarried daughters as well as his married sons along with their wives and children. The compound group may also include a younger brother of the head man with his wives and children (Keesing and Keesing 1971).

The neolocal pattern of residence is the ideal pattern in the United States. Although some couples may live with one set of parents or other relatives, the goal is usually to have a separate residence as soon as possible. The United States is one of the few countries in the world to have retirement villages and nursing homes. These have developed because of our high value on neolocal residency. In most other cultures, the older members of the society would be part of an extended family residence that would care for them.

Among the Navaho Indians of North America, the newlywed couple lives in the household of the bride's family. This pattern of residence is called *matrilocal residence*. Among the Siane of New Guinea, the newlywed couple takes up residence in the village in which the groom was born and raised. This pattern is called *patrilocal residence*. Among the Hopi Indians of North America, the newlywed couple joins the household of the bride's uncle, her mother's brother. This pattern is known as *avunculocal residence*.

One thing we must keep in mind is that these patterns of marriage and residence are the ideals or goals of the various societies that practice them. Not all members of these societies practice the ideal forms. The patterns of marriage and the residence considered ideal by a society may never be attained by some or even most of the members of that society.

Although precise statistics are not available, the observation of anthropologists in the field is that fewer than half of the marriages in societies where polygyny is the ideal are in fact polygynous. In the United States, the ideal is neolocal residence, preferably in a single family dwelling; but many couples live most or all of their married lives with parents or other relatives. What we have discussed in this chapter are patterns, not unbreakable "laws." The student of anthropology must always guard against stereotyping.

God and the Family

The family is the basic unit of every society. It was the first sociological institution. God established the family before He established the church, government, or any other institution. The Bible gives us the basis for marriage and lays out the functions and requirements of marriage and the family. Every culture includes values, traditions, and expectations associated with marriage and the family. The issue facing us is how to relate the biblical teachings to cultural practices.

It is very easy for a Christian to confuse what is biblical with what is cultural. Many of the things we do that we consider to be good Christian behavior are really only good American behavior. Let us take another look at the opening anecdote. Two very different methods of obtaining a mate are present. Which one is biblical?

The only verses that seem to apply to this situation are

2 Corinthians 6:14, "Do not be yoked together with unbelievers. For what do righteousness and wickedness have in common? Or what fellowship can light have with darkness?" and Colossians 3:20, "Children, obey your parents in everything, for this pleases the Lord." It seems that both girls married Christians, so neither was "bound together" with an unbeliever. The Indian girl and boy were obedient to their parents. We will assume the American boy and girl did not go against their parents' wishes. Thus it seems that both marriages were biblical.

As we look at the marriage and residence patterns of other cultures, we need to evaluate them in the light of Scripture and not in the light of our own culture. God's system allows for cultural variation within the biblical guidelines.[4] It is only when the cultural system goes outside the biblical guidelines that change needs to take place. (See figure 8-1.)

The Bible teaches that marriage is basically a total commitment between a man and a woman for life (Gen. 2:24; Matt. 19:4–6; 1 Cor. 7:39). The biblical concept of marriage is basically neither a legal nor a social contract. It is a commitment that is made before God and the family of believers. This commitment does not endure because of the force of law or the threat of social sanctions but because it is made before God.

Although the biblical concept of marriage is basically a total commitment between a man and a woman, the Bible also teaches us that the Christian should live in harmony with the laws and customs of his or her own society (Rom. 13:1–4; 1 Cor. 9:19–23; 1 Peter 2:13–17) unless they violate God's moral laws (Acts 5:27–32). Therefore when the marriage laws, customs, and rituals of a culture are not in conflict with the teachings of Scripture, the Christian in that society should abide by them. In societies where the marriage customs and rituals are associated with pagan religions, the missionary should not attempt to introduce North American customs and rituals. Rather, the missionary should allow the nationals to develop customs and rituals that are consistent with both the national culture and the teachings of Scripture.

God's purpose and plan for the family is spelled out in Genesis 2:18–25. Grant Martin (1976) sees three purposes for marriage in this passage. The first purpose is companionship: "It is not good for the man to be alone" (v. 18). God made humans social beings and saw that man needed the companionship of others of his kind. Marriage provides man and woman with lifetime companionship.

The second purpose is completeness: "I will make a helper suitable for him" (v. 18). Men and women were created equal but different; they complement each other. The noted Hebrew scholar

---

[4] The issue of polygamy will be dealt with in chapter 15.

C. D. Ginsburg, commenting on this passage, says, "Their different characteristics . . . were designed to blend together so as to produce a happy harmony, and *to make both one*" (1970:14).

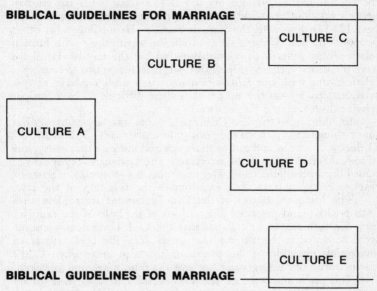

Figure 8-1. CULTURAL RELATIVISM AND BIBLICAL MARRIAGES. As the diagram indicates, there can be variation in marriage form without violating the biblical guidelines. However, when a culture does violate the biblical guidelines as cultures C and E do, it is usually not the whole culture that is in violation of the biblical guidelines but only certain aspects of it. For example, in traditional Samoan society, premarital sex is encouraged in violation of the biblical guidelines, but fidelity in marriage is also encouraged and, of course, that is in keeping with the biblical guidelines.

The third purpose is procreation: "For this reason a man will leave his father and mother and be united to his wife, and they will become one flesh" (Gen. 2:24). In Genesis 1:28 we have God's specific command to the first couple: "Be fruitful and increase in number." Here in the verses from Genesis 1 and 2, we see the sex act in both of its functions, as an expression of oneness and as a means of procreation. It is interesting to see that God created man and woman so that children are conceived during an act of love and oneness. The marriage partnership is God's plan for the conceiving and nurturing of children.

It is worth noting the emphasis the law of Moses puts on the family. For example, in the Ten Commandments (Exod. 20:2–17), the first four commandments (vv. 2–11) deal with the human being's relationship with God while the next six commandments (vv. 12–17) deal with the human being's relationship with other people. The first of these six commandments dealing with human relationships deals with relationships within the family. Until we have the proper relationship with God, it is difficult to have proper relationships with our fellow humans. Also until we have proper relationships within the home, it will be difficult to have proper relationships outside the home.

In addition to the Ten Commandments, the law of Moses has many things to say about the family. Leviticus 18:1–30 and 20:10–21 deal with sex in and out of marriage and indicate that every sort of sexual activity outside of marriage is sin. Leviticus 20:9 speaks of punishing a rebellious child. Deuteronomy 6:4–9 speaks of parents' responsibility to train their children in the teaching of the law.

The historical books of the Old Testament are replete with both positive and negative illustrations of the role of the family.[5] First Corinthians 10:11 tells us that the Old Testament accounts were recorded to be an example to us. The life of David is an interesting example of the problems that can arise when God's instructions concerning marriage and the family are not followed.

The poetical books of the Old Testament also have many things to teach us about marriage and the family.[6] The Book of Job gives us a picture of a godly father praying for his children (Job 1:5). It also gives us a picture of a woman who took her husband for better but not for worse (Job 2:9). The Psalms speak of the blessings of children (Ps. 127:3–5; 128:3). Proverbs speaks of the value and necessity of training children in the home (Prov. 3:1; 4:1; 22:6; 23:13; 29:15). Proverbs points out that to find a wife is to find a good thing (18:22) and that a prudent wife is a gift from the Lord (19:14). It speaks of the enjoyment of sex in marriage (5:18), the value of a good wife (14:1; 31:10), and the misfortune of having a contentious wife (19:13–14; 29:9, 19).

The New Testament also has many things to say about marriage and the family. Jesus spoke of family responsibility (Matt. 15:3–9) and taught on divorce and the sanctity of marriage (19:1–12). Paul also dealt with the family in his Epistles. The seventh chapter of 1 Corinthians speaks about the sexual areas of marriage,

---

[5] The historical books consist of the books from Joshua to Esther, inclusive.
[6] The poetical books consist of Job to Song of Solomon, inclusive.

as does Hebrews 13:4.[7] Paul talked about the husband-wife relationship and the parent-child relationship in Ephesians (5:21–33; 6:1–4). Paul shows how both of these relationships are reciprocal. Peter also mentioned the husband-wife relationship and its reciprocal nature (1 Peter 3:1–7).

As we study the Scriptures, we discover God's purposes and plans for marriage and the family. These purposes and plans are played out in human cultures. It is important for us to recognize that the biblical guidelines for marriage and the family may take different forms in different cultures. It is only as we become familiar with both the Scriptures and culture that we can apply the biblical teachings in a manner consistent with both.

Questions for Discussion

1. How would you define Christian marriage? What are the basic requirements?
2. Is bride price or dowry un-Christian? Explain your answer.
3. What would you do as a missionary if an African man and his three wives accepted the Lord and applied to join the local church?
4. How much should a missionary try to change local marriage customs?
5. How much of our mate-selection system and marriage practices is biblical and how much is only cultural?

Suggested Reading

Bohannan, P., and Middleton, J. 1968. *Marriage, Family, and Residence.* A collection of articles by several noted anthropologists dealing with marriage, family, and residence. The section of articles on marriage forms contains some interesting material.

Cavan, R. S. 1969. *Marriage and Family in the Modern World.* A book of readings on marriage and the family by anthropologists, sociologists, and psychologists. A good section on courtship, marriage, and the family in non–North American cultures.

Evans-Pritchard, E. E. 1951. *Kinship and Marriage Among the Nuer.* A good case study on marriage and kinship in a tribal society. The author has spent many years studying the Nuer, and his familiarity with the tribe is evident. It is interesting to compare the practices of the Nuer with the Hebrews of the Old Testament.

---

[7] We recognize that there is not general agreement over the authorship of Hebrews. We are not asserting Pauline authorship.

Fortes, M. 1962. *Marriage in Tribal Societies*. A collection of four articles dealing with marriage in tribal societies. This is good reading for the student interested in marriage practices in kin-based societies.

Fox, R. 1967. *Kinship and Marriage*. A basic, introductory work on kinship and marriage. Written to be understood by the layman, this book is a good place to begin a study on this subject.

Grunlan, S. A. 1984. *Marriage and the Family: A Perspective*. An introduction to the sociology of marriage and the family from a Christian perspective. This work gives insight into marriage and the family in American culture.

Queen, S. A., and Haberstein, R. W. 1971. *The Family in Various Cultures*. A good overview of the variations in family arrangements found in various present-day cultures as well as a historical perspective. It contains an interesting chapter on the polyandrous Toda family.

9

Kinship

What is man? A man is nothing. Without his family he is of less importance than that bug crossing the trail, of less importance than the sputum or exuviae. At least they can be used to help poison a man. A man must be with his family to amount to anything with us. If he had nobody else to help him, the first trouble he got into he would be killed by his enemies, because there would be no relatives to help him fight the poison of the other group. No woman would marry him. . . . He would be poorer than a newborn child, he would be poorer than a worm. . . . The family is important. If a man has a large family . . . and upbringing by a family that is known to produce good children, then he is somebody and every family is willing to have him marry a woman of their group. In the White way of doing things the family is not so important. The police and soldiers take care of protecting you, the courts give you justice, the post office carries your messages for you, the school teaches you. Everything is taken care of, even your children if you die; but with us the family must do all that.

Without the family we are nothing, and in the old days before the White people came, the family was given the first consideration by anyone who was about to do anything at all. That is why we got along. . . .

> With us the family was everything. Now it is nothing. We are getting like the White people and it is bad for the old people. We had no old people's home like you. The old people were important. They were wise. Your old people must be fools (The soliloquy of an old Pomo Indian of California, Aginsky 1940:43–44).

The family, in its broadest meaning, extends beyond the nuclear family of parents and their children to a whole network of relationships. This larger family network is tied together by kinship. *Kinship* is more than a network of biological relationships; it is also a network of social relationships. It establishes social ties, patterns of behavior, obligations and responsibilities, and patterns of authority. In short, it is a "road map" or structure of interpersonal relationships.

Among the aborigines of Australia, when two strangers meet they do not greet each other until they have determined how they are related so that the proper greeting may be used. If they determine they are not related, they try to kill each other. As might be expected, the aborigines practice exogamy to expand their kinship network.

Kinship relationships are the basis of the social structure in most nonwestern societies. This is true not only in small villages but also among large tribes. The Nuer of the Sudan in Africa number over one hundred thousand. Yet, they have no political or legal authority structure. There is no king, chief, or ruling council. Nevertheless there is social order, economic development, and organized defense. The Nuer social structure is based on a kinship system. The society functions by the obligations and responsibilities of kinship. How can a society this large maintain social order without a political or legal authority system? Does a North American mother call the police to make her son take a bath? No; yet he takes a bath. In the same way the Nuer family has the power and the responsibility to control its members.

Because of the important role kinship plays in understanding the social structure of most non-western societies, a large portion of the work done by cultural anthropologists has been in the area of kinship studies.

Nelson Graburn gives six reasons for the importance of kinship studies:

1. Kinship systems are universal.

2. Kinship systems are always important, though in differing degrees, in the structure of all human societies.

3. In the majority of societies traditionally studied by anthropologists, kinship has been one—if not the major—organizing principle.

4. Kinship systems are relatively easy to identify and lend themselves to fairly simple analysis.

5. In the history of anthropology, the discovery of societies in which kinship was so overwhelmingly important, and so different from our own structures, provided the stimulus for much investigation.

6. Many other aspects of the nature of society had been examined at some length by other social theorists before anthropology became a well-formulated social science—thus, it can be said that anthropologists have concentrated on a subject that other social scientists had tended to neglect (1971:3–4).

Being able to understand and analyze kinship systems is very important to a missionary endeavor. An effective strategy of evangelism and church planting cannot be laid without an understanding of a society's social structure.

Again, regarding the Nuer, whose social structure is based on kinship, E. E. Evans-Pritchard (1940), a Christian anthropologist, who has done much work among them, points out that if one wishes to work among these people he must become a kinsman. If a person is not a kinsman in reality or by mutual acceptance, then he is a potential enemy because without kinship no obligations can be established. Rights, privileges, and obligations are built into the Nuer kinship system, and one must plug into that system to work among the Nuer.

Basis of Kinship

There must be ways of tying the various elements together in any network. In a kinship network, the connecting bonds are called ties. There are three types of kinship ties.

The first is called *affinal ties,* referring to kinship relationships tied together by marital bonds. When a man marries a woman, he is bound to her by an affinal tie. However, now he is related not only to her but also to her parents, her brothers and sisters, and other relatives. In North America we refer to those with whom we have affinal ties as "in-laws" or as "related by marriage."

The second type of kinship ties are called consanguine ties. *Consanguine ties* refer to kinship relationships tied together by biological relationships, that is, by "blood." A son or daughter is tied to his or her parents by a consanguine tie. Brothers and sisters are tied to each other by consanguine ties. An affinal tie is made by contract and may be broken. A consanguine tie is made by birth and cannot be broken.[1] Affinal ties are achieved, whereas consanguine ties are ascribed. You choose your spouse, but not your children, or do you?

The third type of tie is called fictive. A *fictive tie* defines a "socio-legal" kinship relationship, in which a person is legally, ceremonially, or religiously tied into the kinship network. Fictive ties usually represent a consanguine tie such as that of a blood-brother or godmother. A very familiar form of fictive kinship tie in our culture is adoption. When a couple adopts a child, it is as if the child were born to them. Even though a kinship tie may be fictive, it is no less strong. An adopted child has all the rights, privileges, and responsibilities of a natural-born child. Among the Indians of the North American plains as well as some African tribes a relationship known as a blood-brother is used to tie a person into the kinship system. In traditional Latin American society the obligations of a godparent can be as real and binding as those of a biological parent. The Philippines has a similar fictive kinship tie by which one person is called a "sponsor." At the birth of a child, at puberty, or at marriage, coparents or sponsors are named. Children have been known to have as many as seven sponsors at birth. Filipinos seek as sponsors for their children persons who are from their status level or higher levels. These sponsors provide the child with "connections." Power and status are related to family, so the family can be expanded through having many sponsors. Sponsorship is also a way of bringing outsiders into the society.

Diagraming

To help analyze kinship systems, anthropologists have developed a shorthand system of diagraming valuable data for observing and discussing kinship. Although these systems of shorthand and diagraming are similar, there are some differences of usage among anthropologists. We will use Shusky's system, since it is widely used and recognized (1965).

When diagraming kinship systems, males are represented by a triangle and females by a circle. Affinal ties are shown by parallel lines, and consanguine ties are noted by a single line. These symbols can be put together to diagram a kinship system. The diagram for a nuclear family is shown in figure 9-1.

In diagraming a kinship system, a reference point is needed. A diagram usually builds on the kinship of a central person. A man may be one woman's husband, another's brother, and still another's father. This reference is referred to as ego. Ego is shown on

---

[1] In some societies they may be legally broken; but, of course, they can never be biologically broken.

a diagram by shading in his or her symbol (see figures 9-2 and 9-3). While some anthropologists use the male symbol for a neutral or unspecified ego, most use a square.

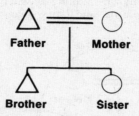

Figure 9-1. THE NUCLEAR FAMILY. The ideal nuclear family as referred to by anthropologists consists of father, mother, brother, and sister. This ideal is used because it demonstrates the most possible relationships using the least number of persons.

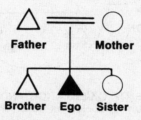

Figure 9-2. THE UNSPECIFIED EGO. Most anthropologists use a shaded square to represent an unspecified ego.

An adult ego is usually a member of two families, the one into which he is born and the one into which he marries. The family that ego was born into is called his *family of orientation*. This is the family that has oriented him in his culture and prepared him for his role in life. The family that that ego forms by marriage is called the *family of procreation*. This is the family where he is involved in procreation. The two families are shown in figure 9-3.

Shorthand

In North America children identify as "uncle" their father's brother, their mother's brother, their father's sister's husband, and their mother's sister's husband.

In order to talk about the same relationships in different cultures, anthropologists distinguish between kin types and kin terms. A *kin type* is an abstract concept that can be described in every culture. A person in every culture can have a father's sister. A *kin term* is a specific term in a specific language that refers to one or more kin types. Although a person in any culture can have a father's sister, only English-speaking people have an *aunt*. Spanish-speaking people have a *tia,* and Norwegian- and Dutch-speaking people have a *tante*.

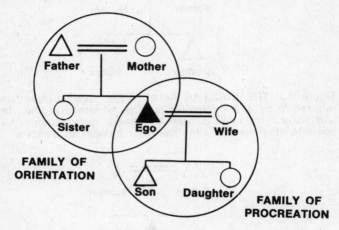

Figure 9-3. FAMILIES OF ORIENTATION AND OF PROCREATION. Note that each person is labeled as he or she is related to ego.

There are two types of kin terms. *Terms of reference* are used to talk about someone. *Terms of address* are used to talk to someone. When I talk about my father, I refer to him as "father," but I address him as "Dad."

As one might imagine, kin types can be cumbersome and very unwieldy to write on kinship diagrams. Imagine trying to fit "father's sister's husband's mother" under a symbol on a diagram. To overcome this problem, anthropologists have formulated a shorthand form of reference. Nine basic symbols account for all kin relationships. Formerly anthropologists used the first two letters of the word as follows:

1. Fa – father	4. Si – sister	7. Hu – husband
2. Mo – mother	5. So – son	8. W – wife
3. Br – brother	6. Da – daughter	9. Ch – child

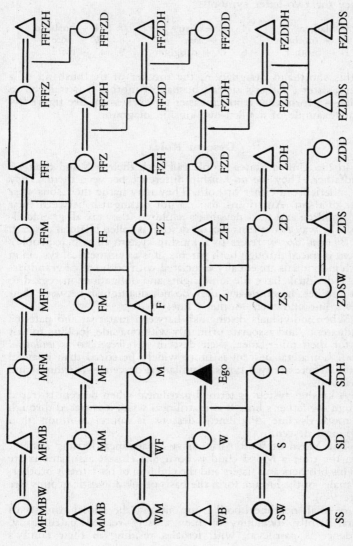

Figure 9-4. EXTENDED KINSHIP DIAGRAM. Note how convenient the shorthand given on page 168 is on this diagram.

but in recent years the following one-letter symbols have come to replace the two-letter symbols:

1. F– father   4. Z – Sister   7. H – husband
2. M – mother   5. S – son   8. W – wife
3. B – brother   6. D – daughter   9. C – child

By this shorthand designation, the mother of the husband of a father's sister ("father's sister's husband's mother") is reduced to FZHM—a form that is much easier to work with. See figure 9-4 for an example of a filled-out kinship diagram.

Descent Rules

In the United States people call both their MF and their FF grandfather. They see no kinship difference between them. They may inherit from either or both. They may name their sons after either of them. Americans also do not distinguish between their sons' children and their daughters' children, they are all grandchildren. The way Americans reckon descent is called bilateral descent.

Bilateral descent refers to a kinship system in which people's descent is traced through both parents. It is a symmetrical system in which individuals are equally associated with both sets of grandparents. Individuals have the same rights and obligations in regard to both families. In summary, they do not distinguish between their father's line and their mother's line.

When individuals distinguish between maternal and paternal grandparents, and associate primarily with one side, looking to that side for their inheritance, their descent is referred to as *unilateral descent*. Unilateral descent is more widely practiced than bilateral descent. There are two types of unilateral descent—patrilineal and matrilineal.

A kinship system is termed patrilineal when descent is traced through the father's line. It is matrilineal when it is traced through the mother's line. Patrilineal descent is more common than matrilineal descent.

The Mossi of West Africa have a patrilineal kinship system. From the time a Mossi child is born, his closest associations are with his brothers and sisters and the children of his father's brother. The males of the lineage form the basis of the domestic groups (see figure 9-5).

A small neighborhood group among the Mossi consists of several family dwellings of men closely related patrilineally. Residence is patrilocal, with females residing in their family's household until they marry. After that they reside in their husband's household. Even though the female resides in her husband's household, she is still a member of her father's lineage and clan. Marriage is exogamous. That is, individuals marry outside their patrilineage. Violation of patrilineal exogamy is considered incest. Cross-cousin marriage is considered desirable.

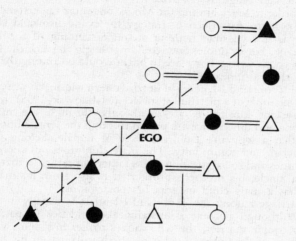

Figure 9-5. PATRILINEAGE MODEL. The members of the patrilineage are shaded, and these are the only persons that ego considers kin. Note that the patrilineage is based solely on consanguine ties, never on affinal ties.

Each Mossi patrilineal residence group acts as a corporate unit in its relations with other patrilineal groups and with the community at large. The patrilineage, as a group, controls all the farmland the lineage owns and allocates its use according to individual need. This also functions as a social control mechanism. Property is passed on through the patrilineage from father to son, or in some cases from older brother to younger brother. All property remains in the patrilineage and assures the economic security of the future generations.

A man's social status is determined by his position within his patrilineage. Authority is generational. The oldest male is the patrilineal elder or leader. When he dies, the next oldest brother becomes the patrilineal elder. When all the brothers of that generation have died, the oldest son of the oldest brother becomes the next patrilineal elder, and the pattern is continued. Village chiefs inherit their position through their patrilineage, as do religious leaders of the Mossi.

The Mossi patrilineage provides a man with his social status, economic opportunity, and position in the political and religious hierarchy. The patrilineal group maintains social order through economic and religious controls.

In order to work among the Mossi, one must understand their kinship system. An effective strategy for evangelism and church planting is not possible without an understanding of the Mossi patrilineage. For example, one would not begin to reach the Mossi through youth work. The place to begin would be among the older men of the patrilineage.

The Trobriand Islanders of northwestern Melanesia provide us with an example of a matrilineal society (Malinowski 1955). In their social system kinship is reckoned only through the mother. Succession and inheritance are passed through the female line. This means that a woman's children, male or female, belong to her family, clan, and community. The male child does not succeed to the dignities and social position of his father but rather to that of his maternal uncle, his mother's brother. It is also from his maternal uncle that a male child inherits his possessions.

Marriage among the Trobriand Islanders is usually monogamous. Although descent is matrilineal, residence is patrilocal. When a couple marries, the wife moves to her husband's village. The village of the husband is his mother's village, not his father's village where he was raised. Even though a Trobriand man is raised in his father's village, his inheritance is in his mother's village and that is where he settles as an adult.

Traditionally, the Trobriand Islanders have not seen the father as having a biological role in procreation. While being aware that sexual intercourse is related to conception, they do not see the father making a biological contribution to the child. They have believed that new lives are placed in the womb by a deceased kinswoman. Because they have seen the children as biologically related to their mothers, kinship has been reckoned through the female line. Even when they come to understand genetics, they still hold to their traditional kinship system, which is functional.

The mother's brother is the male with the real authority over the children. He is the one from whom the boys will inherit. When a boy reaches maturity, he goes to live in his maternal uncle's village where he has his inheritance. It is the uncle that teaches the boy the ways of manhood. When the boy marries, he takes his wife to his maternal uncle's village.

If missionaries were to begin a work among the Trobriand Islanders without understanding the Trobriand kinship system, they could have problems making the gospel intelligible. How would the Trobrianders react to the missionaries' presenting Jesus Christ as the Son of God, or as being of the lineage of David? What about the concept of God the Father?

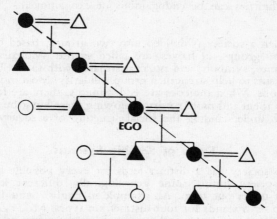

Figure 9-6. MATRILINEAGE MODEL. The members of the matri-lineage are shaded. As with the patrilineage, matrilineage is based on consanguine ties, not affinal ties.

Kin Groups

Three main types of kin groups serve as the basis for the social structure of many societies.

Clan

A *clan* is a consanguinely related group, patrilineal or matri-lineal, believing it has descended from a common nonhuman ancestor. The members of a clan often share a common area of residence. The nonhuman ancestor may be a god, spirit, animal, or mythical person. This nonhuman ancestor is often referred to as the clan's *totem*. Members of the clan may wear a special insignia and have special rituals associated with their totem. Some North American Indians have the famous totem poles to represent the totems of the clans in their tribe.

Phratry

A *phratry* is a group of two or more clans held together either by kinship or by mutual interest. There is some disagreement among anthropologists on this matter. Murdock claims a phratry is based only on kinship ties (1949:47), while Robert Lowie believes they are usually formed on the basis of common interest (1948:338). It is really a semantic argument and the definition given covers both cases. Phratries can be endogamous or exogamous.

Moiety

When a society is divided into two groups, based on birth, these two groups, or halves, are called *moieties*. Moieties usually have names, symbols, and rituals associated with them. These are mechanisms to help strengthen group solidarity. Most moieties are exogamous. When moieties are endogamous, there are fewer ties between them and more rivalry. Knowing these kin groups can be a key to understanding the social structure of a society.

Types of Kinship Systems

No society has a distinct term for every possible kin type. Every society lumps some genealogically different kin types together under one term. An example in English would be *aunt*. This kin term stands for four distinct kin types: MZ, FZ, MBW, and FBW. Among the Sudanese each of these kin types has a different kin term, and the kin term for each kin type differs when used by a male or by a female. A Sudanese boy would call FZ one term, while a Sudanese girl would call FZ another term. Kinship systems are typed by the way they lump together, or classify, different kin types.

There are three basic types of kinship systems. The first, known as the *Hawaiian* kinship system, is a generational system. All close relatives of the same sex and generation are referred to by the same kin term. For example, M, MZ, and FZ are all referred to as "mother." F, FB, and MB are all referred to as "father." Cross-cousins, parallel cousins, and siblings are all referred to as "brother" or "sister." Note that this is a bilateral system. By *bilateral* it is meant that both sides of the family are referred to in the same manner.

The next two kinship systems are linear. They are concerned with distinguishing relatives who are directly in the line of descent from those that are collateral. Under a linear system M is distinguished from MZ, who is collateral. The bilateral linear kinship system, known as the *Eskimo* kinship system, distinguishes collateral relatives from those directly in the line of descent but does not distinguish between patrilineal and matrilineal collaterals. M is distinguished from MZ and FZ; MZ and FZ are not distinguished from each other. Anglo-American kinship is an Eskimo kinship system. One of the distinctions between the Eskimo system and most other systems is that in the Eskimo system no other relatives are called by the same kin terms as members of the nuclear family. This may be because societies with an Eskimo kinship system emphasize the nuclear family rather than the extended family.

The unilateral linear kinship system, known as the *Iroquois* kinship system, distinguishes between matrilineal collaterals, patrilineal collaterals, and those directly in the line of descent. Although these are the three basic types of kinship systems, there are many subtypes and variations. There are systems in which older brothers are referred to by one term and younger brothers by another. In some kinship systems all younger-than-ego male or female kin types are lumped together with one kin term, while older-than-ego kin types are distinguished by kin terms. The variety of types is almost equal to the variety of societies.

An understanding of the kinship system of the group with which missionaries are working could help them devise an effective strategy for presenting the gospel to the group. Missionaries have to begin where the people are. Cultural anthropology gives missionaries the tools to learn about the people and their kinship system.

How to Analyze a Kinship System

In many societies most behavior is regulated by kinship. In order to understand a society so as to be able to live and minister among the people, a person needs to understand the kinship system. The way to begin an analysis of a kinship system is to collect kin terms from an informant and place them on a kinship diagram.

It is important to remember that kinship terms must be collected from both males and females. In some societies the terms used by both sexes will be the same. In others, the terminology used by women will differ from that used by men. It is also important to collect terms from both younger and older informants.

The investigator should talk to as many informants as possible. Most informants will lack certain relatives. One informant may not have a FB. The more informants the investigator talks with, the more gaps he or she will be able to fill. This is a good way to establish the kinship system. Besides, most people like to talk about their relatives and will usually tell stories that are clues to appropriate kin behavior. The investigator will begin to discover the appropriate behavior patterns between any two kin types. The investigator should be alert to discover which kin types ego considers kin and which kin types ego does not consider kin. The investigator should also determine clan membership for each individual in the society.

A good method of practicing this technique at home is to ask foreign students to act as informants for you. Try to analyze their kinship system and then check with them.[2]

Functions of Kinship Systems

As we have already seen, kinship systems are an important part of the social structure in many societies. The kinship system performs many necessary functions in these societies. Reread the Indian soliloquy at the beginning of the chapter and look for the different functions the old Indian attributed to the family.

Socialization

Although it was pointed out in an earlier chapter that the nuclear family usually has the primary responsibility for the socialization of the young, the extended family usually also has an important role in the process. Among the Trobriand Islanders, a boy learns his trade, his clan rituals, and other important things for a useful life from his mother's brother, not his father. The entire kinship system provides models of behavior. Also, certain members of the kinship system have specific roles in certain aspects of the socialization of a child.

Security and Aid

Most societies do not have a social-security system to care for the old or those who cannot work. They do not have old people's homes. They do not have orphanages. They do not have police forces to protect property and life. Then who takes care of the old, the widows, the orphans? Who protects property and life?

The kinship system cares for the old, the young, and the orphaned. It comes to the defense of any of its members who are threatened. It avenges a wronged member. It settles disputes. In short, the kinship system, in many societies, performs the functions we have turned over to our government. Just as a person could not get along in our society without understanding the functions of the government, so an individual could not really get along in many societies without understanding the functions of the kinship system.

---

[2]For a fuller explanation and illustration of analyzing kinship systems, see W. H. R. Rivers, 1910, "The Genealogical Method," *Sociological Review*, 3:1–11, reprinted in Graburn (1971:52–59).

Social Control

In most simple societies, and even in some more complex ones, the kinship network takes the governmental functions of social control. The kinship system punishes wrongdoers, establishes rules, and maintains social order. We will go into more detail on this function of the kinship system in chapter 11.

Old Testament Hebrew Kinship System

Even as an understanding of the kinship system of a society today is necessary to an understanding of that society, so it is important to understand the kinship system of the Hebrews to fully understand them and the message of the Old Testament.

Kinship systems are not static structures but change over time. This is seen also in the Old Testament Hebrew kinship system. A certain period of Old Testament history will have to be chosen to examine the Hebrew kinship system.

During the period of the patriarchs (Abraham, Isaac, and Jacob), the Hebrew kinship system was patrilineal in descent, patrilocal in residence, and clan-endogamous in marriage. The preferred marriage arrangement during the period of the patriarchs was parallel-cousin marriage. The ideal match for a man was the daughter of his father's brother or the daughter of the brother's son of his father's father (see figure 9-7). In Numbers 36:11–12 we find an example of parallel-cousin marriage and clan endogamy:

> Zelophehad's daughters—Mahlah, Tirzah, Hoglah, Milcah,
> and Noah—married their cousins on their father's side.
> They married within the clans of the descendents of
> Manasseh son of Joseph.

The same type of patrilineal, patrilocal, clan-endogamous system with parallel-cousin marriage is practiced today in traditional Arab societies. An Arab man has the first right to his FBD. Because both the Jews and the Arabs are descended from Abraham, they have similar kinship systems. Because the Arabs have remained in the Middle East, little acculturation has taken place, and the kinship system has not changed much in many Arab areas.

One cannot effectively minister to a people until one understands them. A key to understanding many societies is understanding their kinship system. This is true not only among primitive societies, but also among most non-Western advanced societies.

In Japan, many factories operate on a fictive kinship structure, not an organizational structure. Workers are adopted by their foreman, a group of foremen by their supervisor, and so on, to the top of the structure. What you find in the factory is a fictive kinship system with all the behavior patterns and responsibilities of a real one.

To bring men, women, and children into God's family, we need to understand and relate to their family system. In Scripture God uses the family relationship to illustrate our relationship to Him. As we better understand a society's kinship system we will be better able to relate the gospel. If the family is the basic structure of society, then an understanding of kinship is basic to the understanding of society.

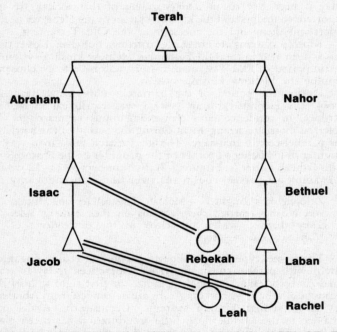

Figure 9-7. PATRILATERAL PARALLEL-COUSIN MARRIAGE. This arrangement was found among the pastoral Hebrews of the Old Testament. This figure gives the patrilineage of Terah, showing the prescribed marriage of Isaac to his patrilateral cousin Rebekah, and of their son Jacob to his parallel-cousins Leah and Rachel. (This diagram is limited to the male offspring through whom the line of descent devolved.) (Hoebel 1972:407).

Questions for Discussion

1. In figure 9-4 what type of marriage is that of ego and his wife?
2. Give the English kin term for each kin type in figure 9-4. Did you have trouble naming any of them? Which ones? Why? What does this tell you about our kinship system?
3. How would you convey the concept of "God the Father" in a matrilineal society such as that of the Trobriand Islands?
4. Referring to the opening anecdote, what were some of the functions of the kinship system of the Pomo Indians? Who performs those functions in our society? Why?
5. Find a person from another culture and try to diagram his kinship system, including the kin terms in his or her native language. Can you tell if it is a generational, bilateral, or unilateral system? How?

Suggested Reading

Bohannan, P., and Middleton, J. 1968. *Kinship and Social Organization*. A collection of readings on kinship and social structure. The first section of readings deals with the historical development of the field and is especially recommended.

Farber, B. 1968. *Comparative Kinship Systems: A Method of Analysis*. A very useful and insightful volume. This work is not easy to read but contains some useful material for the serious student. It has an interesting chapter on American kinship systems.

Graburn, N. 1971. *Readings in Kinship and Social Structure*. A book of readings on kinship and social organization. It includes some classics in the field. Here is a good place for an introductory student to begin.

Merrifield, W. 1981. *Proto Otomanguen Kinship*. Written by a missionary cultural anthropologist, this study focuses on the kinship terms used by an Indian society in southern Mexico. An innovative method of analyzing and diagraming kinship relations is presented.

Murdock, G. P. 1949. *Social Structure*. A classic in the field of kinship. Most later works build on this foundation work. The whole book is highly recommended.

Schusky, E. L. 1965. *Manual for Kinship Analysis*. 2nd ed. A simple, basic, yet thorough introduction to the field. This is an excellent place for a person just getting into kinship analysis to begin. The diagrams and glossary are very useful.

10

Groups and Communities

Mrs. Woodrum, a widow of fifty-five, early one morning jumped to her death from her twelfth-floor apartment on Chicago's north side. Just before she jumped, she saw the janitor working on the balcony across the court in the next wing of the building. Mrs. Woodrum waved to him and smiled. He smiled and waved back. When he turned his back, she jumped.

On her orderly desk, Mrs. Woodrum left this note: "I can't stand one more day of this loneliness. No sound from my telephone. No mail in my box. No friends." Mrs. Jenkins, another widow who lived on the same floor of the large city apartment building, told reporters, "I wish I had known she was lonely; I could have called on her. We could have been friends."

We have defined culture as shared and learned behavior. By its very definition, culture is a group product. To better understand culture, we need to understand group structure and process.

Goldschmidt (1971:286) has suggested three reasons why humans live in groups. The first is the long period of physical and social maturation required by humans. The second is the psychological need for companionship. This is so strong that isolation or solitary confinement is used as punishment. The third is the relative physical weakness of human beings. They are ill equipped without such physical helps as claws, tusks, and hoofs. By cooperation humans control stronger, quicker, and more dangerous animals than themselves and tame many aspects of the environment.

Groups

A *group* is defined as a unit possessing the following five properties: (1) it consists of two or more people; (2) there is interaction or communication between the people; (3) there are one or more symbolic objects present; (4) each person has some kind of relation or orientation toward other persons and toward one or more symbolic objects; and (5) there is "unit awareness" (Taylor 1970:1–2).

Not only must a group contain more than one person, but these people must also interact with one another. Interaction involves the communication of information within a social setting, allowing for the interplay or mutuality of action. One acts in relation to the act of another. The act involves verbal or nonverbal observable behavior. Such behavior takes on significance in relation to objects established as having, or coming to have, meaning within the social setting. These objects have symbolic value within the society and take various forms. They include cultural objects (such as norms, roles, beliefs, and values) or noncultural objects (such as topics of discussion, political issues, and acts of persons).

Thus a person within a social setting is oriented to some person or object within the setting. This orientation may be person-to-person, as in a marriage relationship, or person-to-object, with the person taking a position on a social issue such as abortion or integration.

A group can be distinguished from an aggregation by the above five properties. An *aggregation* is a collection of people who may have one or more of these properties but not all of them. Take, for example, a collection of people waiting for a bus on a street corner in a large city. There are more than two of them. There may be communication when one person asks another when the bus is due. There are symbolic objects: the bus stop, bus fare, the bus, and the norm of waiting at the stop. However, there is no relationship among the people, and they do not have unit awareness.

Sociologists distinguish between two types of groups: primary and secondary. This distinction is also useful to anthropologists. The *primary group* refers to a group that is small, intimate, and informal. The family is an excellent example of a primary group.

Each child must learn a particular set of cultural and linguistic rules in the context of a specific family and local community. This means that his primary social and emotional allegiance is necessarily directed to a small group and its provincial traditions. These local allegiances can, to some extent, be weakened and superseded by wider loyalties later in life; but they are never completely dissolved and, consciously or unconsciously, they continue to shape our behavior (Bock 1969:267).

The *secondary group* refers to groups that are utilitarian, formal, and impersonal. School classes, student bodies, labor unions, and PTAs are examples of secondary groups. A person's primary group associations are usually more important to him than his secondary group associations.

The regularization of interpersonal relations is referred to as *social organization*. All societies have social organization though its form varies from society to society. Social organization depends on the size of the society, its level of technology, its type of kinship system, and many other variables.

All societies consist of a number of groups that may be related to each other in various ways. We may distinguish between *mutually exclusive groups* and overlapping groups. Mutually exclusive groups are groups in which membership in one group excludes membership in another group or groups. For example, if an Australian aborigine is a member of the Fox clan, he cannot be a member of the Rabbit clan. An Indian of the Kshatriyas caste cannot also be a member of the Vaisyas caste. In a college a member of the junior class cannot be a member of the freshman class.

Overlapping groups refer to groups in which membership in one group does not preclude membership in the other group or groups. There are two types of overlapping groups: inclusive and noninclusive. In *inclusive groups* membership in one group means inclusion in another group. For example, to be a member of the junior class at a given school you must be a member of the school's student body. A junior cannot declare himself a nonmember of the larger student body. *Noninclusive groups* are groups where joint membership is neither precluded nor requisite. A member of the college football team may or may not be a member of the college baseball team.

Most clubs and associations in the United States are overlapping, noninclusive. One of the authors of this book was a member of the American Anthropological Association, the Society for Applied Anthropology, the American Sociological Association, and the Association for the Sociology of Religion at the same time. None of these organizations require membership in any of the others nor do they preclude such membership.

The *small group* is a unit or collective that meets all the criteria

for the group plus the following: each person in the group must
receive an impression or perception of *each other* person distinct
enough so that he can, at any time, give some reaction or opinion,
however minimal, to each of the others as an individual. The group
must be sufficiently small in size so that each person can recall one
or more impressions or perceptions of every other person in the
group.

The traditional worship service at most churches meets the
basic criteria for group but not for small group. Probably no
participant in worship could recall one or more things about every
other participant who attended. However, the typical Sunday-
school class could be a small group. The criterion for distinguishing
a small group from a large one is based on the potential range of
perception of other persons and not strictly on a size criterion. In
terms of actual numbers, however, a group is usually considered
small if it ranges from two to twenty persons (Taylor 1970:3).
Typical small groups are families, fraternities, construction crews,
play groups, bomber crews, bridge clubs, athletic teams, boards of
directors, therapy groups, classroom groups, juries, seminars,
hunting parties, and discussion groups.

The study-sharing-fellowship group encountered at times in
the contemporary church is a type of small group that forms in
various settings for specified reasons and for a specified time
period. They are usually not designed to be continuing groups, and
they serve a variety of functions. It is both significant and
interesting to note that twelve disciples gathered around Jesus. He
drew these twelve into a sharing interaction that set them apart in
terms of preparation but not in terms of status. In three short years,
through the sharing-apprentice process, He prepared eleven of
them to take over His ministry and found the church.

A group thus formed is a natural grouping, based on interest
or association. The more it fits the characteristics of a natural
grouping with shared interests or associations, the more effective it
will be. Shared interest or association provides a degree of
compatibility and homogeneity that will support the goals and
processes of the group. When heterogeneity and diversity are
introduced, the small group processes fail to work effectively. For
example, if a member of a Bible-study group wants content and the
group has a sharing format, that person tends to become a
disruptive influence in the group, seeking to move the group
toward a content format. Pressures may be indirect with comments
like, "What's the point of all this talk?" or it may be direct with
comments like, "This isn't a Bible study!" A group can have both
Christian and non-Christian membership and not be heterogeneous
as long as a common interest is shared—a desire to learn what the
Bible has to say to them.

Small groups need not be planned for permanent organization. In fact, a preplanned termination date for reconsideration and reorganization is wise in maintaining vitality and interest in a small group. A large group can be maintained over time, but a small group needs continual evaluation and restructuring.

A plan calling for evaluation every eight to twelve months can help maintain interest in the group. This way people know that if things don't work out, they are free to leave after a set period of time. Three years is probably the maximum length of time a small group should meet with the same membership. Beyond that point, interests begin to diverge and even geographic mobility cuts into the structure of the group. If a group does not plan to reorganize, it is most likely to die when geographic mobility hits.

It is interesting to note that Jesus and his disciples were together for three years. Even during this time there was attrition (Judas' defection) and acts of disloyalty such as Peter's denial. When Jesus was crucified, the group began disintegrating. After Jesus' resurrection and ascension new groups began to form around leaders such as James and Peter. Paul, after his conversion, had a difficult time being accepted by the group. In fact, he seems never to have been fully accepted by the group in Jerusalem. However, the church was shifting from a small group to a large group, and Paul was accepted by the larger group. A study of the Bible from a group dynamics perspective can yield some new insights in our understanding of Scripture.

Small groups have a variety of functions. They can carry out specific tasks, e.g., evangelism of a neighborhood; meet to work on socio-emotional problems; or even form to influence a large group. They can bring their influence to bear by supporting one given individual in interaction within the larger group, or they can bring group pressures to bear on the larger group. The type of group process being discussed here is the socio-emotional group task in which the members enter into a supporting and encouraging role.

The group can participate in a variety of experiences, both planned and unplanned. The group is in basic *equilibrium* as it begins, the members being desirous of making it go and having a good experience within the group. They are ready to sublimate personal wishes for the sake of the group and the members of the group. It is likely that eventually this balance will be destroyed by some misunderstanding or overt act, e.g., gossip about a member of the group or a disagreement that gets serious. Thus, *conflict* results. The conflict may be covered up, or partially resolved, or even replayed at a later date through "role play" to see how the disagreement started, was pursued, might have been pursued, and might have been resolved for the strengthening of the group.

Exchange interaction could thus result in a new rapport within the group with each person becoming involved in his or her own role or in the role of the other. One means of effecting such exchange is through *game theory* utilizing role play, reverse role play, simulations, educational games, and trust activities. Finally, the group can go back to the qualities they are seeking in group interaction and through the *generative process* (logical projection of behavior and activities from a core of concepts or ideas) develop alternative plans that the group can pursue for more effective interaction.

No matter what interests and associations draw a small group together, subcultural differences such as perspective, thought, belief, and practices are prone to interject in the group processes. These differences can result in irritations and distractions that can keep it from fulfilling its purposes. The person working with small groups, especially in crosscultural settings, needs to be aware of the dynamics of small-group interaction.

Communities

India contains over five hundred thousand villages. In these villages live approximately seven out of ten Indian citizens, about one out of every seven human beings in the world. Indian villagers are inventive and conservative, tall and short, friendly and quarrelsome, handsome and ugly, wise and foolish, radical and reactionary. There are no typical rural Indians; there are no typical Indian villages. There are only human beings living in some relationship to the complex pattern of forces and ideas that constitute the civilization of India. To understand a single village and the people in it is to begin to understand India, but it is not more than a beginning.

The community is a corporate body sharing sociopolitical identity. People choose to live together within a certain environment that affords them the substance of life and the convenience of social control. They have an economic base, an authority system, the security of social and environmental protection, and the confidence that they can raise their families to follow them.

Communities develop voluntarily or involuntarily. The internal dynamics of communities call for a balanced relationship, an equilibrium. Insofar as the community affects or achieves this balance, the community is at peace. When this is disrupted for any reason, the community moves into a period of tension that may ultimately lead to its destruction or the emergence of something new and more socially viable for that period. Any society, whether voluntary or involuntary, may be abused by any member or group. Bias or prejudice, selfish interest, and manipulation of social forces may all force a society founded on equality into a basic inequality.

The Household

The household is one type of community core and may, in a given society, serve as a community itself. The basic North American household consists of a father, mother, and children. This is the nuclear family and is not in and of itself likely to serve as a community, but rather as part of a community.

Among the Hopi of Arizona, the core of each household is a group of sisters together with their daughters (single and married) and their daughters' children. The husband is more like a guest and really feels "at home" only in his sister's household.

Among the Tanala of Madagascar, on the other hand, the typical household consists of a man with his married and unmarried sons and their wives and offspring. Such households, containing three or more generations of males, were not uncommon in rural areas of the United States during the nineteenth century.

A Pocomchi household consists of the father, mother, and unmarried children; but one married son may also live in the household for about three years.

Among the Ashanti of Ghana, West Africa, the typical household consists of an old woman, her sons and daughters, and the daughters' children. Here the consanguineal kinship tie overrides the affinal one. Among the Tallensi of Ghana, the core of the household is a group of men; but separate buildings are provided for the wives and young children of a man's married sons. Frequently a separate sleeping room is provided for adolescent boys. In any of these latter cases, the household functions as the community.

Neighborhood as Community

Communities can be classified according to size and function. In agricultural societies, especially those involved with shifting horticulture, *homesteads* or homestead sites may be scattered. Hamlets range from a handful of such homesteads to a score of them. Villages may contain hundreds to thousands of people and be structured with homesteads or hamlets. Towns are sociopolitical entities encompassing oversight of villages, hamlets, and homesteads. The town may be a village that has grown. It may be the prestige center of an area.

The Trobriand village illustrates these concepts. The basic organizational unit of this society is the matrilineal subclan. These subclans are associated with a territory that is passed on from generation to generation and are traditionally associated with the subclan. While Trobriand society is matrilineal, it is patrilocal, so it is the male members of the subclan and their wives that populate the village that serves as the "headquarters" for the subclan. The female members of the subclan reside elsewhere with their husbands.

The village is the center of economic activity, which is organized around gardening. The gardens are corporately owned by the subclan; there is no concept of private land. The leader of the subclan controls the organization of the gardening.

The Pocomchi town is simply a village having a Spanish ruling set. Originally, a fertile area was dotted with homesteads and villages, termed *aldeas*. When the Spanish entered the area, a church was built in the center of the fertile plain at the confluence of the major trails crisscrossing the plain.

The Spanish laid out a grid of streets in rectangular fashion, with the church at the center. The major trails may have remained intact and widened to street width, producing a modification of the grid pattern.

In time, the central part of town was populated by people of Spanish background and other outsiders (e.g., Chinese) who were successful businessmen. They established businesses such as cafes, hostels, and shops. As the town grew, so did the businesses. Thus the Indian people lived on the outskirts of town or in the hills, using the town only as a market center. In the more affluent areas, such as San Cristobal, Alta Verapaz, Guatemala, the Indians live in the mountains but maintain a family homesite within the town limits. So the town appears to be inhabited only on market day.

Much as a peeled orange reveals separate sections, the Spanish background town or city has sections called *barrios*. The community is divided into two or more divisions. Each barrio has a chief responsible to the town mayor or council. Each chief has a degree of autonomy to manage his own affairs and to supervise the social behavior of the barrio. The larger community jurisdiction begins only if trouble arises or a local crime gains more than immediate, local notoriety.

One such community, San Cristobal, Guatemala, has a basic dual economic division: one half the community makes string or cord from the century plant and the other half makes bags of this string. The community is divided into five barrios, much as a pie is divided, from the center to the outskirts. As the town grows, the barrio grows or a new barrio is formed.

The city becomes simply a large town with barrios now named "zones" or *zonas*. Guatemala City, Guatemala, has sixteen official zones and establishes new ones as the need arises. The zones no longer have the same autonomy as do barrios. Rather, they are caught up in a more encompassing and sophisticated political structure of mayor and councilmen. The zones themselves take on a degree of prestige. Some zones are perceived as higher status, others as middle status, and still others as lower status.

Members of the society moving into the city seek a zone where they feel compatible. Otherwise harassment designed to remove them will be applied: they will be reduced to the status level of the zone, or the zone will be brought into a status struggle with the adjacent zones.

The American neighborhood is a collection of peoples who move into adjacent dwellings. It may involve a city block or only a portion of a block. It may entail a number of cross streets if the members of the community feel a loyalty to the community or the members of the community. It may be a subdivision or development, or any part of one.

It becomes a neighborhood, however, only if the people identify it as one. A development or subdivision may never become a neighborhood in this sense because people extend their loyalties out of the community rather than becoming entwined within the community. Within the area of Forest Park, Baltimore, Maryland, the streets of Granada and Rollins became a neighborhood. There was a perception of local community based on expressions of loyalty. Belle Avenue to the north never became part of the neighborhood. House types and homeowners (instead of renters) set it apart. The members of the community related out from the center rather than with others in the immediate vicinity.

Dannybrook is a development, the work of one man primarily, in southwest Dallas. The streets are named for his children. The houses are built on a loop between two creeks. About fifty homes have been constructed as part of the development. The majority of homeowners left other parts of Dallas where there had been an ethnic invasion. The members of the community thus maintain their associations outside the development, and no neighborhood ties or identity have been achieved.

City as Community

The city is department stores, theaters, bright lights, and night life. It is a cultural center and a center for commerce and trade. It has high rises and high crime rates. It is traffic and noise, crowds of people, and unlimited dirt. The city is home to approximately one-third of the people of the world.

When speaking of a city, one is usually talking about a *metropolitan* area, that is, the city and its surrounding suburbs, which are really adjuncts to the city. The United States Bureau of Census defines a metropolitan area as "a county having an urban center of 50,000 or more people and all the contiguous counties that can be shown to have close functional relations with the county containing the urban center" (Hawley 1971:150).

There are more than 230 metropolitan areas in the United States. An example of a metropolitan area is the greater Chicago area, often referred to locally as "Chicagoland." Although the city of Chicago has a population of only about three million, the "Chicagoland" population is over seven million.

An urbanized area is defined as "the central city plus all contiguous area having approximately 500 houses per square mile, or a population density of around two thousand persons (or more) per square mile" (Hawley 1971:151).

Before the era of written history, archaeology (prehistory) shows that humans were living in cities. Village settlements of a few hundred people, usually farmers, were the first stable communities. In some areas, particularly in the "fertile crescent" of the Mesopotamian valley, some of these farming settlements grew quite large. However they did not qualify as cities because all the inhabitants were full-time farmers.

The first cities were not just living areas for farmers but were set off somewhat from agriculture. Two factors were necessary for the beginning of true cities: surplus food and a density of population, with some people freed from food production to engage in manufacturing and trade. Cities came into being because of a change in the social order. In turn, the cities encouraged and hastened this change. The experience of Cain's founding a city, as recorded in the fourth chapter of Genesis, is interesting to compare with the scientific narration of the founding of cities. It was only following the founding of his city that there was recorded the subsequent development of musical instruments and the smelting processes producing bronze.

The changes in the social order that were involved in the development of the early cities included the following:

1. Increased occupational specialization. Instead of each family providing all of its needs, it specialized and overproduced in certain areas.
2. A market for the exchange of goods and the development of a barter economy.
3. The emergence of political leadership and a governmental structure.
4. A management of labor and allocation of resources.
5. Different rewards for different tasks leading to a status system and stratification.

While the above five factors figured in the development of cities, there were three additional factors responsible for the continued growth of cities, as we saw in chapter 6. The first of these factors was the development of money. With the development of tokens of fixed value, which we term money, economies could advance from their barter-based economy, wage labor was possible. Instead of one man making the whole shoe, for example, so that he would have something to barter or trade, several shoemakers could work for one shoemaker, one making heels, another making soles, another making bodies, and still another assembling the shoe. The owner of the business could sell the shoes for cash and pay his workers in cash wages, which the workers could use to provide for their personal necessities.

A second factor responsible for the growth of cities was the development of the alphabet. When humans were able to read and write, further industrial progress was possible. Messages did not have to be carried personally but could be written and delivered by another. This facilitated increased trade and enabled governments to operate more efficiently. The development of writing and reading also led to the development of postal services.

Even with the development of money and the alphabet, the growth of cities would still have been limited were it not for the third factor: technology. As technology advanced, more efficient farming implements were developed, allowing each farmer to produce more food, and thus freeing workers from the land. These people in turn migrated to the cities and entered the wage labor market. As technology increased, the need for wage laborers increased. New factories opened, and the need for skilled artisans, such as blacksmiths, decreased, while the need for laborers increased.

Sex, Age, and Social Function Groupings

Kinship groups are built on consanguineal ties. Because each person may be genealogically related to hundreds of others, most cultures provide *rules of descent,* a set of ordered relations limiting recruitment into the various kinship groups that compose a society. Descent rules are generally divided into *bilateral,* affiliation traced through both parents and relatives of either sex, and *unilateral,* affiliation traced through one parent or relatives of one sex only extending back to the founder of the line.

Bilateral descent groups may be *ego centered* and traced outward by each person to collateral limits, or *non–ego-centered* being traced outward from some prominent individual in each generation. Nonbilateral groups may be unilinear and traced through one relationship only, such as a patrilineal or male–only line, a matrilineal or female–only line, or through double descent permitting the tracing through both equally or by parallel descent in which males affiliate with the father's group and females with the mother's group. Nonbilateral groups may also be multilinear and so traced through a number of affiliations.

Descent groups may involve *moieties* or basic dual divisions in society. These may be divided into phratries, which are associations of clans cooperating together. Clans are divided into lineages, which are generally associated with some specific founder or source and continue relating to that founder or source. Lineages are in turn divided into extended families, and these are divided into nuclear families.

Clans are usually unilinear descent groups tracing descent from a remote, and often mythical, ancestor. They practice exogamy, causing the marriageable child to marry outside the clan. Caste societies, generally associated with India, have castes, rather than clans. These are primarily endogamous, forcing marriage within the caste. They are further associated with traditional occupations. Although they are interdependent because of the strict occupational specialization practiced within a complex division of labor, the castes, ranked in relation to one another, force an isolation and alienation of the castes unparalleled in other social structures in the world.

The Hebrew social system during the prekingdom period consisted of *extended families,* a male patriarch and all those for whom he was responsible. These might include other relatives, his wives, offspring of his wives, and his servants. As the extended family grew, lineages were formed. These lineages grouped into tribes, ultimately twelve of them, each named after a son or grandson of Jacob.

As the society changed to a kingdom under the leadership of Saul and with the express permission of God, the characteristics of social organization shifted from patriarch (first-born male) responsible for a kin-related grouping within tribes, to a king responsible for the whole of the society. The society was still oriented to the male but even this practice experienced change by New Testament times when women could be named as heads of families.

Illustrating age as an organizing principle in group formation, the *Tiriki Age Groups* are organized around seven age levels or groupings: Kabalach, Golongolo, Jiminigayi, Nyonje, Mayina, Juma, and Sawe. Each embraces approximately a fifteen-year age span. Each group passes successively through four distinctive age grades: warriors, elder warriors, judicial elders, and ritual elders. The system is cyclical, each age group being reinstated with new initiates approximately every 105 years.

When a new age group closes, the initiates become warriors, the warriors move into the elder warrior grade, the former elder warriors become judicial warriors, and the former judicial warriors become ritual elders. The initiation spreads over a six-month period. At initiation, a boy receives a spear from his father or uncle and becomes a warrior. At the same time, he is given an ox and thus becomes a herdsman.

The warriors are formally given the responsibility of guarding the land. The elder warriors gradually assume an increasing share of administrative type activities. At public postfuneral gatherings held to settle property claims, one elder warrior is named chairman. His duty is to maintain order, to see that all the claims and counter-claims are heard, and to initiate compromises. However, he is always to seek for and defer to the judgment of the elders in matters that are equivocal or a departure from tradition. Members of this age grade also serve as couriers and envoys when important news needs to be transmitted between elders at different subtribes.

The warriors of the judicial elder age grade fulfill most of the tasks connected with the arbitration and settlement of local disputes. The ruling elders preside over the priestly functions of the homestead ancestral shrine observances, at subclan meetings concerning inheritance and the like, at semiannual community supplications, and at the initiation rites. They also are accredited with having access to magical powers. They are the group that expels or kills witches and calls for the death through sorcery of anyone cursed by the community for violating the initiation secrets or for committing some other heinous crime.

An age-village society, such as Nyakyusa of Africa, carries the age-grade organization to the extreme of forming a village around members of an age-set. Elders donate land to their sons so that the process may continue. Between the ages of five and eleven, the boys sleep in the home of their parents and care for the family cattle. About the age of twelve the boys turn the cattle over to younger brothers and begin to hoe in their father's fields. At this age they depart from their parental homes and live in a village of their own, returning to their own homesteads only for meals. Gradually, the younger brothers mature and join them until the village is closed.

Upon reaching the age of twenty-five or so, the young men marry, bringing their wives into the village and setting up their own homes. Each man receives his own fields from his father and begins eating food prepared by his wife. After a number of villages are established in a territory, full political supervision is ceremonially turned over to the sons, and the fathers step aside.

Illustrating social function groups, the *cofradias* of Central America are socioreligious, voluntary associations assigned to specific saints in the Catholic array of saints. The saints are ranked in importance and thus the attending *cofradias* are also. Each *cofradia* has from eight to fifteen male leaders or *mayordomos* and a set of female counterparts in a separate but linked women's *cofradia*. Each *mayordomo* is elected by the full ongoing membership of the *cofradia* for a two-year period of service. After this time he is to rest a minimum of a year during which time he accumulates the cash reserve needed to enter the *cofradia* and fulfill his responsibilities within it. When he is ready to reenter, he is elected in at a higher rank. He pays dues in keeping with his new rank within a given *cofradia*. The lowest ranked *mayordomo* of the lowest ranked *cofradia* would likely pay about fifty cents a year dues. The highest ranked *mayordomo* in the highest ranked *cofradia*, i.e., that of the town saint, might pay as much as five hundred dollars a year.

Irrespective of rank, however, each *mayordomo* performs the same duties as every other *mayordomo*. By the time a man is forty and has moved through the ranks according to the service and rest plan, he can handle any responsibility assigned him in the society. His rank does not, however, entitle him to order or boss anyone, for each Pocomchi sees himself equal to every other Pocomchi. Thus, decisions are made corporately, and a given decision is delayed until all agree.

The active *mayordomo* plan and execute the festival assigned to their organization by virtue of the saint they patronize. They honor the saint by caring for the images representing the saint. Although the women wash the clothing of the image, the men decorate the altar of their saint in the home of the highest ranked *mayordomo*. The members collect dues and raise money for their respective activities even going so far as to slaughter a cow or dress in women's clothing and parade around town collecting money from each household. Members of the women's *cofradia* prepare the food for the men when they are gathered in service to their saint.

Women and Voluntary Associations

Biological differences have forced social differences on humans in society. That females bear the children whom male and female have conceived forces upon society the need to distinguish their respective roles. From the moment a woman goes into childbirth until she is able to move about freely again, she is unable to do her part, and another must take over. Whether there are other biological differences such as strength or ability have not yet been fully resolved, but at least there is no question about this one difference.

In some societies, the woman is permitted to work right up to her confinement for childbirth. This is the North American plan. Although the woman may take leave of her job, she is still permitted to take care of the house until the moment she leaves for the hospital. In other societies, the woman is confined early but is up and about as soon as the child is born. Among the Black Caribs of Honduras, Belize, and Guatemala the practice of *couvade,* as previously noted, causes the man to go to bed for a number of days following the birth of the child, and the woman is up and about. The North American woman, on the other hand, remains under medical care for a period of time, and it is assumed she will become active in household chores only after satisfactory recuperation. She will return to her job only when her strength has fully returned.

Among the Australian aborigines, females are excluded from religious spheres of rituals and secret societies. Among the Pocomchi, an all-male *cofradia* or brotherhood dominates the religious scene, even to the point of decorating the altar with floral bouquets. The women have their own *cofradia* and hierarchy within it. (It is a "shadow" organization, limited in function and authority and only existing for the sake of the male organization.) They never decide anything nor approve any action without the consent of the male organization. Among the Great Lakes American Indians, however, male and female shamans participate, without distinction, in the medicine lodge. Among the Isnew, non-Christians of the northern Philippines, religious and magical matters are largely handled by female priestesses or seers.

The Hopi of Arizona have a women's association into which all young people are initiated. When children are seven to ten years of age, the parents select a good ceremonial father for them. Up to that time they consider the *kachina* a supernatural visitor. At the time of initiation they are informed that the one in the mask is someone they know but is transmuted into a god when donning a mask.

During the initiation, the child is placed on a sand painting within a ceremonial chamber and whipped by the *kachinas*. After this the *kachinas* whip one another. Then the initiate is warned of the horrible punishment that he or she will suffer for giving away the secrets just learned. The ceremonial parents then take the child home for a feast.

Groups and Ministry

Society functions to bring together people who need to be together and to separate those who need to be separated. At times the system malfunctions and brings together those who become enemies, but more often it separates people who need someone of a different group. Thus it is that each member of a society needs to be trained in effective interpersonal relationships. Ideally this is accomplished by the maturation process within a social context. One of the functions of the primary group called the family is to prepare the child for life in the larger world outside the family. It does this by giving the child practice within the family, in a group where errors and oddities are lovingly overlooked.

The socialization process does not always effectively accomplish its purposes, and frequently one learns inadequate means of relating to another or simply does not use what has been learned. Sometimes one person can ignore another person so completely because of activities and responsibilities defined within the cultural context that a given person will be in effect lost, at least to one person, within the context of culture. Society thus provides the network of communication in which contact may be made; yet a member of that society may fail to make maximum usage of the network and find himself in mental or emotional troubles, as illustrated in the opening anecdote of this chapter.

But just because someone is relating to another does not mean that that person has effective interpersonal skills. The more one learns of effectiveness in interpersonal and intercultural communication, the more one finds he or she needs to learn. Simply following a given theory of interpersonal communication does not guarantee effectiveness in communication. To be effective, communication skills need to leave each communicator as a whole person, viable and vital within the context of each one's culture and able to aid the other within the other's context.

Interpersonal relations are not in effect any different from intercultural relations. In fact, all contact with others is intercultural and calls for interpersonal skills that are at the same time crosscultural. Even twins, as we noted previously, riding in the same stroller, see different things. This seeing of different things is the foundation for producing distinctiveness in cultural development.

Jesus Christ was an effective communicator, expressing Himself both verbally and nonverbally in ways that developed interpersonal relationships for ministry. Jesus formed a small group of disciples and ministered with them and through them. They became the core of the church.

There are various ways of analyzing Jesus' process of developing relationships and small group dynamics. One of those models is the Interpersonal Pyramid. (See figure 10-1.)

Need Satisfaction

Need satisfaction forms the foundation for interpersonal relationships. We have already examined Malinowski's basic needs and have seen how they are met through cultural systems. The opportunity to have immediate needs satisfied is a primary force in motivating people to develop new relationships. Thus unsatisfied felt needs are the initial points for contacting our fellow humans.

Parallel to the initial satisfying investment we make in another person is the benefit we receive as the other reciprocally satisfies our own needs. This is not to imply a cold economic relationship, however. It is simply to point out that both costs and rewards are involved.

It should also be noted that needs are often revealed unintentionally through nonverbal and verbal behavior. This makes it possible to develop a relationship on the felt-need level. Of course, as a relationship cyclically develops on the higher trust level, effectiveness in satisfying should also increase. Increased trust will free the other to intentionally disclose his needs and accept help. This is the principle utilized in a small-group encounter to build a relationship within the church program.

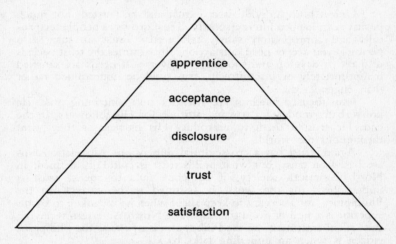

Figure 10-1. INTERPERSONAL PYRAMID. Each higher level of the pyramid represents the successive steps usually encountered as a relationship develops through time—both on the micro level of minutes and on the macro level of years. Relative fulfillment at any level provides an impelling freedom to step up and develop the relationship to the same degree on the next level.

Jesus saw human beings with all their needs—biophysiological, sociocultural, and spiritual—as parts of a whole. His interpersonal lifestyle was aimed at satisfying the needs of the whole person. Nevertheless, He began with the need a person was feeling most urgently.

This is beautifully illustrated by His dealings with the woman at the well. Her response to His ministrations was not "Come see a man who told me what I need to know." It was "Come, see a man who told me everything I ever did" (John 4:29). To her it meant that Jesus knew her. By looking at life from the other's point of view, He was able to scratch a man where he itched and, in turn, free him to grow and give attention to life at higher levels.

Jesus was also willing to be a recipient as well as a giver. By His willingness to allow others to satisfy His needs, He preserved their individual responsibility and self-worth. To be like Jesus is to satisfy the immediate needs of the other whole person to the degree that we are capable of doing so and to allow the other to reciprocally satisfy us.

Trust

Unless both individuals can trust and be trusted, not much positive can happen interpersonally. Trust grows as people reciprocally and appropriately satisfy felt needs. Trust, in turn, also permits even deeper need satisfaction. But at times the trust cycle is difficult to develop and too easy to reverse. If needs are satisfied inappropriately or insensitively, trust will be undermined rather than engendered.

Jesus focused much of His attention on maintaining trust. He nonverbally modeled a trusting attitude for His followers. In the end, He trusted them to reproduce His likeness as they went throughout the world.

Again, trust has a crosscultural dimension. All relationships are based on trust, but what builds trust is culturally defined. In North American society, if someone fails to speak, trust is undermined; for the worst is assumed to be correct. In the Philippines, for a servant to keep silent when he is spoken to by his superior is a sign of good training. The North American receiving the "silent treatment" in the Philippines is upset, as the Philippine citizen is when an underling talks back.

Disclosure

Self-disclosure refers to the process of intentionally making ourselves known to another person significant to us. This level is vital, for we can fully know ourselves only through the process of revealing ourselves to another—and another can fully know us only to the extent that we disclose ourselves to him or her. It is this function that the family primary group fulfills quite naturally and automatically. No one can live in such close juxtaposition without knowing something of the other that he would seek to keep from the outside world.

In relation to the lower pyramid levels, disclosure is free to emerge to the degree that prior trust has already been established. Disclosure, in turn, also increases interpersonal trust and provides a greater depth to our knowing and satisfying another's needs.

People who disclose themselves to others always take a risk. The negative cycle of rejection and hurt coexists with the positive cycle of acceptance and growth. Because the risk of personal damage is real, self-disclosure should not be practiced indecorously. It is appropriate to the degree that the relationship has already developed on the mutual-trust level of the interpersonal pyramid.

We must also be careful to support the self-disclosure of others
in a trustworthy manner. We will undermine the process of self-
disclosure if we

1. do not respond to another's self-disclosure with acceptance.
2. do not respond by reciprocally disclosing ourselves.
3. "overdisclose" far beyond the level of mutual trust established and thereby sabotage the relationship.

Openness is necessary in all relationships. However, culture
defines the levels of openness that is appropriate for a given
situation. It is just as easy to make the mistake of being too open in
a situation as it is to make the mistake of not being open enough.
North Americans tend to be more open in casual relationships than
most Asians. In intercultural exchanges North Americans often
find Asians "secretive," while Asians find North Americans
intrusive.

Acceptance

Acceptance is needed following self-disclosure. It needs to be
applied to oneself as well as to the other. As individuals gain new
self-awareness as a result of self-disclosure, they can react to this
new self-knowledge with either self-acceptance or self-rejection.
Often the easier path is self-rejection. Rejection, or self-denial, of
what I am presently and potentially is a way of absolving the self of
responsibility. However, since Jesus has accepted us just as we are,
the only valid response is self-acceptance. Jesus did not say, "Love
your neighbor and hate yourself." He said, "Love your neighbor as
yourself" (Matt. 19:19).

Also, as an individual gains a new knowledge of another
person as a result of mutual sharing, he or she can respond with
either acceptance or rejection and feedback. However, if Jesus is our
acknowledged model, we dare not reject a fellow-man. Jesus didn't
say, "Do not judge others unjustly." He simply said, "Do not
judge" (Matt. 7:1).

Self-accepting people generally find it easier to accept others.
Individuals who are more self-rejecting also find it more difficult to
accept others. Self-acceptance is a key to accepting others. Self-
acceptance makes it easier for us to practice self-disclosure and
respond positively to the self-disclosure of others.

Healthy self-acceptance also opens an individual to personal
change. Change growing out of Jesus-like acceptance tends to be in
keeping with both one's unique self and in becoming all that God
created one to be.

Jesus' lifestyle was one of continual acceptance. He accepted
Himself, others, and the Father. Although He always rejected
individual sin, He never rejected the individual.

All peoples of the world must learn to accept one another and let this acceptance form a solid foundation under their interpersonal relationships. Each culture defines how this acceptance will be communicated even as it is established.[1] The North American shakes hands with the one he respects and accepts. The Filipino holds hands with the one (even a male) whom he accepts.

Apprenticeship

The apprentice relationship forms the peak of the interpersonal pyramid. The New Testament word *mathētēs* is usually translated "disciple," meaning one who is a student or learner. T. W. Manson has suggested that in Aramaic, which Jesus spoke, the word more precisely meant "apprentice." He states that "Jesus was their Master not so much as a teacher of right doctrine, rather as the mastercraftsman whom they were to follow and imitate. Discipleship was not matriculation in a Rabbinical College but apprenticeship to the work of the Kingdom" (*The Teaching of Jesus,* 240).

Regardless of the word one prefers, when our interpersonal relationships have acquired the characteristics of being satisfying, trusting, disclosing, and accepting, we desire to develop apprentice relationships. The motivation for apprenticing is the altruistic need and affectionate desire to encourage another to grow. It was called the training model in an earlier chapter. It is the patient desire to help another bring his interpersonal potential into actuality.

Apprenticing means that we accept two major responsibilities:

1. We will serve as a model for another with whom we have achieved a deep mutual acceptance. We will allow him to identify with and emulate us, even as Paul suggests, "Be followers of me."
2. We will encourage our apprentice to develop his own apprentice. We will help him serve as a model to another, who, in turn, can then develop his own apprentice.

The El Mamey congregation of the Choco church in Panama was torn with dissension over the government-supported school and its controversial teacher. Gossip, quarrels, and the threats of violence had created severe interfamily tensions. Over and above the central school issues were personal problems of crops damaged by neighbors' animals, unpaid loans and wages, marital infidelities (or at least accusations of attempted seductions), and accusations of sorcery. When overt conflict and permanent damage to the community unity seemed imminent, Pastor Aureliano called a church and community meeting. When the people arrived, they found that the benches in the chapel had been placed not in rows as usual for worship service, but in a circle around the perimeter of the

[1] See Eugene Nida, *Message and Mission,* 215–21.

chapel. The people came in small groups and entered the chapel with obvious discomfort—there was estrangement in the air. But the pastor welcomed them all, opened the meeting with some singing, and then told the assembled group that the time had come to confess offenses, to forgive each other, and to establish peace in the church and in the community. For this part of the service he asked all the people to kneel by their benches facing the outside wall of the building. Thus, setting the example, he personally confessed his anger against the cantankerous schoolteacher and admitted that he also had maligned several men of the community. Then, after having apologized to the offended persons individually and to the people in general, he asked God's forgiveness in prayer. This catalytic self-exposure precipitated an extended session of confession and clarification of difficulties and led to mutual forgiveness and the reestablishment of fellowship. The young church had overcome a crisis that had threatened its very survival.

The above case illustrates application of the interpersonal pyramid on the small-group level. The levels of the pyramid are not to be thought of as rigid. Each step has a fluid relationship with the levels above and below it. A strengthening effect occurs back and forth between levels. Successfully relating at a lower level makes it appropriate and desirable to develop the relationship on the next level to the same degree. Developing on the higher level, in turn, confirms and strengthens the lower levels, which, again in turn, create the potential for an even higher degree of development. Of course, the opposite can also occur. Relationships are not built once and for all. They are gradually developed and must be constantly maintained. Inappropriate behaviors at any level can hinder further interpersonal development, make maintenance of past levels difficult, and even create a reverse process in which the relationship falls apart.

Questions for Discussion

1. What are some primary groups of which you are a member? Some secondary groups?
2. In what ways is the college a community? What type of community is it?
3. Is your church a primary or a secondary group? Which should it be? Why?
4. At what level of the "interpersonal pyramid" should the missionary work? Why?

Suggested Reading

Caplow, T. 1968. *Two Against One.* This work develops the idea that all social interaction is basically triadic in nature because even the behavior of a pair is subject to the influence of an audience. The third party interprets the interaction according to cultural norms. This book presents a unique approach to interpersonal social interaction.

Castell, J. L. 1968. *The Creative Role of Interpersonal Groups in the Church.* An interesting and informative work dealing with the role of small groups in the church.

Davis, J. H. 1969. *Group Performance.* A social and psychological approach to group dynamics. The approach is basically monocultural, but it gives a basic introduction to group processes.

Redfield, R. 1960. *The Little Community and Peasant Society and Culture.* Two essays in one book. The essay on the little community is applicable to this chapter. The author explores the various means by which researchers try to understand human communities.

Snarey, J. 1976. *Jesus-Like Relationships.* A group course in how to develop Christian interpersonal effectiveness. It presents a developmental stage model based on the lifestyle of Jesus Christ and the findings of behavioral science research. Bible studies, awareness games, and readings are used to allow the participants to discover and experience each stage: to satisfy, trust, disclose, accept, and flow.

Wilson, M. 1962. *Good Company: A Study of Nyakyusa Age Villages.* Interesting case study of age groups in a tribal society.

11

Social Control and Government

One day while Wolf Lies Down, a Cheyenne Indian, was away from his lodge, a friend from another camp came to Wolf Lies Down's lodge and took one of his horses and rode off to war. When Wolf Lies Down returned to his lodge, he found one of his horses missing. He also found his friend's bow and arrow in his lodge. His friend had left the bow and arrow as a token to let Wolf Lies Down know who had borrowed his horse.

When a year had passed since his horse was taken, Wolf Lies Down asked the chiefs of his society, the Elk Soldiers, to come to his lodge. He showed them the bow and arrow his friend had left and asked their advice and help in getting his horse back. He asked the chiefs to intercede for him with his friend.

Even though the friend, who had borrowed Wolf Lies Down's horse, was in a far-off camp, the chiefs agreed to intercede. A messenger was sent to the far-off camp to get the friend.

After a period of time, the messenger returned with the friend who was riding the borrowed horse and leading two other horses. When the friend arrived, he asked to see the Elk Soldiers chiefs. When he met with the chiefs, they told him what Wolf Lies Down had told them.

The friend agreed with the account given by Wolf Lies Down. He went on to explain that he had been gone longer than he had expected and when he returned he found that his camp had moved farther away from that of Wolf Lies Down. The horse brought him luck, he added, and pointed out that he had taken excellent care of the horse. He went on to explain that he had been waiting for the two camps to move closer to return the horse. Besides returning the horse he had borrowed, the friend offered Wolf Lies Down one of the other horses he had brought with him and said he could keep the bow and arrow.

Wolf Lies Down, who had also been present, replied that he would take one of the horses and keep the bow and arrow but that his friend could keep the horse he had borrowed. Then Wolf Lies Down reaffirmed his friendship with his friend.

The Elk Soldiers chiefs approved of the agreement and reaffirmed the friendship of their society with that of the friend. Then the chiefs announced a new rule. They declared that from then on no one should borrow anything without asking first. If anyone borrowed anything without first asking permission of the owner, the chiefs would retrieve the borrowed property and have the borrower whipped (Llewellyn and Hoebel 1941).

Every society has some form of governmental system. Each has social mechanisms for social control. Society could not exist without some type of social control. *Government* is the term we apply to a society's mechanisms and structures for the maintenance of that control and communal decision making.

Walter Goldschmidt distinguishes between two levels of social mechanisms for maintaining social control:

> We must distinguish between governance and government. . . . Governance means that pattern of behavior in a society that accords a set of recognized rights for certain people under certain circumstances to enforce their will over the actions of others, whether sanctioned by seniority, kinship, wealth or whatnot. By contrast, government has reference to a special set of institutions by means of which such decisions are regularly rendered; that there are offices, official roles, and sanctions for their support. A government may be defined as that agency which has a monopoly on the legitimate use of force. Many societies perform the functions of governance without such special institutional machinery (1971:420).

Meyer Fortes and E. E. Evans-Pritchard (1940) also see government as a more highly organized system and agree with Goldschmidt that not all societies have government. On the other hand, Schapera (1956) says all societies have government, because every society recognizes certain of its members as having the authority to make communal decisions.

Because every society has mechanisms for making communal decisions and maintaining societal control, we agree with Schapera that every society has government. However, we also see the validity of Goldschmidt's distinguishing between levels of complexity of government. To distinguish between these levels, we will use the terms *informal government* and *formal government*.

Informal government is a system for making communal decisions and maintaining social control based on a kinship, economic, seniority, or some other existing system as opposed to utilizing a separate system set up for these purposes. *Formal government* is an independent system set up for the purpose of making communal decisions and maintaining social control. It is institutionalized, having offices and roles. A formal government has a monopoly on the legitimate use of force.

Origin of Government

Because every society has some form of government, social scientists have speculated on the origin of government. Cultural anthropologists are more concerned with the present than the past. They are concerned with the functions of government in today's societies. However, an understanding of the development of a system often helps in understanding its present functions.

In the seventeenth century Hobbes and Locke suggested the "contract theory" to explain the origin of government. They postulated that, in prehistory, humans saw their need for cooperation with others in order to survive. To maintain a cooperative society, they needed to subjugate some of their individual rights to the rights of the society as a whole. A "contract" was established whereby the members of society surrendered certain individual rights to the group in exchange for certain benefits from the group. Government is the outgrowth of this "contract." It enforces the "contract" and carries out its provisions.

Some anthropologists speculate that government grew out of the family's need to control sex, property, and children. As we have seen, the family is the basic unit of society. For the family to function, there has to be a decision-making process and a system of social control. As groups of families began to live together, they adapted the mechanisms used in individual families for use in the larger group.

Many anthropologists see government as a natural outgrowth of group living. The larger and more complex a group becomes, the greater the need for social controls. Every society, from the most primitive to the most advanced, needs to enforce communal decisions, settle disputes, and protect rights and property. The function of government is to promote the general welfare of the group as a whole.

Social Control

Because culture is learned and shared attitudes, values, and behavior, we expect the members of a culture to behave in similar ways. Members of a culture learn the appropriate behavior for a given situation. Not only do they adhere to that behavior pattern, but they also expect others to adhere to the behavior pattern. For example, we not only drive on the right-hand side of the road, but we also expect others to drive on the right-hand side. These regular and expected patterns of behavior are called *norms*.

There may be four factors that produce normative behavior (Gergen 1969). The first is *maximizing satisfaction*. When a pattern of behavior leads to the maximum satisfaction of the majority of people, it becomes normative. When a society finds a pattern of behavior that meets the needs of most of its members, it will tend to reinforce that pattern. In our society we have found that the exchange of money for goods and services meets the needs of most of our members; so we reinforce this pattern.

The second factor that produces normative behavior is the *value of predictability*. Predictability has great value in the maintenance of society. A person is able to function better when he can predict the behavior of others. It is much easier to drive a car when I can predict that other drivers will stay to the right, stop for red lights, and follow the other norms or rules of the road. Because predictability is so valuable in this situation, we give traffic tickets to violators of these norms.

The third factor is *restraint of power*. Gergen explains:

> If the stronger fully exercises his power, he may be forced into the undesirable activity of monitoring the behavior of the less powerful. The less powerful, on the other hand, is likely to experience poorer outcomes (less satisfaction) should power be used to dictate all his actions. Norms thus become a way of insulating both members of the relationship from unbridled use of power (1969:74).

This factor is illustrated by the patron–client relationship as it was practiced in Benabarre, Spain (Barrett 1974). Several anthropologists have discussed the importance of the patron–client relationship in tying the upper classes to the lower classes in Spanish society (Pitt-Rivers 1961 and Kenny 1960). In Benabarre, before the war, this relationship was a central feature of the social order. One of the major characteristics of patron-client relationships is that this relationship is built on the acceptance of inequality. Powerful and socially superior persons take on the role of benefactors and protectors for persons who are their social inferiors. Their superiority comes from their ability to be benefactors and protectors. The patron becomes a parent figure to the clients and treats them as less than fully mature adults. The patrons recognize their obligation to be generous to the poor and humble. The patron has a sense of *noblesse oblige*. The client reciprocates by working for the patron or in various other ways serving the patron's interests. The patron-client relationship involves obligations on both sides.

An illustration of restraint of power in American society is the recent findings concerning assembly-line workers, management, and productivity. Management can be seen as the more powerful and the assembly-line workers as less powerful. Recent research indicates that when assembly-line workers are allowed to participate in the decision-making process, productivity goes up. For assembly line workers to participate in the decision-making process requires management to practice restraint of power. This restraint of power becomes beneficial to both parties; so this behavior pattern becomes normative.

The fourth factor that produces normative behavior is *secondary gains*. Many times a pattern of behavior becomes rewarding in itself. A student will often read a certain type of literature because it is required. However, the student may find he enjoys that literature and continues to read it even when the class is completed. Norms that may have once been functional, may no longer be functional but are continued as rituals because they are satisfying in themselves. Most of our homes have central heating and have no need for a fireplace, but we add fireplaces because we enjoy them for themselves, not necessarily as heat producers.

Every society has norms by which its members are expected to live. But in no society are the norms always followed by everyone. Therefore, all societies have mechanisms for social control. These mechanisms operate at different levels.

The lowest level of social control mechanisms is folkways. *Folkways* are the manners or customs of a culture, the polite way to do things. They are not enforced by law, and failure to follow them is not considered an act of immorality. An American folkway is the custom of shaking hands when introduced to another person. If a person does not shake hands, he will not be arrested nor will he be accused of being immoral; but he may well be called a boor or a snob and, perhaps, be socially avoided in the future.

Folkways usually cover areas like manners, dress, greetings and other such activities. They are usually enforced by ridicule, avoidance, negative comments, and other such mechanisms. They are usually peer enforced. Folkways are usually the product of cultural traditions. In the United States we drive on the right-hand side of the road. We have carried this over to our walking habits; so usually we walk to the right in a corridor or on a stairway. In the United States if one walks down a hall or up a stairway on the left side, he will not be arrested or called immoral. However, he will be pressured through looks and comments to walk to the right. The observance of folkways makes for smooth interactions in society.

At a more powerful level of social controls are mores. *Mores* are social rules and regulations of a moral nature. In the United States, lying to another person is not illegal, except in courts or in legal documents, yet lying is considered immoral in most circles. While interfaith marriage is not illegal in the United States, many subcultures have mores against marrying outside one's faith. Although in most African nations intertribal marriage is not illegal, it is against the mores of many African tribes.

Robert Lowie describes how some American Indians used scorn and ridicule to enforce mores:

> When a Fox Indian boy in Illinois was taught not to steal and never to abuse his wife, his elder did not hold up to him any tangible punishment here or hereafter nor any abstract rule of morality. The clinching argument was, "The people will say many things about you, although you may not know it."
>
> Gossiping sometimes took special forms of ridicule. An Alaskan youth thus reports his experience: "If you do not marry within your village, they joke about you—they joke so much that it makes it disagreeable." The Crow sang songs in mockery of a miser, a bully, or a man who should take back a divorced wife—the acme of disgrace. Certain kinsmen had the privilege of publicly criticizing a man for breaches of etiquette and ethics, and there was nothing he would fear more than to be thus pilloried. The system was developed by the Blackfoot along slightly different lines. "For mild persistent misconduct, a method of formal discipline is sometimes practiced. When the offender has failed to take hints and suggestions, the head men may take formal notice and decide to resort to discipline. Some evening when all are in their tipis, a head man will call out to a neighbor asking if he has observed the conduct of Mr. A. This starts a general conversation between the many tipis, in which all the grotesque and hideous features of Mr. A.'s acts

are held up to general ridicule, amid shrieks of laughter, the grilling continuing until far into the night. The mortification of the victim is extreme and usually drives him into a temporary exile or, as formerly, upon the warpath to do desperate deeds."

A primitive man sacrifices half his property lest he be dubbed a miser; he yields his favorite wife if jealousy is against the code; he risks life itself, if that is the way to gain the honor of a public eulogy. That is why savages of the same tribe are not forever cutting one another's throats or ravishing available women, even if they lack written constitutions, jails, a police force, and revealed religion (1929:157-68).

The highest level of social controls is that of laws. *Laws* are rules and regulations that are enforced by the state. The state may legitimately use force in their enforcement. Laws usually grow out of folkways and mores. Federal laws enforcing integrated education in the United States went against the folkways and mores of many southerners. At other times, laws are passed that are consistent with the prevailing mores. With time, the mores change but the law remains, creating a conflict. American draft laws were passed at a time when unquestioning patriotism was a more. During the Vietnam War, mores changed but the law remained, creating a conflict situation for many Americans. Another example is the 55 mile-per-hour speed limit passed during the oil crisis in the early seventies. By the mid-eighties there was a glut of oil and prices had dropped drastically. Many began to question the validity of the speed limit and began to violate it. They did not see breaking the law as a moral issue. The law has since been changed in several states.

Many people think that only advanced societies with legislative bodies, written codes, and a judicial system have laws. They see courts, police, correctional facilities, and legal personnel as necessary for a society to have law. However, in this century, anthropologists have come to recognize that all societies, no matter how primitive, have a legal system and laws, whether formal or informal.

In the case study at the beginning of the chapter about the horse of Wolf Lies Down, we see informal law at work. The chiefs acted as a court when they heard Wolf Lies Down's complaint. The chiefs then functioned as the police in sending for the friend who had borrowed the horse. When the friend arrived, the chiefs again functioned as a court. When the issue was settled, the chiefs acted as a legislative body and passed a new law to prevent future incidents of this type. The chiefs then functioned again as police and told how they would enforce the new law among the members of the Cheyenne tribe.

Our discussion so far has emphasized the positive aspects of norms, but there are also costs associated with norms. The benefits come at a price (Gergen 1969). The first cost is related to the need for novelty. Research has indicated that humans have an innate need for novelty (Berlyne 1960). In most societies, the creative members deviate from the norms in some areas. In fact, the idea of doing something out of the ordinary is embodied in the concept of creativity. Norms may stifle creativity.

The second cost of norms is that they are not functional for all members of society. What is best for most of the people in a society is not best for all the members of the society. For example, our public school system is designed for normal children and their needs. Below-average children, who need even more attention than normal children, are shunted to one side while above average children are forced to proceed at the pace of the average child. They may be bored and often may be labeled as troublemakers.[1]

The third cost of norms is that they crystallize inequities. In all societies some groups have certain advantages over other groups. These inequities are crystallized by the norms that develop. An example of this is the caste system in India. The norms associated with caste crystallize the inequities between castes. In our society racial inequities are crystallized by our norms.

The fourth cost of norms is the result of the changing environment. A norm that is functional in one point in time or in one place becomes crystallized and inflexible. When times or places change, the norm may become dysfunctional, but it is unable to be changed. We can see this in many Christian institutions. Rules were made at a time when they served a function. However, times change, and forbidden activities are no longer considered "sinful," but the rules continue.

The norms of a society are embodied in its folkways, mores, and laws. In modern, complex societies there are many sets of norms. No one is bound to all of these sets, but most persons are bound to one or more. However, in these societies there are a few people who are not bound to any set of norms. They are in a condition of normlessness, usually known as *anomie* (Durkheim 1897). Anomie is very rare in simple societies but quite common in more complex societies. In simple societies there are only a few sets of norms, and the person easily fits into them. In complex societies there are many sets of norms, and it is easy for a person to slip

---

[1] See Jules Henry, 1965, *Culture Against Man* (New York: Random) for many illustrations of this.

between sets and be bound to none.[2] The results of anomie are usually criminal behavior, mental illness, or both. Many suicide victims suffer from anomie.

Deviance

While the study of deviance has had a prominent place in sociology for some time, it had not been given as much attention in anthropology. However, recently there have been a number of anthropologists who have dealt with deviance (for example, Swartz 1972; Edgerton 1972; Langness 1972; Plog and Bates 1976; Howard 1986). An understanding of deviance can be invaluable to a missionary. In some societies, the very act of becoming a Christian may be seen by other members of that society as deviant behavior.

What is deviance? It is "behavior that violates normative rules" (Cohen 1966:12). Deviance is the violation of folkways, mores, and laws. Since folkways, mores, and laws differ from culture to culture, behavior that is considered deviant differs from culture to culture. For a man to have more than one wife would be considered deviant behavior in the United States, but it would not be considered deviant behavior among the Nuer of Africa. For a female to weave rugs in Hopi society would be considered deviant behavior, whereas among the Navaho it would be considered deviant for a man to weave rugs. It is important to be aware of the culturally relative nature of deviance. No act is deviant in and of itself, but it is only deviant if it is so defined by the culture.[3]

Merton (1957) has set forth three concepts that were implicit in Durkheim's book *Suicide:*

1. Culture goals—there are culturally taught wants and aspirations.
2. Norms—these are the means that may be legitimately used in pursuit of the culture goals.
3. Institutionalized means—these are the structures set up by society for the achieving of the culture goals in a normative manner.

Merton defined social strain as a sense of frustration, despair, or injustice. He saw strain arising from disjunctions between the three concepts listed above. For example, the culture goals in a

---

[2] See "The Absence of Group Affiliations" by Harvey Zarbough in Walter Goldschmidt's (1971) *Exploring the Ways of Mankind* (New York: Holt) for an excellent illustration of anomie.

[3] This does not mean that culture determines morality in an absolute sense. A culture may see a behavior as normative rather than deviant even though the Bible may condemn that behavior. A behavior condemned by the Bible is sin whether or not a culture sees it as deviant.

society may change without proper norms and means for achieving these new goals. On the other hand, social structure may change, thus frustrating the pursuit of the culture goals. Merton, drawing from Durkheim's concept of anomie (see page 221), sees anomie as arising when there is a stress-producing disjunction between the culture goals and the cultural means of attaining those goals. This strain leads to a weakening of peoples' commitment to the culturally prescribed goals or cultural means of attainment.

Merton (1957) spells out the logically possible ways a person can adapt to disjunction and strain:

1. The person may either accept or reject the cultural goals.
2. The person may either accept or reject the cultural means of goal attainment.
3. The person may replace the cultural goals and means.

Utilizing various combinations of the above choices, Merton presents five modes of adaptation (see figure 11-1). The first mode is *conformity,* the nondeviant mode. The person strives for the culture goals in the culturally approved ways. Merton considers the remaining four modes as deviant.

The second mode is *innovation.* A person accepts the culture's goals while rejecting the cultural means. For example, a student may accept the cultural goal of attaining good grades but may reject the cultural means of studying and attempt to attain the goal through cheating, a deviant behavior. Professional thieves and white-collar criminals are also examples of this mode.

The third mode is *ritualism.* This refers to persons who conform to the cultural means without concern for the culture goals. The means become the end instead of the goals. A biblical example of ritualism is the case of the Pharisees in their reaction to Jesus' healing on the Sabbath (Matt. 12:9–14). For the Pharisees the means had become the end. A modern example is the bureaucrat who follows the rules slavishly even when they are counterproductive.

Retreatism is the fourth mode. In this mode the person rejects both the cultural goals and the cultural means. Examples of this mode are tramps, skid-row alcoholics, drug addicts, and certain American Indians of the Southwest who have turned to the use of peyote, a hallucinogenic plant.

The fifth mode is *rebellion.* In this mode the person rejects the cultural goals and means and replaces them with new goals and means. The basis of rejection and replacement may be either moral or functional. Examples of this mode are political revolutionaries and members of fanatical religious groups. This is a mode in which missionaries and national Christians may find themselves in some societies. If cultural goals and means are in direct violation of

Scripture, the national converts may have to establish new goals and means.

MODES OF ADAPTATION	CULTURE GOALS	CULTURAL MEANS
Conformity	accept	accept
Innovation	accept	reject
Ritualism	reject	accept
Retreatism	reject	reject
Rebellion	replace	replace

Figure 11-1. MERTON'S MODES OF ADAPTATION

For example, in some South Pacific societies premarital sex is encouraged. No one would think of marrying a girl until she was pregnant. Since the cultural goal of marrying a pregnant girl and the cultural means, premarital sex, are in violation of biblical principles concerning sexual behavior and marriage, national Christians in those societies would have to use Merton's rebellion mode of adaptation and replace the cultural goal and means with a new goal and means consistent with biblical principles (not the missionary's culture).

Merton argues that American culture is anomic for two reasons. First, American society overemphasizes the culture goals of success and materialism while underemphasizing the cultural means of attainment. Overemphasis on the goals and underemphasis on the means result in disjunction and lead to deviant behavior in pursuit of the goals. Watergate and the events surrounding it are a classic example of this. A more recent example is the secret sale of weapons to Iran and the sending of profits to the Nicaraguan Contras by members of the Reagan administration. Second, Merton says Americans hold out the same cultural goals to all members of their society but do not provide equal opportunity for those members, and it is in these populations that we find proportionately more deviant behavior.

There are three ways in which deviance may be destructive or dysfunctional for a society or organization (Cohen 1966). First, deviance can have the same effect as the breakdown of a part on a machine. Not all deviant behavior is equally disruptive, just as the breakdown of different parts on a car are not equally disruptive. If a car radio breaks, the driver can still operate the car safely. If a tire goes flat, he cannot. But even here there is a difference between a blowout and a slow leak. Some deviant behavior is more disruptive than other types.

The second dysfunction of deviant behavior is that it undermines morale. If deviance becomes too prevalent, especially if it is not sanctioned, people begin to question the value of "playing by the rules." When deviant behavior results in a proportionately larger reward than normative behavior, morale is undermined.

The third dysfunction of deviant behavior is that it undermines trust. When a person "plays by the rules" of a society or an organization, he has made an "investment." If he does not believe he will get a "return" on his "investment," he may "pull out of the game." Even criminal activity is based on trust. An illegal bookmaker stays in business because his clients trust him. He pays off on wins. If the gamblers did not trust the bookmaker, they would not place bets with him and he would be out of business. All social relationships are built on trust. The undermining of trust undermines social relationships.

Cohen goes on to point out that deviance is not always disruptive in a society or organization; in some cases it may make a positive contribution. He suggests seven functions (or beneficial results) of deviance. One function that deviance may perform is to cut through red tape. When rules are established in societies or in organizations, not every possible eventuality can be foreseen. In some instances the rules may be counterproductive, and deviating from the rules may be in the best interest of the society or organization. In many complex organizations, if everyone followed every rule to the letter, the organization would cease to function.

A second function that deviance may perform is to act as a "safety valve." It allows persons to release tensions before there is an excessive accumulation of discontent. Practical jokes, pranks, pillow fights, TPing (toilet papering), and other forms of relatively harmless activities have served this function on college campuses for years. Another form of this behavior is computer "hacking." While some forms of "hacking" can be criminal, many engage in it only as a prank.

A third function of deviance is to clarify rules. When rules are first established, they are often fuzzy around the edges. Experimentation around these edges, until something is labeled deviant, helps to clarify the rules. For example, a business establishment may require its employees to dress "modestly." What is modest? When some persons dress in certain ways that are labeled "immodest," it helps clarify what "modest" is.

A fourth function that deviance may perform is to unite the group—against the deviant. It is well known that "nothing unites a group like a common enemy." The deviant within a society or an organization becomes an "enemy" within.

In Judges 20 there is an example of this function of deviance. In chapter 8, we discussed the account of the Levite from Ephraim who went down to Bethlehem to retrieve his concubine. Returning to Ephraim, he spent the night in Gibeah of Benjamin. There his concubine was gang-raped and killed. The Levite informed the other tribes of Israel about the rape and murder. All the other tribes united to punish Benjamin for this act of deviance.

Fifth, the deviant may again unite the society or organization, but this time in his behalf. The members of a good family stand behind each other even when one of them has done something wrong. In fact, a deviant act by one member of a family may rally the family around that person.

There is also an illustration of this fifth function of deviance in the account of the Levite who allowed his concubine to be raped and murdered. In Judges 20:12–13 the other tribes of Israel came to the tribe of Benjamin and asked them to turn over the men responsible for this act. However, the people of Benjamin rejected the demand of the other tribes and united around the men of Gibeah. In this case the Benjaminites rallied around the deviants and tried to defend them.

A sixth function that deviance may perform is that of providing a contrast. "Good" behavior always stands out better when it is contrasted to "bad" behavior. Deviants provide a contrast that makes conformists feel good. The censuring of the deviant is a backhanded reinforcement of the conformist's behavior.

The seventh function of deviance is that of a warning signal. Often a rise in deviant behavior is an indication that something is wrong somewhere. Jesus Christ deviated from the religious norms of His day, and this deviation was a warning that there was a problem with these norms (Matt. 12:1–14). Jesus used the mode of adaptation Merton calls rebellion, where the old goals and means are rejected and replaced with new ones. The goals of the pharisaical religious system were worldly, centering around recognition and honor, but the goals of Jesus' system were spiritual— service and true worship. Christians tend to defend the status quo and label deviance as bad. We need to be sensitive and discerning and be aware when deviance is warning us that change is needed.

The missionary needs to be aware that in many countries it is considered deviant behavior for a national to become a Christian. This is especially true in Islamic countries where the sanctions for this type of deviance may be severe. An understanding of deviance and its functions as well as dysfunctions can aid the missionary in developing an effective strategy for evangelism and church planting on the field.

Basis of Government

Many anthropologists recognize two bases on which government is organized: (1) kinship and (2) territoriality.

Kinship

Most primitive societies have a governmental system based on kinship. The unit of organization may be the extended family, the clan, the lineage, or the moiety. The leadership may be patriarchal or collective. In many kinship-based systems the leadership is a collectivity of the heads of the various households or clans.

The Bushmen of the Kalahari Desert of Botswana have a governmental system based on kinship. They are hunters and gatherers and usually organize into bands of twenty-five to fifty persons, often consisting of members of a single extended family. The leader is usually the head male of the dominant extended family. His functions consist primarily of directing the band's movements, presiding at ceremonial functions, and leading the band in warfare. The leader's authority is not absolute, but rests on tradition and his personality and ability to lead.

Not only small groups or societies have kinship-based governments. The Nuer of the Sudan in Africa, numbering approximately 200,000, is one of the largest tribes in that part of Africa; and yet, according to Evans-Pritchard (1940), they have no overall tribal government. Their government is based on their kinship system. Each clan polices and governs itself. In times of war, clans join together for mutual defense, but otherwise each clan is independent. Since there is no overall tribal government, disputes between clans are usually settled by feuds.

Territoriality

The second organizing principle on which government is based is territoriality. In practice, most kinship-based governments are also territorial. However, their basis of organization is kinship rather than territory. Most modern states are based on territory. All persons residing within a given territory come under the government of that territory regardless of kinship. A child born within the territory of the United States becomes a United States citizen regardless of the citizenship of the parents. However, even governments based on territoriality recognize kinship as a basis of government in some circumstances. For example, if a married American couple gives birth to a child outside the territory of the United States, that child is still a United States citizen.

Types of Government

We have talked about informal and formal government. In reality, governmental systems do not neatly fall into one of two categories but rather find their place somewhere on a continuum from family-based systems to modern states.

Clan

In a clan-based governmental system the largest governmental unit is the clan. Government is based on kinship and is quite informal. The kinship structure and the governmental structure are the same.

The Arunta of Australia provide an example of this type of system. They live in hunting and gathering bands, usually consisting of small migrating families. However, these families see themselves as part of a larger clan group. This group is exogamous and patrilocal. Their system of social controls is built around folkways. Enforcement is by ridicule and threat of banishment, though the threat is rarely carried out.

Multiclan

The governmental unit in a multiclan governmental system is a group of clans. Hottentots of South Africa have such a system. They are primarily a pastoral people who herd cattle and sheep. Organized into multiclan groups of about five hundred to twenty-five hundred persons, each multiclan group is completely autonomous from other multiclan groups of Hottentots.

In each group, one clan is considered senior to the others. The chief of the multiclan group comes from this senior clan. The office of chief is hereditary, passing from father to son. The heads of the other clans in the group constitute a ruling council. Although the power of the chief is great, his authority is ultimately subject to the ruling council.

Tribal

Although a multiclan group may be a tribe, a tribe does not have to be based on kinship. It may be composed of totally unrelated groups. Therefore we will define a tribe as a group of individuals who share language, culture, and territory and see themselves as an autonomous unit.

Tribal governments are usually headed by chiefs. While it may appear that chiefs have unlimited power, they usually have to answer to a tribal council, a kin group, or ultimately the gods. In some societies a chief may be subject to magic if he abuses his power. Such was the case among the Temne of Sierra Leone in Africa. A man could use "swearing medicine" against the chief if he was wronged by him, thereby attempting to harm the chief for abusing his power.

State

According to Hoebel (1972:523), the state is a governmental unit based on three elements: (1) territoriality, (2) cultural organization, and (3) centralized government with strong coercive powers. The state is characterized by such features as a bureaucracy, political specialization, taxation, and a military force.

Old Testament Hebrew Governmental System

In the Old Testament we are able to trace a people's transition form a clan to a state. Under Abraham, Isaac, and Jacob, the Hebrews were a clan. They were a nomadic, pastoral clan with a patriarchal form of government. From the time Jacob and his twelve sons entered Egypt until the Exodus, the Hebrews made the transition from a clan to a multiclan group. When the children of Israel left Egypt, they left as a multiclan group.

When the Hebrews arrived in Palestine, they were assigned to territories by clans. Under Joshua, the Hebrews continued as a multiclan group. With the death of Joshua, each clan developed into a tribe. During the period of the Judges, each tribe functioned autonomously. When there was threat of attack from the outside, some of the tribes fought together.

During the time of Samuel, Israel began its transition from tribal government to statehood with the anointing of Saul as king. However, it was not until Saul asserted his authority and threatened force against those who would not comply that the last vestiges of tribalism were put away and true statehood was achieved (1 Sam. 11:6–11).

Government and Missions

An understanding of the government of the missionary's host society is very important. When missionaries enter another society, they work within a new and different cultural system. It is just as important for missionaries to become familiar with the folkways and mores of the new culture as it is for them to become familiar with the laws of the new society. They should be sensitive to cultural cues from the nationals. Usually the nationals will not tell missionaries they have done something impolite, crude, or more seriously offensive. Missionaries must be aware of the folkways and mores and be sensitive to cues or feedback they receive from the nationals. Missionaries need to learn to observe and, if appropriate, ask questions.

An understanding of the governmental system is a valuable asset in a church-planting ministry in a new society. American society has a democratic system of government. Most American churches reflect that system. A vote is taken to call a pastor, to elect church officers, and to decide important issues facing the church. Americans take that form of government, both in their churches and in their country, for granted. In fact, they assume that democracy—and only democracy—is the Christian way.

The Bible does not lay down a clear pattern for church polity. What few glimpses we get of the government of the early church do not necessarily reveal a democratic process. In Acts 14:23 Paul and Barnabas appointed elders for the churches. In Acts 15 a church council decided matters of faith and practice.

When missionaries plant a church in another culture, a decision must be made about the type of church polity to be established. If the missionaries decide, they will probably set up a democratic system similar to that of their home church. If the nationals are to decide, they will set up an indigenous system, which most likely will not be democratic, since democracy is not extensively practiced outside the West. If missionaries impose a democratic system on the people, they will find the nationals electing the oldest male, or the wealthiest person, or only people from a certain clan, or whichever person would have had the leadership if they had set up the system following their own cultural model. Also, if the missionaries introduce a system of church polity that is alien to the culture, the church may quite likely become impotent in its government and weak in its witness, as the church members have no precedent by which to operate.

In any culture, the church polity should be that with which the nationals feel comfortable and can best function. Any functional system that does not violate biblical principles or cultural folkways and mores should be acceptable. The missionary should avoid the danger of trying to establish a democratic system of church polity in a culture that has no history of democratic government. If people have not had experience with democracy, it will probably not work.

Questions for Discussion

1. What type of social control mechanisms were practiced in your home? What type of government did your family have?

2. What are some more examples of folkways and mores in our culture? How are they enforced?
3. Some examples were given of conflicts between mores and laws. Can you think of any others? How did they develop?
4. What type of church polity is practiced in your home church? What is the basis for this system? What assumptions underlie it?
5. In what ways may deviance be functional? Give some examples from situations with which you are familiar.

Suggested Reading

Fortes, M., and Evans-Pritchard, E. E. 1955. *African Political Systems*. A collection of papers describing the political systems of various African societies. Several of the chapters give an insight into the changes in African political systems under colonialism.

Hoebel, E. A. 1954. *The Law of Primitive Man*. Illustrates the functions of law in primitive societies.

Mair, L. 1962. *Primitive Government*. A good treatment of government in underdeveloped societies. This book contains a good section on government without a state. The introduction has an excellent discussion of the anthropological use of the word *primitive*.

Nadar, L. 1969. *Law in Culture and Society*. Deals with the interrelationship of law and culture, the function of law, and its role in society.

Schapera, I. 1963. *Government and Politics in Tribal Societies*. Deals with government and politics in tribal societies. This work is recommended for those who anticipate a ministry in a tribal society.

Swartz, M. et al. 1966. *Political Anthropology*. A collection of readings on political anthropology. The readings deal with the dimensions of conflicts in political action, authority and authority codes, politics and rituals, and political fields and their boundaries. The last sections contain some especially interesting selections.

12

Religion

The Great Boss is the one who takes care of my sheep;
I don't want to own anything.
The Great Boss wants me to lie down in the field.
He wants me to go to the lake.
He makes my good spirit come back.
Even though I walk though something the missionary
    calls the valley of the shadow of death,
    I do not care.
You are with me.
You use a stick and a club to make me comfortable.
You manufacture a piece of furniture right in front
    of my eyes while my enemies watch.
You pour car grease on my head.
My cup has too much water in it and therefore overflows.
Goodness and kindness will walk single file behind me
    all my life.
And I will live in the hut of the Great Boss until I die and am
forgotten by the tribe.[1]

---

[1]The Twenty-third Psalm as it would be literally translated for the Khmu tribe of Laos. This translation appeared in the *Wichita Eagle* (January 7, 1960) as part of an interview with the missionary anthropologist Dr. William Smalley.

As we have seen in the preceding chapters, there are several social institutions universal to all cultures. Another social institution found in all cultures is religion. Every known society practices some form of religion. What do we mean by religion? As we have seen, anthropological usage of words often differs from their popular usage. To anthropologists the term *religion* refers to the shared beliefs and practices of a society. These beliefs and practices form the doctrines and rituals of the religion.

The beliefs of a society are usually codified, either orally or in written form. These codified beliefs make up the *doctrine* of the religion. The elementary form of belief is the myth. The term *myth,* when used as a technical concept by anthropologists, differs from its popular usage. *Myth,* as used by anthropologists, is a value-free term denoting neither falsity nor truth. Myths are distinct from folklore and legends. Myths deal with the supernatural and are primarily concerned with the origins of man and the material universe. James Down shares with us the Navaho origin myth:

> *Dine,* the Navajo term for themselves, means literally "People of the Surface of the Earth." The origin myth of the Navajo describes the ascent of the ancestors of the People of the Surface of the Earth to the surface and the adventures and miraculous happenings that led to the establishing of traditional Navajo life. It could be considered an allegory describing the wanderings of the Athapaskan-speaking peoples and their eventual arrival in the Southwest. It incorporates elements of mythology that are almost universal in the New World. Some themes even appear to have relations to myth elements common in Asia. Certain aspects of myth and ritual reflect association with other Southwestern people, especially the Hopi and other Pueblo tribes. Still other things are unique to the Navajo or at least to the Southwestern Athapaskans.
>
> Before there were Earth Surface People, there were, and are, the Holy People who once lived in the lowest of twelve worlds below the present surface of the earth. The Holy People are holy because they are powerful—not because they are perfect. It was in each instance some act of mischief or malice that forced the Holy People to move into a higher world. Usually one among them practiced witchcraft against the others and forced the move. In each world there were adventures and events that still have effect on the people of today. Practices were established, knowledge was created, and even special types of people appeared. For instance, in the third or fourth world (there is disagreement in the different versions of the myth) there appeared hermaphrodites or transvestites, men who dress and act like women. Such people today and in the past are somewhat venerated

by the Navajo and considered to have potential supernatural power. In the last world but one, men and women quarreled bitterly and decided to live separately, each sex on the opposite side of the river. The men, according to the myth, lived quite harmoniously, learning the skills of women and even inventing some important household implements and techniques. The women, on the other hand, after getting off to a good start, were unable to suppress their sexual urges. Details vary, but it would seem that they engaged in homosexual intercourse and also had intercourse with monsters. From these relations there sprang a whole series of monsters who were to plague the Navajo for a long time—some of them even today. Eventually the sexes reached a rapprochement and rejoined each other to live in traditional harmony. But soon a great flood began to fill the eleventh world, and the Holy People were forced to scramble up through a hollow reed to the surface of the earth.

On the earth, the natural objects were formed, the landscape shaped either by powers of the universe or by the Holy People themselves. Death appeared for the first time.

Prominent among the Holy People were First Man and First Woman, who were created from two ears of corn and who are felt by some to have created the Universe (or at least First Man is given the honor). But their important role is that of mother and father of Changing Woman, the most important figure in Navajo mythology. Her conception and birth were miraculous affairs, but the original pair raised her and trained and allowed her to mate with the Sun and with Water. This mating or matings (it's difficult to know) produced two sons, twins, who grew up to seek out their father the Sun and receive from him weapons and knowledge that allowed them to slay the monsters plaguing the earth and The People. The record of their victories is written in the landscape of the Navajo country. Prominent mountains, lava flows, and other natural features are identified with the carcasses of slain monsters (1972:96-97).

Since myths deal with origins, they are foundational to the belief system of a society. Sacred books usually contain the myths of the religion as well as other codified beliefs.

Along with the beliefs of a religion, there are also accompanying practices that make up the rituals of the religion. Anthropologists divide religious rituals into two types: rites of passage and rites of intensification.

Rites of passage mark an individual's passage from one stage in the life cycle to the next. The rite lets both the individual and the society know the individual has advanced from one stage to the next. Certain stages in the life cycle are marked by religious rites in almost all societies. These include birth, puberty, marriage, and death. In Christianity, birth is marked by christening, by baptism, or by baby dedication; puberty is marked by confirmation or its equivalent. Marriage involves a religious ceremony marking the passage into responsible adulthood, and death is marked by a funeral.

Rites of intensification are rituals that bring the community together, increase group solidarity, and reinforce commitment to the beliefs of the group. Communion is an example of a rite of intensification in Christianity. Some rites function as both rites of passage and rites of intensification, such as the baptismal service in Christianity.

Functions of Religion

Religion is found in all societies because it meets universal (social and psychological) needs. There are, perhaps, six basic cultural functions of religion (O'Dea 1966). The first is *psychological*. Religion provides support, consolation, and reconciliation. Human beings are relatively powerless in controlling their destiny. Despite their best-laid plans, sickness, natural disaster, and other circumstances beyond their control make the future very uncertain as the following paragraph indicates:

> Life is one big puzzle. You bend every effort on the hunt and fail while a lazy good-for-nothing brings home plenty of food. Your comrades on a war-party are killed, but *you* escape. Neighbor X looked hale and hearty when he suddenly fell dead. Why does cousin Y always win at button, button, who's got the button? Why did his wife bear twins? What's the meaning of that owl hooting about the lodge night after night? All this is strange, some of it uncanny. There is supernatural power floating about; the universe teems with it. By hook or by crook you had better get some if you want to live safely, gain social position, win at gambling, or prevent *your* wife from bearing twins. You have to solve an equation with an infinite number of unknown quantities, and unfortunately your happiness, your life and death depend on finding the right answers. So tread softly in the universe. If you follow the trails charted by the wise men of old, they will lead to happiness—provided Force Number 1,678,872 does not upset their calculations (Lowie 1929:215).

Religion provides emotional support to face the uncertain and often hostile future. When a Jagga of East Africa goes on a journey or has an important decision to make, he offers a sacrifice to the ghost of an ancestor. The Baganda of East Africa study the entrails of a bird before making a decision. The Mapuche Indians of Chile offer prayers and sacrifices to the ancestors and to *ñenechen,* the supreme being.

When the future brings failure and disappointment, religion provides consolation. For example, in Tepoztlán, Mexico, when a child dies, religion provides consolation (Lewis 1960). The funeral of a child differs from that of an older person. The people of this area believe the child's soul goes directly to heaven and hence the funeral is supposed to be a happy occasion. This happiness is symbolized by happy music. A boy is dressed like San José, and a girl like the Virgin of Guadalupe. The feet are fitted with socks and sandals lined with gold paper. The face is covered with a veil, and a crown of paper flowers is placed on the head. The hands and feet of the child are tied together with ribbons when the body is laid out. The ribbons are untied at the grave. To provide water for the soul on its journey to heaven, a small, painted gourd filled with water is placed by the body. Children of the same sex as the child who has died carry the litter. As the body is brought out of the house, the bell of the *barrio* chapel is rung.

When a man becomes alienated from his society, religion provides a means of reconciliation. In our culture criminals are usually alienated from society. If that person gets "religion," often he is more quickly accepted back into society. Some of these may have been genuine conversions, but the point is that there were sociological results also.

The second function of religion is *transcendental;* it provides security and direction. The world is constantly changing. History brings about many changes in the human condition. In an everchanging world people look for a reference point from which they can orient themselves in the ebb and flow of history. Religion provides an absolute reference point from which people can cope with a changing world.

The Yoruba of Nigeria look to Odua as the creator of the earth. He is considered the progenitor of all the Yoruba. Yoruba kings consider themselves direct descendants of Odua and receive their status and authority from him.

The third function of religion is *sacralization;* it legitimizes norms and values. Every society has its own way of doing things and its own group goals. Every society also faces the problem of getting individuals to subjugate their personal goals to the group's goals. Religion legitimizes the group's goals and the means of achieving them.

For example, eternal reward and punishment in the afterlife are used by the Yoruba as an inducement for proper or socially approved behavior. The Yoruba believe they have three souls, and when a person dies, all three souls travel to heaven (Bascom 1969).

In heaven the ancestral guardian soul gives account for all the good and bad deeds done on earth by the person. *Olorun*, the judge in heaven, judges a person's deeds in the same way those deeds are judged at a court on earth. If people have been kind and good and have behaved properly on earth, then their souls are sent to *orun rere*, the "good heaven." If people have not behaved properly on earth, engaged in bad magic, been cruel or wicked, murdered or robbed, or beaten or poisoned others, their souls are condemned to *orun buburu*, the "bad heaven," where they are punished. Both heavens are located in the same part of the universe. Evil deeds are punished there and any wrongs done on earth are made right.

The Yoruba word *orun* refers to both heaven and the sky. Although the Yoruba believe that the afterworld is near *Olorun*, the sky god, they also believe the dead travel there by foot. They believe the dead must cross rivers and climb mountains and buy food to eat on the way. The money for food comes from money their relatives spend at the funeral. They believe the unkind and wicked will meet dangerous animals on the way, encounter swollen rivers, and be forced to climb mountains so slippery that it will take years to climb them. They also believe the wicked will spend all their food money before they arrive and will be hungry on the journey.

The fourth function of religion is *prophetic;* it criticizes norms and values. This function of religion is the counterpart to sacralization. Although religion legitimizes those norms and values that are consistent with the beliefs of a society, it also condemns those norms and values that are not. The Hebrew prophets are one of the clearest examples of this function of religion, and it is from them that this function derives its name.

In traditional Navaho religion, all of nature is seen as being in balance. Problems are the result of disturbing this balance. The Navaho sees the universe as a whole or of one piece. Everything is nature or natural and is part of the universe, including man. Since man is part of the natural universe, he must adhere to the laws of the universe. These laws are pretty well known to the Navaho, if not in complete detail, at least in general form. He knows how to act at different times and in different situations to maintain the order and balance of the universe. For example, if a Navaho puts his shoes on the wrong feet, it may bring about his death. This is not because the act is seen as a sin, but because he has, for an instant, disturbed the order of the universe. Many of the older Navahos believe that the lack of rain in recent years resulted from the younger men cutting their hair in the styles of the young white men. They believe that long hair encourages rain because that is the natural order of things. They see the results of various actions as both understandable and inevitable.

This account illustrates the prophetic function of religion. When the Navahos depart from the Navaho way, they are condemned and warned of the supernatural penalties that will have to be paid.

In most Latin American countries, three types of marriage are common. The first type is a Roman Catholic marriage performed in the church by a priest. The second is a civil marriage performed by a government official. The third is common-law marriage, a consensual union between a man and a woman. Common-law marriage is quite frequent in Latin America. Although common-law marriage is the norm in many areas of Latin America, it is condemned by a church that recognizes only church marriages.

The fifth function of religion is *identification*. It tells us who we are. "Religion gives the individual a sense of identity with the distant past and the limitless future. It expands his ego by making his spirit significant for the universe and the universe significant for him. In these ways religion contributes to the integration of personality" (Davis 1948:531–33).

The more rapid the social change in a society, the more important identification becomes.

This function operates among the Mapuche Indians of Chile. The hierarchical nature of divinity and the process of progressing from man to divinity, which are both central to the Mapuche world view, are illustrated by the connecting role of the ancestral chiefs. They believe that the spirits of the chiefs walk with the sons of the gods. The Mapuche see themselves as directly connected to the gods (Faron 1968).

The Mapuche Indians see themselves as descended from their ancestors, who still exist as spirits. When an Indian dies, he joins his ancestor as a spirit. The Hindus of India believe in reincarnation. They believe they came from God and progress through a series of reincarnations. Their goal is to rejoin God. The Hindu concept of God is impersonal and pantheistic.

The sixth function of religion is *maturation;* it marks the individual's passage through life for him and his society. Since life is sacred and related to the supernatural, this function marks stages of life. It is ritualized in the form of rites of passage.

When a child is born among the Yoruba of Nigeria, it is sprinkled with water to make it cry. No one present at the delivery says a word until the baby cries. They believe this would cause the child to be impotent or barren. A woman buries the placenta in the backyard. On this spot the baby is washed with a loofah sponge and rubbed with palm oil. The child is then held by its feet and shaken three times so it will be brave and strong. Its head is gently

226 CULTURAL ANTHROPOLOGY

touched to the ground so the child will not hurt itself if it should fall later in life (Bascom 1969).

Puberty is marked by rites of passage in many societies. Among the Kalapalo Indians of Brazil, the ritual is marked by a three-to-five-year period of seclusion. Among the Kaguru of East Africa, circumcision is part of the puberty rites for males. In many Roman Catholic societies, puberty is marked by confirmation. Jewish people mark puberty for males with a bar mitzvah.

In most societies, the marriage ritual marks a person's entrance into responsible adulthood as illustrated by the ceremonial wife-capture among the Barabaig of East Africa (Klima 1970). Before dawn on the morning the groom is to capture his bride, a group of friends go with him to the bride's homestead. Advance arrangements have been made, usually with either the bride's brother or mother, to remove the thorn bushes used to guard the kraal gate. The strategy used in the wife-capture is referred to as *lugod*, which is the same term for a raid or a war maneuver. The object of these maneuvers is to put around the bride's neck a string of blue and red beads which have a magicoreligious significance. After the bride has been captured, she does not associate with the young girls any more, and all her ties with the group of young girls with whom she formerly associated are severed. Now her place is with the married women and their groups.

Animism

Even as religion is universal so there is a universal belief in spiritual beings. The nineteenth-century English anthropologist Sir Edward Tylor, in his study of preliterate cultures, coined the term *animism* to describe the religions of these peoples. The term comes from the Latin word *anima*, meaning breath or soul. Tylor observed that the religions practiced by preliterate societies had certain features in common. These people generally believe they are constituted of two elements. (1) the body, or flesh, and (2) the soul. The soul concept is key to understanding animism. These preliterate peoples believe that not only individuals have souls but also animals and plants do. The souls of humans, animals, and plants continue to exist after the physical being ceases to exist.

Besides the souls of natural beings, preliterate people also believe in supernatural forces. R. R. Marett, another early anthropologist who studied religion, borrowed the Melanesian world *mana* to refer to the these supernatural forces. *Mana*, which can indwell humans, animals, plants, and inanimate objects, is an impersonal force that can be good or evil. Extraordinary feats are usually explained in terms of *mana*. Great deeds in battle, a large kill in a hunt, the ability to heal people, and other outstanding accomplishments are usually attributed to the *mana* a person possesses.

Another feature of many of these religions is totemism. *Totem* is an Ojibwa word used by anthropologists to refer to the spiritual unity between an animal or plant and a social group, often a clan or other kin group. The people believe they are spiritually related to their totem. This relationship is not evolutionary, as if they had evolved from the totem, but rather a spiritual relationship where they see their source of life as being the same as that of the totem.

Totemism is practiced among the aborigines of Australia, who believe in the preexistence of spirits. A person's spirit resides with the totem until it is time for its birth. If an aborigine woman gives birth to a second child before an earlier child is weaned, she leaves the second child in the bush to die. To the aborigine, the second child's spirit arrived too soon. It will now return to the totem and come back as a child at the proper time.

Another concept found in many of these religions, as well as in modern religions, is taboo. *Taboo* is a Polynesian word for supernatural injunctions against certain behavior. The breaking of a taboo may be an offense only against the supernatural or it may be against both the supernatural and society. Taboos are usually enforced by the supernatural but may be enforced by society. Taboos serve at least three functions. First, they keep the faithful in line. For example, the Mormon church excommunicated a woman for publicly supporting the Equal Rights Ammendment, which was opposed by the church. Second, they establish lines of separation to delineate the group and increase group solidarity. We often see this in extreme fundamentalist groups who view all other Christians, including Evangelicals, as apostate and separate from them. Third, taboos are used to help maintain social controls, as for example, the incest taboo discussed in chapter 8.

Religion and Magic

A distinction should be made between religion, magic, and science (Malinowski 1954). Every society, no matter how primitive, has a science or technology. Magic begins where science or technology leaves off. The Trobriand islanders, for example, use magic in growing yams.

The islander knows he must dig the soil to plant his yams. He knows how deep and how far apart to plant them. He knows he must weed his yam patch. He knows how to do all these things. They are part of his technology. However, there are aspects of yam growing that his technology cannot control, such as rain, insects, and climate. Because his technology cannot control these factors, the Trobriand islander turns to magic in an attempt to control them.

It seems clear that there is a distinction between religion and magic (Frazer 1941). Both begin with a belief in the supernatural, but they differ in their orientation to the supernatural. In religion, man recognizes the superiority of the supernatural. The attitude toward the supernatural is one of submission, reverence, and adoration. Man serves the supernatural in religion.

In magic man seeks to control the supernatural. He believes that if he uses the proper formulas, he can get the supernatural to do his bidding. While religion is the worship of the supernatural, magic is the manipulation of the supernatural.

Frazer (1953) distinguishes two types of magic: imitative and contagious. *Imitative magic* involves procedures in which the desired end is depicted or acted out, such as hunters shooting arrows at a model of their prey before setting out on a hunt. In *contagious magic* one first obtains some portion of a person, such as fingernail clippings, or a substance associated with a person, such as an item of clothing. This material is then subjected to a procedure believed to affect the person in a particular manner such as causing him or her to die, to be cured, or to fall in love. In most societies spiritual and nonspiritual techniques are closely related. Wherever uncertainty and anxiety enter into human life, spiritual techniques flourish.

Magic works often enough to convince the practitioners it is real. There are three possible ways to explain the occurrence of magic. First, it may simply be coincidence or chance. Almost anything will work a percentage of the time. The more time allowed, the greater the probability of its working.

The second explanation is psychological. If a person believes an event will occur, the person will act on that belief. That action may help insure the occurrence of the event. This is referred to as *self-fulfilling prophecy*. If bad magic is practiced against another person, and if that person believes in the magic, the person will be so overcome with fear that he will get sick or die. Psychologists refer to this phenomenon as *somatic compliance*.

The third explanation for the efficacy of magic is demonological. The Bible clearly speaks of a spirit world. Satan and his demons have supernatural power. They are not more powerful than God, but their powers supersede human powers. However, we must realize that although it may appear that the practitioners of magic are controlling the supernatural, it is probable that they are being controlled by demons. Of course, this explanation is not accepted by those who do not believe in the supernatural.

Magic used for antisocial or aggressive purposes is called sorcery. *Sorcery* is used to harm persons physically, socially, economically, or spiritually. This seems to have been the case in the "hex death" reported at Baltimore City Hospital in 1967:

> A midwife informed the mothers of three baby girls born near the Florida swamps that a spell had been placed upon their daughters who would all die young: the first, before her 16th birthday, the second before her 21st birthday, and the third, before her 23rd birthday. Years passed. The third young woman was admitted to a hospital in apparent congestive heart failure. She was in a state of panic and was hyperventilating. When questioned at length by a physician several days later, she broke down and related the outcome of her hex. The first girl died in an auto accident during her 15th year. The second was at a nightclub celebrating the end of the hex on the evening of her 21st birthday when a fight broke out and several shots were fired. One ricocheted off a piece of furniture and killed her. The third girl died two days before her 23rd birthday, presumably of congestive heart failure (Wintrob 1972).

Christianity, Religion, and Missions

Is Christianity unique or is it just a religion among religions? Anthropologically, it is the latter. Anthropologists are supposed to practice value-free science. They are not supposed to make value judgments. They are to describe, categorize, and, if possible, make generalizations; but they are not to evaluate. To the anthropologist every religion is equally valid, and every religion performs basically the same functions in every society. But the Christian views his religion as not only unique but also exclusive (John 14:6; 1 Tim. 2:5–6).

An anthropological study of comparative religions shows that all religions perform the same cultural functions. How can this be explained in the light of our belief in the uniqueness of Christianity? First, we need to remember that the human race is the result of a special creative act of God. God created humans as biological, psychological, sociological, and spiritual beings with needs in all four aspects. Because all people have common needs, the cultural systems they develop to meet these needs will have common functions. This includes their religions.

God created humans with a set of psychological and spiritual needs that can find their complete satisfaction only in Him. Biblical Christianity, as opposed to any cultural form of Christianity, is the only system that will completely meet those needs. Other religions are counterfeits of the real thing. Like counterfeit money, they work for a while, but in the end they fail to pass the test of authenticity.

Although we refer to Christianity as biblical Christianity, we must realize that it is never found apart from a culture; it is always a part of a culture. The Christianity of the New Testament was a part of the culture of the Greco-Roman world of the first century. Today we find American Christianity, Colombian Christianity, and Nigerian Christianity. There is no such thing as plain Christianity. Christianity always expresses itself through a culture. It is unique in that it can be expressed equally well in any culture. It is the one religion that can meet people's needs in any society.

When missionaries bring Christianity to other cultures, they must keep two anthropological concepts in mind. First, the people to whom they are bringing the gospel already have a religion that meets their cultural needs. It is an intregal part of their culture. Their religion gives them identity and direction in their culture. Second, missionaries bring with them the Christianity of their culture. It is a form of Christianity that is functional in the missionaries' culture. Missionaries have learned their religion in the context of their culture.

If missionaries are to introduce Christianity into other cultures effectively, they will need to follow a three-step strategy. First, they will have to study the religion of the culture in which they are serving. This involves more than understanding the philosophical basis of the religion, its theological concepts, and its sacred writings—though these are very important. Missionaries must also understand the cultural functions of the religion of society. One starting point for analyzing a religion's cultural functions is O'Dea's six cultural functions of religion. Understanding the cultural functions of a religion within a society is the first step in introducing Christianity to those people.

The second step is for missionaries to understand the cultural functions of Christianity within their own culture. Missionaries should see how Christianity meets O'Dea's six functions in their society. This will help them deculturalize their Christianity.

This leads to the third step: recasting Christianity in cultural forms to meet needs in the other culture. This involves much more than just replacing one culturally oriented belief system with a new cultural belief system. Christianity is a real and vital experience with the living God. The end product of a missionary strategy is not conversion, but the planting of a dynamic church with maturing believers who are reproducing themselves. The work of the Holy Spirit must continue in a person's life after conversion. However, people do not live in a vacuum. They are part of a culture. If Christianity is truly the universal religion, it will meet people's needs in every culture.

Questions for Discussion

1. List all the rituals practiced by your church. Which are rites of passage and which are rites of intensification?
2. In our culture, how does Christianity meet each of the six cultural functions listed in this chapter?
3. Are there any taboos in Christianity? What are they?
4. Three explanations for magic were given. Which of these reasons best explains each of the three deaths in the case study about the three girls who were "hexed"?
5. Is there such a thing as a Christian culture? Can there be Christianity apart from culture?

Suggested Reading

Durkheim, E. 1954. *The Elementary Forms of Religious Life*. A classic study in primitive religion. This book examines animism, naturism, totemism, myth, and ritual in primitive societies. Durkheim sees religion as a social phenomenon.

Goode, W. J. 1951. *Religion Among the Primitives*. Goode has written a good basic introduction to this area of study. The chapter on religion as an object of scientific study is highly recommended.

Lessa, W. A. and Vogt, E. Z. 1965. *Reader in Comparative Religion*. A collection of articles dealing with religion and culture.

Levi-Strauss, C. 1962. *Totemism*. A functionalist perspective of totemism. This book also looks at totemism from the perspective of the practitioner. It may be a little too technical for the beginning student but it is insightful for the serious student.

Mair, L. 1969. *Witchcraft*. A basic treatment of witchcraft. Mair utilizes a functionalist approach in her discussion of witchcraft. The book deals with the ideas and practices of those people who take the existence of witchcraft for granted.

Malinowski, B. 1948. *Magic, Science, and Religion and Other Essays*. A collection of Malinowski's writings on religion. The main essay deals with magic, science, and religion. The book also includes an essay on myth in primitive psychology and one on spirits.

Evans-Pritchard, E. E. 1956. *Nuer Religion*. A good description of Nuer religion. Their religion is similar to that of many other African tribal societies and makes an interesting case study.

13

Anthropological Research

Mary sits under a swaying palm tree on the beach overlooking the Pacific Ocean as it rolls up on a Malayan island. Next to her sits a young mother feeding her baby and telling Mary about some of the traditions of her people.

Harold sits at a table in the broiling sun outside a hut in Kenya, Africa. Equipped with a piece of paper and pencil, he asks an African youth to draw a picture of a person.

Carl sits at the edge of a clearing in a tropical rain forest watching an Indian wedding ceremony. He carefully notes who sits where and who speaks with whom.

Linda carefully types into a personal computer kinship terms and relationships she gathered among the Pueblo Indians the previous summer. She has already entered a program that will help her analyze the data.

What do Mary, Harold, Carl, and Linda have in common? They are all involved in anthropological research.

The Scientific Method

The scientific method (see pages 35–39) is a way of approaching the real world in an objective and systematic manner. Basic to the scientific method is the process of making observations about the regularities in properties or behaviors and then forming hypotheses about the processes involved or the patterns revealed. If the hypotheses hold up under further study, one begins to arrive at a working knowledge of the process or behavior. A hypothesis that appears to handle adequately observed phenomena is termed a *working hypothesis*.

The working hypothesis becomes highly refined when dealing with inanimate objects and their properties and processes, as in chemistry or physics. However, when dealing with the behavior of animals or man, the scientific investigator must be content with hypotheses that explain a large percentage of the phenomena, though perhaps not every aspect.

The process of observation, forming hypotheses, and testing them is illustrated in the following account. One of the authors traveled to the Philippines and moved into the home of a Filipino couple. He observed the age and condition of their home and noted that they had an automobile—an older compact model—and they employed three part-time house girls. Based on observations of the possessions and lifestyles of other families, he hypothesized that they belonged to the lower end of the wealthier members of society.

Yet these observations made the author aware only of the family's relative wealth. He still needed to determine whether the society was organized around a class system or a status system of social stratification. This was important to know if he was to analyze social interaction. In a class system people will relate to anyone they perceive as being of the same class and they will ignore minor variance in actual wealth. However, in a status system a person must know accurately the wealth and social position of others in order to know how to relate to them. If one is above another in status, that person will be able to influence the other. But, if one is below the other in status, it will require the help of others to influence the other. Therefore, the author needed to develop a hypothesis regarding relative wealth.

He was invited to live in the Filipino home. This invitation alone could be part of the complex behavior of hospitality in a class system or a status system. The fact that he was invited to stay one or two months suggested the behavior of status. Another system might have necessitated his being a relative, family friend, or paying guest.

Other hints to a status system were given in the behavior of visitors to the house. The parents of the host went anywhere, but other relatives stayed in the living area and were not admitted to the sleeping area. Some people came no farther than the front door and were never invited in. Others remained at the gate through their entire transaction with the household.

Even the method of presenting the author to friends and

acquaintances suggested this was a status system rather than a class system. His introduction to friends and acquaintances was selective. He would be introduced only to select individuals.

Working with the hypothesis that the society was a status system the author sought to determine his own relationship to the family. Being perceived by them as higher in status, how was he to maintain that status? One way was by riding only on "first-class" public transportation. Also, how might he influence them without manipulating them unfairly through the social system? This could be accomplished by quietly granting them favors for which they could take credit, reinforcing their own status in relation to the status of others.

The hypothesis of relative wealth within a status system of social stratification could be tested at any time. For example, the guest admitted to riding a third-class bus and enjoying the experience. The perceived attitude of openness by the household quickly changed to a situation of coolness toward the guest. This improved only when he promised to ride first-class buses in the future. Such behavior would not be characteristic of a class system, where discipline is in keeping with proper socioeconomic behavior rather than proper stratified behavior.

Anthropological Research

Whereas psychological research deals primarily with experimental design and sociological research with surveys, questionnaires, and statistical validation, anthropological research is primarily concerned with observation as a participant in the culture. Field investigators work within the context of the research setting. They are a vital part of the setting. They record their findings in relation to their participation in the setting under observation. This approach is called *participant observation;* that is, researchers participate in the setting. The resultant research findings are not as rigidly controlled as in psychological experiments nor are they of the same statistical validity as sociological findings. Nevertheless they do reflect the whole and the relation of each part to the whole, and so they form a sound foundation for other more rigorous and precise research methodologies. The techniques of experimentation and statistical validity give an accurate picture of the part studied but seldom give the relation of the part to the whole nor an understanding of the whole. Anthropological investigators cannot risk seeing only a part of the culture lest their findings distort the whole culture they are studying.

It is not by chance, therefore, that this research approach is referred to as field work. Researchers must live in the middle of their field to understand how the parts of the culture fit into the whole. For example, a linguist can begin learning a language away from the actual area where it is spoken because it can, at least in the beginning, be learned in isolation. Nonverbal culture is so complex, however, that if one is not where people are expressing themselves nonverbally as well as verbally, one does not perceive the entire meaning and is frequently miscued.

Field workers have intimate knowledge of one culture—their own. Their efforts at researching another culture primarily take the form of comparing it with their own culture. If researchers are functioning as true behavioral scientists, they will usually be objective in comparing the two cultures. Such objectivity permits them to value and respect each culture for its own structures and patterns of interaction. Researchers who place high value on certain aspects of their own culture tend to look down on those aspects in the other culture and impose a subtle feeling of superiority. Or else researchers may view those aspects of the other culture as superior, and by doing so create other problems.

Behavioral scientists through their education and research training have discovered the structure and interaction patterns of their own culture and this enables them to become increasingly aware of the structures and patterns of interaction in other cultures. The more societies the researchers have lived in and studied, the better equipped they are to test for and search out alternative structures and patterns of interaction.

For example, North Americans entering Philippine society become aware of Oriental influences and North American influences quite readily. However, unless they have lived in and studied Latin culture, they might very easily miss the subtle, but powerful, Latin influence on the culture, especially in interpersonal relationships.

Although the British school of social anthropology has tended to ignore the place of history in researching a society, cultural anthropologists tend to use both history and observation in seeking a total understanding of a people. For example, when one of the authors did field work in the Philippines, he studied the history of the islands. He found that Spanish explorers, bringing Spanish culture, came to the Americas and from Mexico traveled on to the Philippines. They were followed by Spanish priests who used Manila as a center for sending priests to the rest of Asia. The Spanish ruled the Philippines until the Spanish-American War, when it came under American control. However, the centuries under Spanish rule left their mark on the culture. There are many similarities between Latin culture and the culture of the Philippines. Both societies have status systems of stratification, for example.

A synchronic study—the study of one time period, especially the present—can be undertaken with a minimum of references to history. In this approach the researcher seeks to understand the dynamics and the patterns of interpersonal relations, as well as the religious, economic, political, and governmental institutions at a particular moment in time.

On the other hand, diachronic studies—i.e., those following a historical perspective—attempt to uncover development and change through time, historical antecedents of structures and behaviors, and trends and fads in sociogeographic regions at different time periods. These studies are concerned with questions of origin and source of process, of temporal or regional comparisons, and of hypothetical future developments.

Earlier we spoke about the statistical methodology of sociology. Recent trends in both sociology and geography have seen a cross-fertilization of research methodology. In sociology, men such as Howard Beeker and Erving Goffman have used participant observation. A whole new field based on participant observation has developed in sociology. It is known as ethnomethodology. Meanwhile, anthropology is adapting the statistical methodologies of sociology. Walter Goldschmidt has been active in utilizing sociological approaches in anthropology.

As we pointed out in chapter 2, one of the main differences between anthropology and the other behavioral sciences is anthropology's comparative approach. As more anthropological data is being collected, statistical techniques are proving to be valuable tools in the evaluation of this data. With the statistical methods of sociology being applied to crosscultural studies, old-line anthropologists have accused those who use these statistical methods of being little more than comparative sociologists. However, statistical analysis in anthropology is now well entrenched in the discipline. These statistical methods are proving to be very fruitful, and today most graduate departments of anthropology require their majors to take course work in statistics.

Along with statistics, another research tool being introduced to anthropology is the computer. Although computers have long been used to calculate statistical data, new uses are being developed. One new use is in the area of linguistics. Computers are being used to analyze languages and in some cases even being used in translation work. Wycliffe Bible Translators are among the pioneers in these new computer techniques. Computers are also being used for simulation and game theory. This allows the anthropologist to simulate various social phenomena and observe the hypothetical results.

Research Design

Once the larger concerns of the whole culture have been properly researched and evaluated, parts can be handled through any research methodology available to the behavioral scientist.

Experimental design is a methodology used to control various factors in an experimental situation. Experimental design involves two or more groups. All factors, except for one, are held constant in each group. The varied factor is called the *independent variable*. Another factor is observed to see how it varies with the independent variable. The observed factor is called the *dependent variable*. In an experimental design only the independent variable is changed or varied. All other things are held constant; so if the dependent variable changes or varies, then it must be a result of the variation in the independent variable.

Small group studies have shown that a group of people brought together and given a task will form some sort of leadership among themselves.

Suppose we wanted to know if the sex of the group members affected the type of resultant leadership. We could design an experiment to find out.

Five male and five female subjects could be matched according to age, race, education, and any other relevant factors. All factors would be constant. The males would be put in one room, the females in an identical room, and each group would be given an identical task. Sex type would be the only variable factor. If there was variation in the type of leadership that developed (the dependent variable), then, all things being equal, the sex composition of the group must have affected the type of leadership that was formed.

Of course, the only place all the factors can be controlled is in a laboratory. Psychologists have the advantage of being able to conduct much of their research in the laboratory, but anthropologists must conduct most of their research in the field, where they do not have control of all the factors. However, the anthropologists can utilize what is called a quasi-experimental design. A *quasi-experimental design* is a methodology similar to an experimental design except that the researchers cannot control all the factors, though they try to maintain as much control as possible.

Suppose anthropologists wanted to know which would facilitate better learning—coeducational or sexually segregated literacy classes in rural Mexican villages. They might try to find two villages as nearly alike as possible in population, wealth, educational resources, and any other relevant characteristics. Then they would set up a coeducational program in one village and a segregated program in the other, monitoring the results. This would be a quasi-experimental design because there would be no way to match every factor perfectly; but the closer the match, the more valid the results.

"Steel Axes for Stone Age Australians" is a classic example of quasi-experimental design gone sour (Sharp 1952). The experiment was not set up by a researcher but was established through chance by missionaries.

In one Australian aborigine group, missionaries introduced steel axes so that the aborigine could be more efficient in his life. Instead, his whole society was destroyed, including the physical and material culture. Instead of becoming more efficient, the aborigines had more time to sleep and loaf. Axes were originally only male possessions, but the missionaries gave them also to women and children. This resulted in the breaking down of the authority structure. Other aborigine groups served as the control group and showed that a society in which the steel axe was not introduced would not disintegrate to the same degree.

Such experiments are best handled on the individual or small-group level where the result can be watched more closely and adverse side effects can be controlled. When experiments are carried out in the larger society, forces may be set in motion that could in time destroy the society and cause its uniqueness to be lost.

Survey design involves the study of a sociogeographic area for certain specified interests such as language characteristics and burial practices. In this study a survey questionnaire is administered by the researcher, and the data collected is studied statistically for correlations between areas or zones. Surveys can be used to gather information on almost any subject: religion, family, occupation, residence, child rearing, and others.

A linguistic survey involves the use of a word list; a cultural-specific questionnaire, including a broad variety of nonlanguage questions for studying cultural practices and correlating findings with language usage; nonstructured interview tests in response to lead questions (e.g., How do you make your living?); and life histories of key informants.

Clinical design involves applying sound anthropological principles to some setting in a society calling for change. The Vicos project was set up by an anthropologist from Cornell University. A farm was bought and divided among landless Indian peasants. They developed the land and became the landowners. Although certain aspects of the project were poorly handled and some intentions misfired, the program revealed that the Indians could handle their own affairs and develop land if given an opportunity.

Research Tools and Mechanisms

Archiving is still the most extensively used research tool in the study of culture. Use is made of any repository of evidence, information, or organized body or records. A library and its book depository and archives are the most available sources. Nonlibrary sources include private papers, letters, office records, and permanent records of schools, churches, and organizations. One looks to books, journals, indexes, files, newspapers, encyclopedias, files of expeditions, and records of experiments and studies for source material bearing on the subject of interest. Without much study of the archives and the available materials of research, field studies may fall short of expectations and contribute little to the ongoing literature of the field.

One of the finest sources for anthropological material is the Human Relations Area Files at Yale University in Connecticut. Many major universities are tied into the file by computer. Although it has potential usefulness, the file has not been as fully used by missionary researchers as it might be.[1]

Participant observation is the primary research tool of anthropologists. In part this is because anthropologists are usually studying people never before studied and only minimally observed. The people are probably illiterate or marginally literate; so formal questionnaires are useless. Little has been written about them, and what has been written is probably only in the form of travel notes, which are not very useful in studying the lifeway and social organization of the society.

Nonparticipant observation is the outside view. The investigators remain outside the society, being simply travelers or visitors. They view what is happening in terms of what can be seen and in terms of what is known—likely from outside the system of the society. From this vantage point they are able to see some aspects of the society objectively but are likely to compare all they see with their own culture, thereby losing a degree of objectivity. A value judgment may be made at certain points, blocking one from viewing and understanding the whole.

Participant observation, on the other hand, provides observers with an inside view, as long as they have a model that will allow them to take what they see and integrate it into a picture of the whole culture. Kenneth L. Pike refers to this as the *emic* view, the view of the society from within, the way the people themselves see their universe and organize it.

However, in participant observation researchers run the risk of becoming too closely identified with the people they study and may

---

[1] For more information on the files, see the works by Ford, Moore, and Murdock listed in the "Suggested Reading" at the end of the chapter.

lose perspective. What they do gain, though, is a perspective that allows them to appreciate both the way the people live and the people themselves. It is this view that one must have in working with the people in any program of social or religious change. Many Bible translation projects fail because the translators do not work with the language within the cultural context in which the language is spoken. As a result, the translations become artificial and fail to communicate to the people.

Researchers need to allow themselves to become associated with a social role in the society and to establish in this context a position from which they may observe the society. Then they are able to observe as participants rather than as outsiders and are less likely to be obtrusive.

As mentioned earlier in this chapter, when one of the authors was conducting a study in the Philippines, he lived in the home of a high-status Filipino. From this position he was able to observe every social stratum throughout the community. Had he lived in a lower-status home, this would not have been possible because the higher-status living situations would not then have been open to him. The selection of an observation position will affect the results of a study because it affects the perspective of the observation.

Interviewing is face-to-face research carried out by the use of asking formal questionnaires or informal questions of an informant or respondent. Directive interviews involve asking questions of respondents. These questions guide them in a series of insight responses, starting from a point selected by, and proceeding in a direction determined by, the researcher.

Nondirective interviewing, on the other hand, simply gets the responder talking and allows the conversation to develop naturally. The nondirective interview is more likely to tap thoughts and feelings rather than ideas and projections. The material gained is valuable in discovering the mental structure of the person within the society.

Specific interview mechanisms involve such techniques as probe questions, genealogies, conversations, life histories, and the ranking of people, ideas, and artifacts.

Projective techniques are also utilized by anthropologists. A projective technique is a psychological instrument that measures subconscious aspects of behavior. Its value lies in its ability to allow and encourage a wide range of responses from a subject. Many times it gives data on many dimensions or aspects of subconscious behavior, and it draws out much useful data from the subject without revealing the purpose of a specific test.

The Rorschach test has probably been used more than any other projective technique in crosscultural research (Barnouw 1963). The test was developed in 1922 by a Swiss psychiatrist named Hermann Rorschach. Rorschach experimented with thousands of different inkblots and eventually came up with the ten cards that are still used today. The ten cards are a series of bilaterally symmetrical inkblots. Half of the inkblots are black on white and the other half use some color. All ten cards are always used in the same order when administering the test. The Rorschach analyst examines the response of the person being tested for clues to their personality structure. The process of analyzing Rorschach responses is quite complex and requires special training.

Another widely used projective technique is the thematic apperception test (TAT). In administering the TAT, the researcher shows a series of pictures to the person being tested. The person is asked to make up a story about each picture. The story is to include what led up to the scene in the picture, what the people in the picture are feeling now, and how the story will end.

Still another widely used projective technique is the Draw-A-Person test (DAP). The persons being tested are given a pencil with an eraser and a blank sheet of 8 1/2" x 11" paper. They are then instructed to draw a person. Instructions are purposely vague so that the sex and age of the person in the drawing will be determined by those being tested. After the subjects have drawn a person, they are given another piece of blank paper and are asked to draw a person of the opposite sex from that of the person drawn first. Analysis of the drawings involves looking at the age, sex, size, and other important characteristics of the person drawn to get clues about the personality of the person who drew the picture.[2]

The availability of technical aids has increased over the past decades so that now anthropologists have available to them an array of sophisticated research tools that were undreamed of at the turn of the century. Battery-powered, miniaturized, high-fidelity tape recorders and lightweight, portable video recording equipment are available. With zoom lenses and directional microphones, one can record activities hundreds of feet away without appearing to intrude on the situation. There are also portable personal computers with the capacity to process and store all of the researcher's data.

Improved transportation, particularly small aircraft, allows field researchers to arrive at their study sites in a matter of hours rather than days or weeks. Modern communication systems are able to link researchers with any part of the world in a matter of minutes. Personal computers and software packages have progressed to the extent that the most sophisticated statistical analysis of data may be completed in a matter of minutes right on the field.

[2]For a fuller treatment of the use of projective techniques in crosscultural research see G. Lindzey 1961, *Projective Techniques and Cross-Cultural Research* (New York: Irvington.)

There is no doubt that the present opportunities in research include open attitudes, adequate field opportunities on the whole, remarkable response potential for significant findings, adequate methodologies, and remarkable equipment to complete the task of field research. The world is a researcher's paradise.

Before research can begin, researchers need to decide what they are looking for and which research methods to use. For this step they will ask, How should the data be gathered? What research methods and models will be used? The researchers will want to test the research methods they have chosen so they will be certain that the methods will produce the desired data. Many research projects have been well under way in the field before the researchers discovered they were using the wrong methods to obtain the data desired.

For example, a researcher seeking to determine the social group in whose language he was to do Bible translation surveyed the three largest centers of the language, but he overlooked a small community with a prestigious dialect in the language area. The translation was only of limited use because it was not in this important dialect. The researcher had used a shallow survey technique rather than one extending in depth and breadth. He lost much time attempting to provide a translation available to all the people he wanted to reach.

Finally, to make an analysis of the data and draw conclusions, the researcher asks, What did I find? How will I code and tabulate the data? How can I analyze the relationships between the variables? What are the implications that can be drawn from the data? Wise researchers present their data simply and accurately. They will use charts, diagrams, tables, or any other means to make their results easy to read and understand.

Steps in Research

Step One: Focus on the Problem or Issue

In beginning research it is wise to ask, What am I attempting to do? What is it all about? A brief summary statement of the reason for research is appropriate. It not only becomes a useful statement in reporting research findings, but it can be referred to again and again during research to be sure the work is relevant to the purpose. This will not be the finished summary, only a preliminary point of view.

A research project to be undertaken in the Philippines had the following beginning summary:

1. To look for influences of Spanish culture that are likely to

be reflected as much in the social structure as in the artifactual record.

2. To examine the social dynamics operating to draw people into groups and to separate one group from another. If there is Spanish influence here, it will show in extended family organization. Groups will form around relatives and separate at points of family division.

3. To try to uncover what is blocking church growth, leaving churches small (twenty to forty adults) and limiting church-to-church interaction.

Little else was known about the field at the beginning of the project, but this was enough to guide research activities and keep the project "on track."

Step Two: Literature Review

Once a summary of interest and intent is ready, it is wise to check the available literature. The researcher needs to consider questions such as the following:

1. Who else has researched this area?
2. What have they found?
3. What must I avoid in setting up a new project?
4. What can I build on for my own program?

Such insights from available literature can save valuable time in the field and make the total project of that much greater value.

In this Philippine research project, the investigator utilized library materials with the following guidelines:

1. Search out, in reference works, all available facts about the area of investigation.
2. Begin reading descriptive analytic works on the area by reputable professionals. Respect them but don't assume complete accuracy.
3. Limit the reading of historical and theoretical treatises— some of this is useful but much develops biases that are difficult to overcome.
4. Set aside materials for later perusal once field work has begun.

The researcher's counterpart was on location in the Philippines and had already developed an excellent bibliography. Once on the field, these words were read and reread for research ideas. Many insights were gained from fresh research approaches. The entire bibliography was again reviewed as the final research report was being written.

Step Three: Hypotheses/Purpose

The questions appropriate to this step are the following:

1. What am I attempting to test?
2. What am I attempting to verify or demonstrate?
3. What do I predict I'll discover?

This is the time for making preliminary hypotheses. These should be made in observable and countable terms. If this is not done, the hypotheses cannot be tested. Depending on the research design, some preliminary hypotheses may be less amenable to testing, such as studying aspects of "national character," or they may demand highly controlled testing, such as analyzing specifics of a kinship system. Because the Philippine project involved a larger cultural study of national character and social structure, the hypotheses needed to be refined as experience was gained and data was collected. One of the hypotheses developed out of this project was the following:

> Hypothesis: The system of social stratification operating is one of status, not socioeconomic class or some age-related system (status is assigned the role, not the person; see chapter 7).

> Test: Any respondents questioned will be able to list ten of their associates in order of importance and prestige. They will accomplish this task with a minimum of hesitation. They will also be able to place themselves in the list at their perceived rank in relationship to the others listed. They can do this with a minimum of perceived embarrassment. (Note: This would not be true in a class system. A member would need a specific category such as "politics" before he could rank political leaders in order of importance. Of course, this would not be true in an age-grade system, for there rank order of importance would be by age. The list would be an age-prestige list, not a social-status list.)

Twenty such lists were collected. Each was checked with the other, and all were checked with the control list prepared by the field investigator. The lists correlated at a 90 percent level of accuracy.

This ranking procedure was one of many utilized to test the hypothesis of status stratification.

Step Four: The Sample

For this step the researcher becomes involved with the population studied. The questions relevant to this stage are, Who or what should I study? How can I obtain a representative sample? What percentage of the population need I concentrate on? It is important that characteristics of the population, the sample, and the situation be given. This step is usually carried out simultaneously with step three.

Step Five: Analysis and Conclusions

In the Philippine study the mission organization requesting the study had approximately twenty churches. Of these, four were studied to determine patterns of intergroup relationship. In all churches studied, no more than two extended families were represented by name. Of these, one family was related by marriage to the first and simply assumed a subordinate role. Based on the result of this study, the mission was able to modify its strategy to fit the culture.

Beginning Research Procedures

The beginning students of anthropology may not have the training to accomplish sophisticated research involving statistical validity derived from carefully controlled research approaches, but it is possible for them to immediately utilize the approach of participant observation and begin making field notations that may in time permit the description of the culture.

The following are some preliminary research procedures:

1. *What is worn.* Record clothing seen and unseen. Seek to determine how the people themselves react to what falls into the category of clothing. (What some consider clothing, others do not.) Be aware of patterns or combinations of patterns in cloth style as well as color combinations that are worn by different people. Become aware of how the people perceive appropriateness of clothing for a social event and try to discover their individual emotional response to their own clothing. They will have some feeling as to whether they are well dressed or poorly dressed, properly dressed or not properly dressed. Do this for each person encountered, being aware of age and generation differences.

2. *Irritations and surprises.* Keep a list of each irritation encountered, however slight, along with each response that surprised you. After a few weeks of listing, examine each item for clues to crosscultural difference. It is wise to compile the list daily and especially important to record irritations and surprises following each encounter in the community under study.

3. *Map of each locality.* Walk or move throughout the sociogeographic locale, remembering details of land-

marks, streets, architecture, and other environmental aspects. In many areas of the world, until you are known in the community, it is wise to actually draw the map at your place of residence. In an area where you are known, you may draw it as you go. Take further excursions to check details of the map.

4. *Biological-sociological display of the community.* Pay attention to the function of each structure encountered in the community. Relate each structure to the biological needs that society attempts to meet. (See Malinowski's seven basic needs in chapter 2, p. 41.)

5. *Natural resources display.* In the same way, display the area's natural resources in relation to their use in filling the above-stated biological needs.

6. *Sociogram.* Keep accurate records of the following:

   a. Who is with whom and in what occasion or setting. For example, A may be with B, but not with C.
   b. Where you meet those to whom you are introduced and where you meet the accidental acquaintance. One may only and always encounter A in the living room of the house whereas B may be encountered in any room of the house.
   c. Who greets whom and how. In some areas of the world, it is proper for a man to greet an older woman, but not a younger woman, when he encounters her.

7. *Kinship map.* Begin eliciting proper names within the community. Ask each how one refers to another and how he or she addresses the other. Once the kinship network is determined, inquire into expected and appropriate behavior, including responsibilities and opportunities. It may be proper for a man to be seen on the trail with his wife's mother but not with his wife's sister. (See chapter 9 for further details on kinship diagramming.)

8. *List of artifacts.* Keep a master list of all objects observed in the community. Record a description of the appearance and use of each object. What are their functions?

9. *Information sources.* Trace lines of contact and communication within the locale. Keep accurate track of where you get different types of messages and from whom you receive each. Who talks with whom?

10. *Cognitive research.* Start with the question, "This is a . . . ?" when showing a native speaker an artifact, a situation, or anything that can be named. This question is then followed by the next question, "Is this a . . . ?" while

showing a similar item. This process assists in determining the categories of thought of the people being studied.

11. *Diary or journal.* A diary is useful for recording emotional responses to experiences. A journal or log is useful for recording details of personal and community schedules of events and activities.

Anthropological Research and Missions

Professors Engel and Norton, in their book *What's Gone Wrong With the Harvest?* (1975), point out that one of the major breakdowns in communicating the gospel, in any culture, is a lack of understanding of the audience. In order to communicate our message to other people effectively we need to understand them and their needs. Professor Engel has followed up this work with a book on communication research, *How Can I Get Them to Listen?* (1977).

Ethnocentrism leads us to believe that other peoples have the same cultural needs, wants, and desires that we have. We tend to see their culture in terms of our own culture. We often do not really understand the people to whom we are trying to minister. Anthropological research can help us to better understand those peoples among whom we will be ministering.

Although many of the techniques discussed in this chapter are beyond the scope of the missionary without advanced specialized training in social research, at least three of the techniques discussed may be utilized by all missionaries. The first is literature research. Just about every society that a missionary may find himself or herself in has been the subject of social research. A missionary should be familiar with the relevant literature about the people among whom he or she will be ministering. One warning must be given about literature research. All cultures change, and in developing countries this change may be rapid. This means that some literature may become out of date rather quickly. However, this literature may still be useful in understanding the people's past, and the past is often the key to understanding the present.

The next research technique that a missionary may find useful is interviewing. Several techniques for interviewing were discussed earlier in the chapter. The student will find more help in several of the works listed at the end of this chapter.

The third research technique is one the missionary should be constantly engaged in—participant observation. Schatzman and Strauss' *Field Research* (1973) is an excellent little volume in this area.

Throughout his or her whole career, the missionary should be engaged in research in order to better know and understand the people among whom he or she will be working. As we come to know a people better, we will be better able to make the gospel relevant to their needs and to see them come to new life in Christ and grow in that new life.

Questions for Discussion

1. Which research techniques would be most useful to the missionary entering a new culture? Why?
2. What is the difference between participant observation and nonparticipant observation? Give an illustration of each at the school you are attending.
3. How would a student utilize principles of participant observation research to achieve the top grade in a course?
4. If you were attending a school or church for the first time and wanted to understand the leadership system, what would be your research strategy?
5. How could a pastor utilize anthropological research in ways profitable to his church in areas of church growth, education, evangelism, and worship?

Suggested Reading

Babbie, E. R. 1986. *The Practice of Social Research* (4th ed.). A helpful introduction to social research methods. This book contains several chapters on various modes of observation and discusses analyzing data.

Blalock, H. M. 1970. *An Introduction to Social Research*. A good basic introduction to social research. The chapter on exploratory and descriptive studies should be most helpful for those involved in missions.

———. 1972. *Social Statistics*. A good basic text in social statistics. This book takes a "cookbook" approach rather than a mathematical approach, but mathematical explanations are included for those who are interested. Most of the statistics can be calculated with only a knowledge of simple algebra and a calculator. Illustrations make explanations clear and practical.

Brislin, R. W.; Lonner, W. J.; and Thorndike, R. M. 1973. *Crosscultural Research Methods*. A limited overview of the field of crosscultural research. This work contains useful chapters on questionnaires and survey methods and also contains a section on statistical techniques.

Engel, J. 1977. *How Can I Get Them to Listen?* A recent work by Professor Engel from the Wheaton Graduate School. This is a follow-up to the work he coauthored with Dean Norton, *What's*

Gone Wrong With the Harvest? This book is an excellent introduction to basic communication research. It covers research techniques, sampling, instruments, analysis, and how to utilize research findings.

Ford, C. 1967. *Cross-cultural Approaches: Reading in Comparative Research.* A collection of readings dealing with crosscultural research.

Horvath, T. 1985. *Basic Statistics for Behavioral Sciences.* An introductory text covering the basic statistical tests used by behavioral scientists. It is research oriented.

Lindzey, G. 1961. *Projective Techniques and Cross-cultural Research.* A good reference for those interested in the crosscultural use of projective techniques.

Madge, J. 1965. *Tools of the Social Sciences.* Recommended reading for those interested in research.

Moore, F. W. 1966. *Readings in Cross-cultural Methodologies.* A collection of readings dealing with crosscultural research. The whole book is highly recommended to any person interested in seriously studying another culture.

Murdock, G. P. 1966. *Outline of Cultural Materials;* 1967. *Ethnographic Atlas.* These two works, which draw on the Human Relations Area Files, give basic ethnographic data on over 850 different societies. An excellent research source that has often been overlooked by missions.

Pelto, P. 1970. *Anthropological Research.* A basic introduction to anthropological research. The chapter on the emic and etic approaches to observation is very useful.

Schatzman, L., and Strauss, A. 1973. *Field Research.* An excellent introduction to observation in the field. It is a how-to-do-it manual.

14

Biblical Authority and Cultural Relativity

An American missionary couple went to British Columbia to minister among the Kwakiutl Indians. The work was not progressing as rapidly as the couple had hoped, and the village chief was not cooperative. When their first child, a handsome son, was born, they named him after the chief, thinking this would flatter him and gain his cooperation.

Much to their surprise, when they announced the baby's name, the Indians branded them as thieves and forced them to leave the village. The couple did not know, until too late, that the Kwakiutl Indians consider a person's name private property. It is one of their most prized possessions. No one takes another's name unless it is willed to him.

Can a given behavior be right in one culture and wrong in another? If so, are there any absolutes? Does not the concept of cultural relativity challenge the absolute authority of Scripture? Many Christians find the concept of cultural relativism disturbing. This is because they confuse it with the concepts of ethical or moral relativism. In this chapter we will look at the distinction between

Note: Much of this chapter is taken from Stephan A. Grunlan and Milton Reimer, eds., *Christian Perspectives on Sociology* (Grand Rapids: Zondervan, 1982), chapter 3.

251

cultural relativism and ethical or moral relativism. We will also see how one can hold to biblical authority and be a cultural relativist. In fact, we believe only a cultural relativist can truly hold to biblical authority. A cultural absolutist makes his or her own culture the authority. We will begin by defining our terms and develop our model of biblical authority and cultural relativity.

Cultural Relativity

William Graham Sumner, in his classic work *Folkways,* defined ethnocentrism as the "view of things in which one's own group is the center of everything, and all others are scaled and rated with reference to it" (1906:13). Basically ethnocentrism is the practice of making one's own culture and its norms and values the standard by which all other cultures are judged.

Sumner went on to define cultural relativism[1] in the following way: "Everything in the mores of a time and place must be regarded as justified with regard to that time and place" (1906:65). In other words the concept of cultural relativity is the position that ideas, actions, and objects should be evaluated by the norms and values of the culture in which they are found rather than by another culture's norms and values. Also the norms and values of each culture should be evaluated in the light of the culture that they belong to. As Sumner says, " 'Good' mores are those which are well adapted to the situation. 'Bad' mores are those which are not so adapted" (1906:65).

The concept of cultural relativity implies that "any cultural trait is socially 'good' if it operates harmoniously within its cultural setting to attain the goals which the people are seeking" (Horton and Hunt, 1976:59). While most anthropologists hold to the position of cultural relativity, at least as a methodological approach, there has been some criticism of the position.

One of the criticisms of cultural relativity is that it has little value in resolving crosscultural conflict. It is said that if two cultures are in competition or conflict, to use the term *good* to describe the actions of both does nothing to resolve the conflict. In fact, in any conflict the anthropologist must sit back and see which participant wins over, or dominates, the rival. In other words, pushed to its extreme, cultural relativity would seem to advocate that might makes right, or that the doctrine of the survival of the fittest is moral.

A second criticism of cultural relativity is that the concept itself is said to be ethnocentric. The concept is a Western idea and

---

[1] The terms *cultural relativism* and *cultural relativity* are used interchangeably in this chapter.

reflects a Western bias. A thing is good if it is functional or efficient: Functionalism and efficiency are Western values. Related to this Western concept is the problem of who determines if something is operating "harmoniously within its cultural setting to attain the goals the people are seeking." The whole process can quickly become quite subjective with a Western bias.

Another criticism is that, as some have argued, cultural relativity is actually self-contradictory. Cultural relativity implies that all values are cultural and therefore relative. Yet "cultural relativism itself posits a fundamental value: respect for cultural differences" (Broom and Selznick, 1977:73). Cultural relativists state that all cultures are equally good and should be respected equally. Cultural relativists have in fact made an a priori judgment of all cultures based on a value from their own culture: equality.

Finally, it may be argued that cultural relativity leads to ethical relativity. As Broom and Selznick point out, "It is sometimes said that cultural relativism precludes the belief that some values are good for all humanity" (1977:73). Horton and Hunt state, "Sociologists are sometimes accused of undermining morality with their concept of cultural relativism" (1976:59). To use an extreme example in order to demonstrate the moral dilemma of cultural relativity, let us suppose an anthropologist studied the Nazi extermination of Jews during World War II and found that this policy operated "harmoniously within its cultural setting to attain the goals which the people are seeking"; then, according to the definition of cultural relativity, it would have to be called good. Yet few, if any, anthropologists would want to call the Holocaust good. Cultural relativity seems to leave us without a basis for human morality.

Biblical Authority

Although cultural relativity seems to leave us without a universal morality, Christians claim a universal moral standard in the Word of God, the Bible. As the National Association of Evangelicals states it, "We believe the Bible to be the inspired, the only infallible, authoritative Word of God."

God created humans as spiritual, biological, psychological, and sociological beings. Humans have developed cultures to meet the needs arising from their nature. While cultures vary, humankind is one and is responsible to God. God has revealed Himself to humankind through creation, through the spoken word (prophets and apostles), through the written Word (Scriptures), and preeminently through the incarnate Word, Jesus Christ. The written Word is the testimony to the spoken word and the living Word. Richard Quebedeaux points out that Evangelicals accept Scripture as *both* history and revelation. They view the redemptive historical events recorded therein as the mighty acts of God, culminating in the life, death and resurrection of Jesus Christ. But for them, the Bible also embodies the divinely given Word of God as spoken by the prophets, and which interpret Christ's earthly kingdom of God (1974:74).

The Scriptures are both divine and human and are, as Quebedeaux says, "at the same time the words of God *and* the words of man recorded in a specific historical [cultural] time and context" (1974:75). God, by inspiration, worked through the human authors as products of their cultural situations. As George Ladd puts it, "The result is not a mere product of history or religious insight: it is a normative, authoritative, divinely initiated and superintended account of who God has revealed Himself to be and what He has done for man's salvation" (1966:216). The importance of the doctrine of inspiration is to impute authority to the biblical principles and teachings.

In speaking of the inspiration and authority of the Bible, we must remember that the Bible derives its authority from God; it is the Word of God. As Edward J. Young points out:

> The Scriptures therefore are writings which found their origin in God; they are the very product of His creative breath. It is this, then, we mean when we speak of the inspiration of the Bible (1957:21).

Biblical Authority and Cultural Relativity

Several criticisms were earlier leveled against the concept of cultural relativity. It also appears to be diametrically opposed to the concept of biblical authority. One might ask, Is there any place for a concept such as cultural relativity in a Christian world view? Several evangelical social scientists believe there is.

Both Eugene Nida (1954) and Charles Kraft (1979) see ethnocentrism and cultural relativity as two ends of a continuum. They claim that if we go to the ethnocentric end of the continuum, we absolutize human institutions; and if we go to the cultural relativity end of the continuum, we relativize God and the Bible. Nida therefore posits a position, which Kraft adopts, of "relative relativism" and Nida describes it as follows:

> In contrast with the absolute relativity of some contemporary social scientists, the Biblical position may be described as a "relative relativism," for the Bible clearly recognizes that different cultures have different standards and that these differences are recognized by God as having

different values. The relativism of the Bible is relative to three principal factors: (1) the endowment and the opportunities of people, (2) the extent of revelation, and (3) the cultural patterns of the society in question (1954:50).

In further explaining the three principal factors of his "relative relativism," Nida turns to the Scriptures for illustrations. He points out that the Bible teaches that rewards and judgments are relative to a people's endowment and opportunities. He cites the parable of the talents in Matthew 25:14–30, as well as this statement from Luke 12:48: "From everyone who has been given much, much will be demanded."

Nida says the Bible teaches that people are responsible to God according to the extent of revelation they have received. To support this point he cites Jesus' upgrading of the Old Testament positions on retribution for evil and divorce in Matthew 5, as well as Luke 12:47–48, which says, "That servant who knows his master's will and does not get ready or does not do what his master wants will be beaten with many blows. But the one who does not know and does things deserving punishment will be beaten with few blows." Nida is not suggesting that people may be saved apart from the gospel or that those who have never heard the gospel are not lost.

Nida also sees the Bible relative to different cultures. To support this point he cites 1 Corinthians 9:20–21:

> To the Jews I became like a Jew, to win the Jews. To those under the law I became like one under the law (though I myself am not under the law), so as to win those under the law. To those not having the law I became like one not having the law (though I am not free from God's law but am under Christ's law), so as to win those not having the law.

In concluding his discussion of "relative relativism," Nida defends his position by saying that it

> is not a matter of inconsistency, but a recognition of the different cultural factors which influence standards and actions. While the Koran attempts to fix for all time the behavior of Muslims, the Bible clearly establishes the principle of relative relativism, which permits growth, adaptation, and freedom, under the Lordship of Jesus Christ. The Bible presents realistically the facts of culture and the plan of God. . . . The Christian position is not one of static conformance to dead rules, but of dynamic obedience to a living God (1954:52).

Marvin Mayers (1987 [2nd ed.]) has also attempted to integrate biblical authority and cultural relativity. He sees ethnocentrism and cultural relativity as antithetical ideas. Mayers has developed a paradigm that involves two sets of opposing concepts. The first set includes cultural absolutism (ethnocentrism) and cultural relativism. The second set of concepts includes biblical relativism (that the teachings of Scripture are relative) and biblical absolutism, or biblical authority (that the teachings of Scripture are authoritative). Mayers' paradigm involves pairing either concept from one set with either concept from the other set, giving the possibility of four combinations as listed: (1) biblical relativism and cultural absolutism; (2) biblical relativism and cultural relativism; (3) biblical absolutism and cultural absolutism; (4) biblical absolutism and cultural relativism.

Mayers sees each of these four combinations resulting in four distinct positions that are shown in this diagram:

		BIBLICAL	
		RELATIVISM	ABSOLUTISM
	ABSOLUTISM	Situation Ethics	Traditionalist
CULTURAL			
	RELATIVISM	Antinomian	Mutual Respect

Mayers labels persons who hold to a position of biblical relativism and cultural absolutism as situation ethicists. In this position, when Scripture and culture clash, culture is absolute and Scripture is relative; and therefore Scripture yields to culture. The major proponent of this position is Joseph Fletcher, who writes:

> The situationalist enters into every decision-making situation fully armed with the ethical maxims of his community and its heritage, and he treats them with respect as illuminators of his problems. Just the same, he is prepared in any situation to compromise them or set them aside in the situation if love seems better served by doing so (1966:26).
>
> The situational factors are so primary that we may even say, "Circumstances alter rules and principles" (1966:29).[2]

---

[2]Fletcher would no doubt argue that he is not abandoning Scripture but that he is appealing to love, the highest principle in Scripture. However, his position absolutizes the situation, for he allows the situation to determine what serves love; he relativizes the Bible by going against its teachings if that serves love in a

Mayers goes on to label the person who holds to the position of biblical relativism and cultural relativism as an antinomian. The antinomian is bound neither by the Scriptures nor by culture. The antinomian acts without principle. This person will equally violate scriptural principles and cultural mores when it furthers his or her ends.[3]

The third combination is biblical absolutism and cultural absolutism, and Mayers calls a person holding this position a traditionalist. Traditionalists apply the Scriptures to a situation in their own culture. They absolutize the solution in a form compatible with their own culture and make this absolutized form the standard for evaluating all other cultural forms. For example, an American traditionalist would take his or her subcultural form of worship and make it the standard by which all other subcultural forms of worship would be evaluated. The traditionalist would argue: I follow the Bible and this is how I do it; therefore, deviation from how I do it is deviation from the Bible. The traditionalist easily becomes a legalist. The tendency of a traditionalist, once he or she has absolutized a cultural form, is to give that form precedence over the Word of God.

The fourth combination, that of biblical absolutism and cultural relativity, according to Mayers, leads to a position of mutual respect. Mutual respect allows each person to follow the Scriptures in a manner that is compatible with the individual's culture. Mayers argues that there can be mutual respect of cultures only with biblical absolutism. He writes:

> The approach of biblical absolutism and cultural relativism affirms that there is a supernatural intrusion. This involves act as well as precept. Even as Christ, through the incarnation, became flesh and dwelt among us, so precept or truth becomes expressed in culture. However, even as the Word made flesh lost none of his divineness, so precept loses no truth by its expression via human sociocultural forms. It is always full and complete as truth. So long as sociocultural expression is approached crossculturally it can be recognized as truth as well. The moment truth is wed to one cultural expression there is high potential for "falsehood" in any other culture. More seriously, since any given culture is in

situation. The issue is, Which best informs us on what best serves the principle of love, culture itself or culture in obedience to Scripture? Fletcher has opted for culture itself.

[3] While it is certainly true that a person holding this position could be an antinomian, we recognize that there are other possibilities. A person holding this position could also be a situationalist. Also, a person could disregard the Scriptures, hold to cultural relativity, and still maintain a highly moral and ethical lifestyle by his or her culture's standards.

the process of change, there is an even higher potential for falsehood within the culture that locks truth into one expression (1974:233).

After having examined two different models for integrating the concepts of biblical authority and cultural relativity, we see that these two concepts appear more compatible than one might at first believe. Building on Mayers' model, one can argue not only that the position of biblical authority and cultural relativity can integrate the concepts, but also that only a person who holds to biblical authority can truly practice cultural relativity, and vice versa. The position of biblical authority and cultural relativity is able to answer each of the criticisms of cultural relativity raised earlier in this chapter.

One of the criticisms of cultural relativity is that it has little value in resolving crosscultural conflict. That is because the actions of persons from each culture in the conflict, according to cultural relativity, are to be evaluated in the light of their own culture. Therefore, there is no common ground for evaluation and resolution. However, with the position of biblical authority and cultural relativity, there is the common ground of the Bible. The Bible as God's Word rises above both cultures, that is, its teachings are supracultural. Thus it becomes the basis for evaluating the actions of each culture as well as the basis for resolving the conflict.

Another criticism of cultural relativity is that it is, in fact, ethnocentric. Since no person is culture-free, the values of the person's culture will always influence the determination of what is good or harmonious in a culture. However, the position of biblical authority and cultural relativity makes possible—at least in theory—the potential for a nonbiased cultural relativity (an ideal that probably never will be fully attained). This is so because the basis for what is good does not come from the values of any culture but rather from the supracultural principles found in the Word of God.

The third criticism of cultural relativity is that it is self-contradictory. Cultural relativity begins with the assumption that all cultures are equally good, equality itself being a cultural value. In contrast, the position of biblical authority and cultural relativity would see all cultures as (1) adequate for meeting the needs of their members,[4] (2) manifesting human sinfulness, and (3) potential vehicles for God's interaction with humanity (Kraft, 1979:52). The values for this position are drawn from the Scriptures rather than from any specific culture.

The fourth criticism is that cultural relativity leads to ethical relativity. The only basis that cultural relativity has by itself for

[4]God has created humans with basic needs that must be met. A culture that did not meet these basic needs would cease to exist.

making moral evaluations is functionalism. However, the position of biblical authority and cultural relativity has a supracultural standard, the Word of God, by which moral judgments may be made in all cultures. The position of biblical authority and cultural relativity calls for biblical principles to be applied directly in each culture. If the principles come by way of a second culture, the model may be violated and result in ethnocentrism. This is why training in cultural anthropology and crosscultural communication is so valuable to missionaries.

As an illustration of this point, see again the opening anecdote about the missionaries in British Columbia. The cultural norms for naming children in the United States differs from those among the Kwakiutl Indians of British Columbia. In the United States given, or first, names are considered to be in the public domain. Anyone may name a child Robert, Mary, Frank, or Sue regardless of whether any other person has that name. Among the Kwakiutl Indians, names are considered private property, and no one may give to a child the name of a living person. As people die, their names may be given, or willed to others. We may inquire how one determines if the act of naming a child after a person still living is right or wrong. The following questions, adapted from Mayers (1987 [2nd ed.]:255), can serve as a guide in the process of evaluation:

1. What is the cultural norm? (This is the expression of cultural relativity.)
2. Is the norm in keeping with biblical principles? (This is the expression of biblical authority.)
3. Is the action in keeping with the norm? (This defines the situation.)
4. Does the action violate either the norm or biblical principles? (This is the integration of biblical authority and cultural relativity.)

Let us see how these four questions help us as we think about the action of naming a child after a living person in each of the two cultures.

1. What is the cultural norm? Given names in the United States are in the public domain and may be freely used. Among the Kwakiutl Indians names are private property, and one may not use another's name.
2. Is the norm in keeping with biblical principles? The Scriptures teach respect for the property of others (Exod. 20:15, 17; Mark 10:19; Rom. 2:21; Eph. 4:28) but do not prescribe what things are or are not to be considered private property. This is left up to each culture. Neither the United

States norm nor the Kwakiutl Indian norm violates biblical
principles.[5]
3. Is the action in keeping with the norm? In the United
States, naming a child after a living person is in keeping
with the cultural norm. Among the Kwakiutl Indians it
would violate the norm.
4. Does the action violate biblical principles? In the United
States, naming a child after a living person does not violate
biblical principles, but among the Kwakiutl Indians it
would do so because they consider a name private property.

This illustration demonstrates that an action may be right in
one culture and wrong in another. It is important to note that it was
not the culture that determined the rightness or wrongness of the
action; rather, it was the biblical principles. Each culture defined the
situation (cultural relativity), but it was on the basis of the biblical
principles (biblical authority) that the action was evaluated.

Let us apply this model of biblical authority and cultural
relativity to another case study. A young missionary couple with a
well-known mission board had just finished language training.
They were on their way to a small Central American country to
which they had been assigned for a church-planting ministry.

They arrived at a small rural town on the border, their
crossing point to their new field. They had checked up on all the
laws covering imports and were bringing in only those items that
were legally permitted. They had filled out all the paperwork, had
honestly declared everything, and had nothing to hide. They were
prepared to pay the required duty fees.

They were expecting a missionary couple who had been in the
country for several years to meet them when they arrived early in
the morning. However, there had been a mixup, and the missionaries were not there. By 10:30 that morning they decided to go
through customs. They approached the customs official on duty
and asked about getting their outfit through customs. He told the
young missionaries that it was close to lunchtime and that they
should come back after lunch. By mid-afternoon the official
returned. After some small talk, the official told them it was too
late in the day and they should return first thing in the morning.
The next day the official told them it was too hot and they should
come back the next day when it might be cooler.

By this time the young missionary couple was thoroughly

---

[5]Not all cultural norms are in keeping with biblical principles. Even as
humans are sinful, so are their cultures. For example, the norms for divorce in
the United States seem to be at odds with the biblical concept of marriage.
When cultural norms violate biblical principles, the Christian is responsible to
the biblical principles.

frustrated. They did not know what to do. The only other North American in town was a representative of an American oil company. They went to see him. Although he was not a Christian, he was very helpful to the young couple. He told them that the official was stalling for a "bribe." He told them that if they did not pay, it would take weeks to get through customs. He explained that the going rate was about 1,000 pesos (about $20.00 in American money). What was the young missionary couple to do? To help this couple we need to answer our four questions.

1. What is the norm? In North America to give money to a government official under any circumstances is considered a bribe, therefore the oil company representative saw it as a bribe. However, in some Latin countries government officials are paid low salaries because they are expected to supplement their salaries with tips. In that country paying an official to perform legal duties is viewed as giving a tip.[6]

2. Is the norm in keeping with biblical principles? In Hebrew the word for *gift* and *bribe* are the same. It is the context that determines whether it is a gift or a bribe. The Old Testament makes it quite clear that a bribe is money given to get an official to do something illegal (1 Sam. 8:1–3; Prov. 17:23; Isa. 33:15; Amos 5:12; Micah 7:3). Therefore money given to someone for doing what they should do is viewed as a gift or tip. In our culture we tip people for various services performed.

3. Is the action in keeping with the norm? Yes, in that culture it is acceptable to tip government officials. While we do not tip government officials in our culture, it would be ethnocentric to say they should not be given a tip in other cultures.

4. Does the action violate biblical principles? No, the Bible teaches that "a wicked man accepts a bribe in secret to pervert the course of justice" (Prov. 17:23). Since the tip would be given openly and would not be for subverting justice, it would not violate the biblical principle.

As we have seen, the model of biblical authority and cultural relativity allows a person to remain faithful to biblical principles while operating in another culture. In fact, it is only the cultural relativist who can truly remain faithful to the biblical principles. The cultural absolutist or ethnocentric person, while claiming to remain faithful to the Bible, is actually remaining faithful only to his or her own culture. The fact that biblical principles can find their own expression in each culture is another evidence for the

---

[6] It is possible to bribe officials in these countries. A bribe is money given for doing something illegal.

inspiration of Scripture. The effective missionary will always keep in mind that the Word of God is absolute whereas cultures are relative.

Questions for Discussion

1. Why do you think people confuse cultural relativism with ethical and moral relativism? How would you explain the difference to someone?
2. What problems do you see with Nida and Kraft's concept of "relative relativism"? What are its limitations?
3. Can you give examples from your church or other setting where people were traditionalists, practicing cultural absolutism with biblical absolutism? Which really has the greater authority in this view, the Bible or culture? Why?
4. In chapter 1 we asked, Does culture determine if a given action is right or wrong? How would you answer that question after reading this chapter? Why?
5. The authors claim that only a cultural relativist can be a true biblical absolutist. Do you agree or disagree? Why?

Suggested Reading

Hesselgrave, D. J. 1978. *Communicating Christ Cross-culturally*. A former missionary to Japan and professor at Trinity Seminary, the author deals with the issue of cultural relativity and biblical authority. Chapter 30 is particularly instructive.

Kraft, C. H. 1979. *Christianity in Culture*. An argument for the position of relative relativism. This book contains an excellent section on God and culture.

Mayers, M. K. 1987 (2nd ed.). *Christianity Confronts Culture*. A presentation of the model of biblical authority and cultural relativism. The book contains a number of case studies that will allow the student to apply the model.

15

Anthropology and Theology

When an automobile manufacturer produces a new automobile, he also prepares an owner's manual. The manufacturer has designed and built the car; so he knows what type of fuel and lubricants are best for it. He knows the tire pressure that will give the best performance. He knows at what speeds it is best to shift gears. In short, the manufacturer knows better than anyone else how to operate the car. He has written the owner's manual, not to keep people from enjoying the car, but to guide them in getting the most out of the car. God designed the universe and created human beings to live in it. Since God designed and created people, He knows best what they need to function. God's "owner's manual" for the human race is the Bible. It was given, not to keep us from enjoying life, but to help us get the most out of life.

The Bible is a most remarkable book. It has been around for over twenty centuries, and throughout these centuries millions of people have been led to God by its message of faith. The Hebrew rituals of the Old Testament period pointed to Christ, and the New Testament taught a personal faith in Jesus Christ. The Bible has also been used as a book of theology and doctrine through these centuries. Theologies and doctrinal statements have been formulated and presented to members of the body of Christ as the final truth. In the process, people have overlooked the biblical message that deals with how to relate effectively with other people. To many, it has often been enough to just grapple with the statements of doctrine and simply "know" the truth. What theologians have often overlooked is that religion is lived on a sociological level rather than a theological level. Anthropology adds a new perspective for theologians as they look into God's Word for direction in developing a relationship with God and relationships with other people.

Anthropology in the Bible

The Bible contains facts that relate to zoology, geology, astronomy, history, and the data of many other disciplines, including theology. However, the Bible deals with all of these disciplines as they relate to humans. Although God is the central character of the Bible, the revelation about Him is geared to needs of humans.

If theology is the queen of sciences, then anthropology is the crown princess. Because humans are the apex of God's creation, it is in the study of them that we can learn of God. The Creator may be known in His creation. The Bible teaches us that human beings were made in God's image (Gen. 1:27). We know this does not refer to a physical image because the Bible tells us that God is spirit (John 4:24), nor does it refer to the fact that a human is a "living soul" (Gen. 2:7). The Hebrew word for soul is *nephesh* and is used 756 times in the Old Testament. Usually *nephesh* does not refer to the spiritual part of human but rather to the physical. It is used in reference to the creation of animals (Gen. 1:20, 21, 24, and 30), and the animals were not created in the image of God. What, then, does "the image of God" mean?

Genesis 9:6 says, "Whoever sheds the blood of man, by man shall his blood be shed; for in the image of God has God made man." According to the Old Testament, an animal did not have to be killed if it killed another animal (Exod. 21:35–36). An animal is not responsible for its actions but a person is. This gives us a clue to the meaning of "the image of God." People are rational and responsible social beings. This is what is meant by their being created in the image of God. God created them to have fellowship with Him (Gen. 1:26–27; 2:18–23; 3:8).

As we study humans as social beings, as well as spiritual beings, we learn more about God, because people were created in the image of God. In fact, in the Bible God shows us what He is like by using illustrations from various human social relationships. He uses the social relationships of the family and compares Himself to a father (Matt. 5:45) and a mother (Isa. 66:13). He uses the social relationships in the legal system and compares Himself to a judge (Rev. 18:8) and a lawyer (1 John 2:1). God uses the economic system and compares Himself to the owner of a vineyard who goes out and hires laborers (Matt. 20:1–16). As we can see, God uses human social relationships to reveal Himself to us. As we study human social relationships, we can understand God better. Human beings are social creatures as well as spiritual creatures created in God's image; therefore as we study mankind (anthropology) we learn more about God.

Anthropology is the study of humans and any study of them should begin with their origin and purpose. Only when we correctly understand humankind's origin and purpose can we correctly understand humans. In chapter 2 we presented our position of functional creationism, a perspective that views God's creation as functional. Each part serves a purpose; creation is an integrated whole. Functionalism also is a perspective that underlies much of cultural anthropology. Anthropology views the various aspects of society as functional and society itself as an integrated whole.

Functional creationism also views the Bible and its proscriptions as functional. God's rules for living are not capricious but functional (see opening anecdote). For example, God did not limit sexual activity to the family setting, between husband and wife, arbitrarily. His rules concerning human sexual activity are functional. As was pointed out in chapter 8, the Communists in Russia discovered, through experience, the functional nature of this proscription.

While functional creationism is more concerned with the functions of creation than with attempting to date Creation, this is a question of great interest and one on which anthropology may be able to shed some light.

In the seventeenth century, James Ussher, the Archbishop of Ireland, calculated the date of the creation of man to be 4004 B.C. This date is found in the margin of many editions of the King James Version, including the popular Scofield Reference Bible (original edition). How did Archbishop Ussher arrive at this date? He dated Abraham as having lived a little after 2000 B.C. Most modern scholars would agree with this dating of Abraham (Harris 1971:68; Archer 1964:203–4; Unger 1954:105–18). He used the genealogy in Genesis 5 to calculate the time from Adam to Noah and the genealogy in Genesis 11 to calculate the time from Noah to Abraham. Ussher's calculations are based on the assumption that the accounts in Genesis 5 and 11 are complete chronological genealogies. A cursory reading of these passages might lead one to believe that this is the case. After all, the passages appear to say that

A lived so many years and begat *B,* and *B* lived so many years and begat *C,* and so on. It seems complete, with no apparent gaps.

Evangelical Christians usually take the Bible literally. Hermeneutics is the science of interpreting the Bible. One of the basic rules of evangelical, Protestant hermeneutics is the principle of interpreting a passage in the light of the culture in which it was written: What did it literally mean to those to whom it was written (Ramm 1956:136; Berkhof 1950:113–32; Mickelsen 1963:159–77)? How did the people of Moses' day understand the genealogies in Genesis 5 and 11?

We will look at three lines of evidence that seem to indicate that these genealogies were not meant to be, or understood to be, complete chronological genealogies. Rather, they were meant to be used to trace ancestry and family line. The first line of evidence is found in the passages themselves. This is the internal evidence. The second line of evidence will be found in other parts of the Bible. This is the biblical evidence. The third line of evidence will be information from outside the Bible that sheds light on the culture of that period and helps us understand these passages. This is the external evidence.

It is apparent that the purpose of these passages is not that of chronology. Genesis 5:32 reads, "After Noah was 500 years old, he became the father of Shem, Ham, and Japheth." Genesis 11:26 reads, "After Terah had lived 70 years, he became the father of Abram, Nahor and Haran."

If we take these two verses literally, Shem, Ham, and Japheth were triplets and so were Abram, Nahor, and Haran. However, we know that Abram was born many years after his father was 70 years old. Genesis 11:32 says Terah was 205 years old when he died. Acts 7:4 states that Abraham left Haran after his father Terah's death and Genesis 12:4 records that Abraham was 75 years old when he left Haran. That means Abraham could not have been born until Terah was at least 130 years old.

What Genesis 5:32 and 11:26 are most likely indicating is at what age these men began to have their families (Harris 1971:69). In fact, Genesis 11:27–32 seems to indicate that Abraham was the youngest of the three brothers because he survived the other two. Thus, the internal evidence seems to point out that the purpose of the genealogies was not to establish chronology but rather lineages.

Turning to the rest of the Bible, we find some clues to the purpose of genealogies in Jewish culture and how they were understood by the people of that culture. In 1 Chronicles 7:20–27 at least eleven generations are listed in the genealogy from Ephraim to Joshua, but 1 Chronicles 6:1–3 lists only four generations in the genealogy from Levi, Ephraim's uncle, to Moses, Joshua's contemporary. There must have been more than four generations between

Levi and Moses. The descendants of Levi numbered twenty-two thousand in Moses' day (Num. 3:39). It was often the practice in ancient Israel to trace genealogies through only the more important people in the line (Harris 1971:69). The purpose of the genealogies was to establish lineage, not to account for every person and year in the line.

As we continue to look at the biblical evidence, we see that this procedure was still being practiced in the Jewish culture of Christ's day. In Matthew 1:2–16, where the genealogy of Christ is listed, four wicked kings (Ahaziah, Joash, Amaziah, and Jehoahaz) are left out. Because they are mentioned both in 2 Kings and 2 Chronicles, Matthew would have been well aware of them. In fact, in Matthew 1:1 he says that David is the son of Abraham and Jesus is the son of David. Again, we see that the purpose of the genealogy was not to account for everyone in the lineage but to establish the lineage.

It appears that the word *begat* (KJV) or the phrase *became the father of* (NASB) in Hebrew is not always used to indicate a literal biological link (Archer 1964:187). In several instances grandfathers are spoken of as having *begotten* a grandson. For example, Matthew 1:8 (KJV) says Jehoram *begat* Uzziah, but we know from 2 Chronicles that Jehoram begat Joash who begat Amaziah who begat Uzziah. In 1 Chronicles 7:13, Bilhah's grandsons are spoken of as her sons, as though she begat them.

Our third line of evidence comes from outside the Bible. Moses, the writer of Genesis, was raised and educated in Egypt, where that culture had a great influence on him. The term *father* was often used to indicate lineage and succession rather than procreation as Egyptian literature reveals:

> In the Egyptian story "King Cheops and the Magicians" (preserved in the Papyrus Westcar from the Hyksos Period), Prince Khephren says to King Khufu (Chepos), "I will relate to thy majesty a wonder that came to pass in the time of thy father, King Neb-ka." Actually Neb-ka belonged to the Third Dynasty, a full century before the time of Khufu in the Fourth Dynasty (Archer 1964:371).

It seems then that the Genesis account does not indicate the date of Creation. Any attempt to date Creation must come from extrabiblical evidence. Some of this evidence shows that Creation took place well before 4004 B.C., the date suggested by Ussher:

> Corroborative evidence . . . is given by the fact that we have practically continuous records of ancient Egypt and Mesopotamia back to 3000 B.C., that is . . . well before Ussher's date for the flood. Also there are examples of many cities showing continuous inhabitation through periods long

before that—to about 7000 B.C. in the case of Jericho. Made
of mud and brick and lying as it does in the valley of the
Jordan, Jericho would have been washed away, or at least
seriously affected by the flood. But no problem exists if the
flood is dated at some time near 10,000 years ago. . . . This
is a critical date in world history and the remains of all settled
human habitation come after it (Harris 1971:70)

There is a diversity of opinion among secular scholars as to
when humans first appeared on earth. There is an equally wide
diversion of opinion among evangelical scholars as to when
Creation took place. Rather than add to the many dates already
suggested for Creation, we would prefer to make an appeal for
openmindedness and toleration on this issue. Evangelicals need not
and should not be divided on this issue. We all hold to the Bible as
the inspired and authoritative Word of God. We all see God as the
Creator of the universe and humankind. As we stated in chapter 2,
we do not believe the purpose of the Genesis account of creation is
to tell us when or how, but rather who and why. Our mission as
Christians is to make the Creator and His plan of salvation through
Jesus Christ known to all His human creation. Let us be tolerant on
the issue of the date of creation and united on the mission of the
Creator.

Anthropology and Hermeneutics

As we have stated, one of the basic principles of evangelical
Protestant hermeneutics is to interpret a passage in light of the
culture in which it was written. Cultural anthropology gives the
Bible student the conceptual tools for understanding the cultures in
which the Bible was written and, hence, to better understand the
biblical message.

The following illustrations demonstrate how an understanding
of the cultural situation surrounding a biblical passage sheds light
on the meaning of the passage. We will begin with an illustration
that has application on many mission fields. First Timothy 3:2, 12
and Titus 1:6 say that deacons and elders should "be the husband of
but one wife." Missionaries ministering in polygynous societies
have at times misused these verses in two ways.[1]

First, they have often tried to apply these verses to all
Christians when the passages are clearly dealing with elders and
deacons. The second misuse of these verses is even more serious. In
these passages Paul is, most likely, not even dealing with the issue
of polygyny but rather with the nature of the marriage relationship

---

[1] As was pointed out in chapter 8, polygyny is practiced in many of the
world's societies.

and possibly with the issue of divorce and remarriage. How can we know what Paul is or is not referring to in these passages? The cultural situation in which Paul wrote can shed some light here.

For all practical purposes, polygyny was not being practiced by the Jews, the Greeks, or the Romans of Paul's day.[2] Because polygyny was not an issue in Paul's day there is no reason to believe that he was referring to polygyny. In the context of these passages, it is the quality of marriage and family life that is being emphasized. It is interesting that the Old Testament never condemned the practice of polygyny but only regulated it (Exod. 21:1–11; Lev. 18:17–18; Deut. 21:15–17). In fact, the law of levirate marriage may even have required polygyny in some instances, though this is not certain (Deut. 25:5–10). Our purpose here is not to defend or condemn polygyny but to demonstrate how anthropology can help in the interpretation and application of Scripture.[3]

Why did Abraham try to pass off Sarah as his sister (Gen. 12:10–20; 20:1–18) and why did Isaac do the same with Rebekah (Gen. 26:7–11)? An understanding of the culture helps to explain this strange behavior.

Many of these contemporary societies were matrilineal. In a matrilineal society, a man's wife is not of the same lineage as he is, but his sister is. Property and wealth in matrilineal societies are passed down the female descent line but are usually controlled by the males. Because males control the property and wealth but females establish the line of inheritance, the brother-sister relationship is more important than the husband-wife relationship. In ancient Nuzi, upper-status men at times adopted their wives as sisters for legal purposes. In this way the wife became part of the noble line and had the rights and status of nobility. Perhaps Abraham and Isaac were taking advantage of this social mechanism to protect both themselves and their wives (Harris 1971:11).

In Judges 3:24 we find Eglon's servants thinking he was in his upper chamber "covering his feet" (KJV). First Samuel 24:3 records that Saul went into a cave to "cover his feet." What does the expression "to cover his feet" mean? How do we interpret these passages? Again, we find the answer by observing their culture. In that culture men wore robes. In order to relieve themselves, they lowered their robes, which "covered their feet."

In Genesis 31 Rachel hid her father's household idols. Why did she do this? Why was Laban so anxious to recover them? Again Nuzi culture sheds light on this incident. According to Nuzi law,

---

[2]While many families and marriages (Jewish, Greek, and Roman) are mentioned in the New Testament, not one of them was polygynous. In John 4, the Samaritan woman's sin was not polygyny but adultery through divorce and remarriage.

[3]We personally believe God's ideal is one man and one woman.

the possession of the household idols indicated the right of inheritance. Rachel wanted the household idols so that Jacob and her sons would receive the inheritance. Laban wanted them back to preserve his inheritance for his sons.

Understanding the culture of an area can often help us understand a passage written about that area. This is the case in understanding Revelation 3:14–18. Laodicea lay about eighty miles inland from Ephesus and about forty miles southeast of Philadelphia. It was named after Laodice, the wife of Antiochus the Second.

In the first century A.D., Laodicea was a major banking center. It was also a great garment center famous for its woolen robes. Laodicea was also a medical center and may be the place where Luke received his medical training. Along with being a medical center, Laodicea was a pharmaceutical center specializing in the manufacture of an eye salve.

The city had no internal water supply. It received water by viaduct from the hot springs in Hieropolis, a short way to the north. Water was also piped in from cold springs to the south. By the time the hot water from the north reached the city, it had become lukewarm as had the cold water from the south.

This cultural information gives us insight into Revelation 3:14–18. When the Lord said that the Laodicean Christians were neither hot nor cold but lukewarm (v. 16), He may have been comparing them to the city's water supply. Hot and cold, in this case, are not contrasting but rather parallel illustrations. Hot water is useful and refreshing. Cold water is useful and refreshing. But lukewarm water is neither useful nor refreshing. The Lord was telling them they had lost their usefulness. They, like the city's water supply, were unsatisfying.

When the Lord said that they were poor, blind, and naked (v. 17), He may have been referring to the industries of Laodicea. The Laodicean Christians were trusting in their material wealth rather than in the Lord. Although physically they may have possessed gold, eye salve, and robes, spiritually they were poor, blind, and naked. The Lord told them to buy gold from Him, to come to Him for white robes, and to get eye salve from Him so that they would be able to see spiritual things (v. 18). The Lord used the culture of Laodicea to communicate with the Laodiceans.

Contributions of Anthropology to Theology

Anthropology has numerous contributions to make to theological studies. First, through the crosscultural perspective, it allows us to look at other people and social groups as "valid." At least two lifeways are always in focus rather than just that of the scholar. The scholar sets aside his or her own lifeway to enter the social system operating in the biblical cultures. That is, the scholar tries to understand the Scriptures and their teachings in light of the relevant cultures. The scholar then returns to his or her own lifeway in relation to and in comparison with the biblical cultures. The scholar looks for the divine principles behind the forms in the biblical culture so that those divine principles may be applied in the scholar's culture. Finally, the scholar must become familiar with the language and culture of his or her audience so that the biblical principles may be applied in the host culture.

The second contribution of anthropology comes from the concept of functionalism, particularly as applied to creation, as in the theory of functional creationism. Other disciplines stress the origin and source of people and things—and thus of the universe. Through the structure-function approach of cultural anthropology, the function of the whole system, or the function of any component part of the system, may be examined from a functional perspective. Thus the question of the first chapters of Genesis is no longer seen only as one of origin and time sequence but also of function. We can now begin to see the function each part of the universe has in relation to the whole—or any part of the body in relation to the whole—or any part of society in relation to the whole.

In the ecological system light provides the energy for growth. Green plants provide oxygen and air purification, and humans are responsible for the maintenance of the system. Humans are the only created beings with the intelligence sufficient to maintain the effective balance in the system since they were made in the image of the Creator and were given the command "have dominion over" all that God had made.

Third, only anthropology, apart from the Bible, offers insight into the origin of humans as distinct from animals. The form and expression of Homo sapiens is distinct from those of any simian and mammal or any other nonsapien primate that ever existed. It is this distinction that marks humans off from the rest of creation. Cro-Magnon man and those following had all the mental, social, emotional, and spiritual potential spoken of in the early chapters of Genesis. There is evidence of art, metal working, and musical expression in the artifactual remains of this form of Homo sapiens.

Sapiens are set off from other creatures by their extensive ability to symbolize through language and to develop social structures and organization. This leads to the ability to utilize nonverbal culture and to abstract spiritual insights. These abilities allowed them to know God as well as their fellow humans. This is what is referred to so clearly and succinctly in the Bible as the "image of God."

Fourth, anthropology allows us to see the great potential of the industrial and urban revolutions. Just a glimpse of this potential is given to us in the experience of Cain, who founded the first city. Within a few generations there was the development of herding— the movable community food supply—the development of musical instruments, and the use of metal. Thus in these early accounts we see the promise of maximum expression of man's God-given abilities. Humans did not need to spend their entire lives in the quest of food as other animals do. They could be craftsmen, musicians, or whatever they desired. Because a few people could provide food for many, it freed others to pursue other skills and crafts. This had considerable import in the modern mission movement. The age of specialization has freed some people to pursue, full-time, the task of evangelization.

Fifth, anthropology helps us to be cultural relativists while we remain biblical absolutists. We have already dealt with the validity of distinct societies as well as the sociocultural perspective growing out of this concept. For example, Jesus lived in an event-oriented society; yet He can have maximum impact in our time-oriented society. He enters the heart. He does not seek to change the culture except as it changes through the regeneration of the hearts and lives of its members. We can thus come to an understanding of biblical cultures and our own culture and know how each compares and relates to the other. Moreover, we can know, in our own culture, that the Spirit will influence our lives in keeping with the eternal truths and intents of Scripture. Cultural anthropology makes it easier for us to enter other cultures and realize that the eternal truths and intents of Scripture, under the guidance of the Holy Spirit, may take different forms from those in our own culture or the biblical cultures.

Finally, anthropology can provide valuable insights for the development of an evangelical theology that is truly intercultural. Why is there a need for an intercultural evangelical theology? Because the church of Jesus Christ is multicultural, we need to develop a theology that is intercultural, a theology for the whole church.

Kraft in his article "Can Anthropological Insight Assist Evangelical Theory?" (1977) has suggested four specific areas in which an anthropological perspective can aid in the development of an intercultural theology.

The first suggestion is that a scholar must distinguish between the data with which he or she works and the interpretation of that data. Anthropologists, as well as other scientists, are careful to distinguish between the data and the theoretical model with which they approach the data. They also distinguish between the data and their interpretation of the data. It is also important for theologians to distinguish between their data and their theoretical models and interpretations.[4] Because theologians often work with sacred data (biblical documents), it is easy for them to begin to see their theoretical models and interpretations as sacred as well.

The theologian must realize that while the biblical data is sacred and infallible, the theoretical models and interpretations are human and fallible. Not only are the theologian's models and interpretations human, they are also bound by culture. Without realizing it, most theologians are using Western (usually Greek) philosophical models to interpret the biblical data. They need to realize that there are other valid models for interpreting the Scriptures. For example, African and Middle Eastern philosophical models are able to provide valuable insights into understanding the Old Testament and many parts of the New Testament. Because African and Middle Eastern cultures are closer to the Hebrew culture of the biblical periods than Western cultures, the insights provided by their philosophical models should be incorporated into our theological processes.

The second suggested area in which anthropological insight can aid theologians is that of relevance. In general, theologians concern themselves with problems and issues on a philosophical level whereas most people live on a behavioral level. Most theology is done in the language and concepts of metaphysical philosophy. Theologians need to begin to approach their problems and state their conclusions in behavioral terms. Theologians need to use the language of the behavioral scientist as well as that of the philosopher.

The third suggested area in which anthropological insight can aid theologians is that of distinguishing between form and meaning. This, we believe, is the key contribution of anthropology to the theological process. This is the very heart of the approach that combines biblical absolutism and cultural relativity. The distinction between cultural forms and their meanings is critical to the development of an intercultural theology. The theologian needs to realize that cultural forms are important because of their meaning to a particular people and not in and of themselves. Cultural forms derive their meanings from their cultural context and can be fully understood only in that context. A cultural form retains its meaning only in its own culture; once it is transferred to another culture, it takes on another meaning.

The cultural forms in the Scriptures must be understood in the context of their own culture. Cultural forms found in the Scriptures are not sacred; it is their meanings that are sacred. Indeed all cultures are relative, including the biblical cultures. The theologian, in developing an intercultural theology, must discover the meaning

---

[4]This includes missionaries and pastors as well as seminary professors.

274   CULTURAL ANTHROPOLOGY

(which is absolute and authoritative) that lies behind a given cultural form in Scripture. Then a theologian in any given culture can look for the cultural form in his or her culture that conveys the same meaning. Anthropological insight can aid the theologian in distinguishing between the cultures of the Bible and the teachings of the Bible.

Fourth, anthropological insight can aid the theologian in understanding the needs of people so that he or she can address these needs rather than just the needs of other theologians. This suggestion is related to but distinct from the second suggestion. The second suggestion was that theologians begin to deal with problems on the behavioral level as well as the philosophical level. This suggestion is that theologians use anthropological research methods to raise the proper questions and to find out what the problems of the people are.

One of the authors of this book has worked with a local church in developing a questionnaire that was administered to the congregation. The questionnaire was designed to discover the people's felt needs and how well, or how poorly, the church's programs were meeting those needs. The pastor used the results to develop a ministry that would address the needs of the congregation.

We are familiar with a professor at a Bible college who, each semester, gives his classes a questionnaire to find out what their thinking and level of knowledge is so that he can make his class relevant to his students' needs and at the same time cover the assigned material. In our teaching we have used both questionnaires and personal interviews for this same purpose.

All of the research methods discussed in chapter 13 can be used by theologians. Besides doing their own research, theologians can take advantage of the research done by others. For example, several years ago Zuck and Getz (1968) did a massive research project on the beliefs, attitudes, and behaviors of teenagers in evangelical churches. These findings have much to say to theologians, and yet there was very little theological reaction to their findings. The Harris, Roper, and other national polls often ask questions of moral, ethical, and religious interest. The National Opinion Research Center at the University of Michigan annually polls a national sample. These questionnaires almost always include religious questions.

If we are going to reach the world for Jesus Christ, we must make the gospel relevant to the people of the world. By this we do not mean that we change the message. We have only one message (1 Cor. 15:3–4). But we need to discover what people's needs are and be able to demonstrate how the gospel relates to their needs in their cultural setting.

Conclusion

Anthropology must never become the work of the church or missions. It must always remain a tool. As a tool, anthropology can be a valuable instrument in the mission of the church. Anthropology can contribute to our better understanding of ourselves and others as well as of God and His Word. As we better understand ourselves and God's Word, we can more effectively apply Scripture's teachings to our lives. As we better understand others, we can more effectively apply Scripture's teachings to their needs.

It is our prayer that a working knowledge of anthropology will contribute to making each of us a more fit vessel for the Holy Spirit to use.

Questions for Discussion

1. How can anthropology help a person better understand the Bible?
2. What is the relationship between anthropology and theology? In your opinion, does a theologian need a behavioral science background? Why?
3. How much knowledge of biblical cultures is necessary in order to understand the Bible? What implications does this have for missions?
4. Now that you have engaged in the study of cultural anthropology, how important do you think course work in cultural anthropology is for prospective missionaries? Why?
5. In what ways has your study of cultural anthropology affected the relationship between your faith and your culture?

Suggested Reading

Archer, G. L. 1964. *A Survey of Old Testament Introduction.* An introduction to Old Testament times and cultures. Dr. Archer utilizes the latest archaeological finds. This book gives a good understanding of the background of the Old Testament.

Harris, R. L. 1971. *Man: God's Eternal Creation.* The chapters on the nature of human beings, their origins, Creation, and Old Testament culture are excellent. All of this book is highly recommended.

Mayers, M. K. 1987 (2nd ed.). *Christianity Confronts Culture.* An application of anthropological concepts and biblical principles to the task of crosscultural evangelization. Mayers' book offers a good example of anthropology and the Bible in practice and makes an excellent follow-up to this volume.

Ramm, B. 1954. *The Christian View of Science and the Scripture.* Somewhat out of date but still an excellent resource. The chapters on biology and anthropology are highly recommended. This book takes an intellectual approach from an evangelical perspective.

Tenney, M. C. 1965. *New Testament Times.* Gives a good basic background to the cultural, political, and geographic setting of the New Testament.

Unger, M. F. 1954. *Archaeology and the Old Testament.* An older but not out-dated work that still provides good background to the Old Testament and its culture. It demonstrates how archaeology can help us understand past cultures.

GLOSSARY

Acculturation—the process by which individuals acquire the knowledge and skills that enable them to function to some degree in a second culture

Achieved status—a status obtained through choice and achievement

Adjudication—the process involving delegating decisions to others

Affinal ties—kinship relationships by marriage

Aggregation—a collection of people who do not have the properties of a group

Animism—primitive peoples' religion based on a belief in a spirit world

Anthropology—the study of man as a biological, psychological, and sociological culture-bearing being

Archaeology—the study of the artifacts of prehistoric societies

Artifact—any portion of the material environment deliberately used or modified for use by man

Ascribed status—a status that society assigns to an individual, usually based on characteristics of birth such as race and sex

Assimilation—the total adaptation to a new culture

Avunculocal residence—a living arrangement by which a married couple lives with the brother of the wife's mother

Behavioral sciences—those sciences that study human behavior, including anthropology, psychology, and sociology

Bilateral descent—descent traced through both parents

Clan—a consanguinely related group, patrilineal or matrilineal, believing in a common descent

Clinical design—the application of anthropology to a social problem

Cognitive anthropology—the study of the organizing principles underlying behavior

Community—a corporate body sharing sociopolitical identity and a geographic area

Compartmentalization—a psychological process by which a person boxes off conflicting things from each other

Consanguine ties—kinship relationships based on biological relationships

Container—a tool used to store matter or energy for a length of time while preserving it from loss or contamination

Contextualization—the developing of a theology from within a culture

Converter—a tool that changes one kind or form of matter or energy into another

Cross cousin—the child of one's parent's sibling of the opposite sex

Cultural anthropology—the branch of anthropology concerned with the study of existing human cultures

Cultural determinism—the approach to human behavior that sees culture as the determining factor of behavior

Cultural relativism—the approach to an interpretation and evaluation of behavior and objects by reference to the normative and value standards of the culture to which the behavior or objects belong

Culture—the learned and shared attitudes, values, and ways of behaving of a people; also the artifacts of the people

Culture complex—a cluster of related culture traits seen as a single unit

Culture shock—the reaction experienced by an individual who comes to live in a new and different culture

Culture trait—the smallest unit of culture; individual acts characteristically done by members of a culture

Dependent variable—the observed factor in an experimental study

Deviance—behavior that violates normative rules

Dialect—a variation of a language

Discourse—the process of structuring phrases, clauses, and statements into meaningful units

Economics—the production, distribution, purchase, and consumption of goods and services

Educational anthropology—the comparative study of socialization and enculturation processes

Enculturation—the process by which individuals acquire the knowledge, skills, attitudes, and values that enable them to become more or less functioning members of their society

Endogamy—a sociological rule requiring a person to select a mate from within a culturally defined group of which both are members

Eskimo kinship system—a bilateral, linear kinship system

Ethnocentrism—the practice of interpreting and evaluating behavior and objects by reference to the standards of one's own culture rather than those of the culture to which they belong

Ethnography—the descriptive study of human societies

Ethnohistory—the cultural history of a people

Ethnology—comparative ethnography

Ethnoscience—a linguistic approach to the study of nonverbal culture

Ethnotheology—a discipline concerned with the deculturalization and contextualization of theology

Exogamy—a sociological rule requiring that potential mates come from different culturally defined groups

Experimental design—a methodology used to control various factors in an experimental study

Extended family—a living arrangement in which two or more related nuclear families share a household

Family of orientation—the family one is born into

Family of procreation—the family one forms by marriage

Fictive ties—socio-legal kinship relationships

Folkways—low-level norms such as customs and manners

Foraging—food acquisition by gathering naturally growing foodstuffs

Formal government—an independent system or social institution set up for the purpose of governing

Fraternal polyandry—a marriage arrangement in which a woman marries a man and his brothers

Functional equivalent—something in one culture that performs the same function as something else in another culture

Government—a society's mechanisms and structures for the maintenance of order and communal decision making

Grammar—the structure of language

Group—a unit of two or more people involved in communication and interrelationship and having "unit awareness"

Hawaiian kinship system—a bilateral, generational kinship system

Horizontal status—a status on the same level or having the same rank as another

Horticulture—intensive types of agriculture involving killing certain plant growth and planting other plant growth with higher food value

Hunting—the catching and killing of wildlife for food

Hypothesis—a statement to be tested by a scientific methodology

Idiolect—an individual usage of a language

Incest taboo—the prohibition against mating with or marrying a close kinsman

Inclusive groups—groups in which membership in one group means inclusion in another group

Independent variable—a factor that is varied in an experimental study

Informal government—a governmental system based on an already-existing system such as the kinship system

Iroquois kinship system—a unilateral, linear kinship system

Kinesic communication—the transmission of messages by body movements

Kinship—a network of family relationships

Kin term—a specific term in a specific language used to refer to a kin type

Kin type—an abstract concept of a relationship that can be described in every culture

Language—verbal, systematic, and symbolic communication

Laws—rules and regulations that are enforced by the state

Levirate marriage—an arrangement by which if a man dies childless, his brother marries the widow

Mana—supernatural nonpersonalized forces in animistic religions

Marriage—a pattern of norms and customs that define and control the relationship between a man and a woman, designating them as legitimate sex partners

Matrilineal descent—descent traced through the mother's line

Matrilocal residence—a living arrangement in which a couple lives with the wife's family

Mechanism—arrangements of media designed to transmit or modify the application of power, force, or motion

Media—tools used to transmit matter or energy through space while preserving their essential qualities

Medical anthropology—the application of cultural criteria to the practice of medicine and response to medical, clinical, and educational practices

Moiety—the division of a tribe into two groups, based on birth

Monogamy—a marriage arrangement in which each individual has only one mate

Mores—social norms of a moral nature

Morphemes—meaningful units of sound of a language

Morphology—the organization of the basic sounds of a language into meaningful units

Mutually exclusive groups—groups in which membership in one group precludes membership in the other group

Neolocal residence—an arrangement by which a couple lives apart from both partners' families and sets up a new household

Noninclusive groups—groups in which joint membership is neither precluded nor requisite

Nonverbal communication—the process by which a message is sent and received through any one or more of the sense channels, without the use of spoken language

Norm—regular and accepted patterns of behavior

Nuclear family—a husband and wife and their immature children

Overlapping groups—groups in which membership in one group does not preclude membership in the other group or groups

Parallel cousin—the child of one's parent's same-sex sibling

Participant observation—systematic observation while participating in a society

Patrilineal descent—descent traced through the father's line

Patrilocal residence—a living arrangement in which a couple lives with the husband's family

Peasant economies—subsocieties of a larger stratified society that is either preindustrial or semi-industrial

Phonemes—distinct sounds used in a language

Phonology—the study of the sounds of a language

Phratry—a group of two or more clans held together either by kinship or by mutual interest

Polyandry—a marriage arrangement in which a female has more than one husband

Polygamy—a marriage arrangement in which a person has multiple mates

Polygyny—a marriage arrangement in which a male has more than one wife

Primary group—a small, intimate, and informal group

Primogeniture—a system of inheritance in which the family's wealth and position is passed on to the firstborn son

Proximic communication—transmission of messages that utilizes space

Quasi-experimental design—a methodology similar to that of using an experimental design but in which the researcher cannot control all the factors

Rationalization—a psychological defense process by which an individual recasts a difficult situation into one that is acceptable

Religion—the shared beliefs and belief practices of a people. These may or may not be supernatural in character

Rites of intensification—religious practices that increase group solidarity and commitment

Rites of passage—religious practices that mark an individual's passage from one life stage to another

Role—the behavior, attitudes, and values associated with a particular status

Role conflict—conflict between the demands of a single role or between roles

Role-set—an array of roles that accrue to a particular status

Rules of descent—a set of ordered relations limiting recruitment into various kinship groups

Secondary groups—utilitarian, formal, and impersonal groups

Selector—a tool used to discriminate among several inputs

Skill—the acquired ability to apply a given technique effectively and readily

Small group—generally a group of no more than fifteen individuals

Social class—those people on a social scale who see themselves as equal and are seen as equal by others on the scale

Social organization—the regularization of interpersonal relations

Society—a social organization made up of a group of people who share a geographical area and a culture

Sororal polygyny—a marriage arrangement by which a man marries a woman and her sisters

Sororate marriage—an arrangement by which if a woman dies childless, her sister marries the widower

State—a governmental unit based on territoriality, cultural organization, and formal government

Status—a position or place in a social system with its attendant rights and duties

Stratification—a hierarchy of statuses

Subculture—a cluster of behavior patterns related to the general culture and yet distinguishable from it

Survey—a research technique involving collecting data by systematic questioning of individuals

Switch—a valve with a finite number of positions

Syntax—the way a language combines words to make a meaningful statement

Technique—a set of categories and plans used to achieve a given end

Technological systems—those parts of culture that enable humans to produce objective changes in their physical and biological environment

Technology—the sum total of all the social customs by which a people manipulate entities and substances of all kinds

Terms of address—terms used to address persons

Terms of reference—terms used to talk about persons

Tools—devices for transmitting, transforming, or storing energy

Totem—a nonhuman "progenitor" of a clan

Trap—a tool that is a selector combined with a container

Tribe—a group of people who share a language, culture, and territory and see themselves as an autonomous unit

Unilateral descent—descent traced through only one parent

Urban anthropology—the crosscultural study of urbanization

Valve—a device that passes different kinds or quantities of input at different times

Vehicle—a tool used to transmit stored objects, energy, or information through space

Vertical status—the hierarchical ordering of statuses

BIBLIOGRAPHY

Adeney, M. 1975. Do Your Own Thing: As Long as You Do It Our Way. *Christianity Today*. Vol. 19, no. 20: 11–14.

Aginsky, B. W. 1940. An Indian's Soliloquy. *American Journal of Sociology* 46:43–44.

Archer, G. L. 1964. *A Survey of Old Testament Introduction.* Chicago: Moody.

Babbie, E. R. 1986. *The Practice of Social Research (4th ed.).* Belmont, Calif: Wadsworth.

Baliki, Asen. 1970. *The Netsilik Eskimo.* New York: Natural History.

Barnett, H. G. 1960. *Being a Palayan.* New York: HR&W.

Barnouw, V. 1963. *Culture and Personality.* Homewood, Ill.: Dorsey.

Barret, D. B. 1968. *Schism and Renewal in Africa.* Oxford: Oxford U Pr.

Barrett, R. A. 1974. *Benabarre: The Modernization of a Spanish Village.* New York: HR&W.

Bascom, W. 1969. *The Yoruba of Southeastern Nigeria.* New York: HR&W.

Basso, E. B. 1973. *The Kalapalo Indians of Central Brazil.* New York: HR&W.

Beals, A. R. with G. Spindler and L. Spindler. 1967. *Culture in Process.* New York: HR&W.

Beattie, J. H. 1965. *Understanding an African Kingdom: Bunyoro.* New York: HR&W.

Beidelman, T. O. 1971. *The Kaguru: A Matrilineal People of East Africa.* New York: HR&W.

Bendix, R., and Lipset, S. M., eds. 1966. *Class, Status and Power.* New York: Free Pr.

Benedict, R. 1934. *Patterns of Culture.* Boston: Houghton.

Berelson, B., and Steiner, G. A. 1964. *Human Behavior.* New York: HarBraceJ.

Berkhof, L. 1950. *Principles of Biblical Interpretation.* Grand Rapids: Baker.

Berlyne, D. E. 1960. *Conflict, Arousal, and Curiosity.* New York: McGraw.

Birdwhistell, R. L. 1970. *Kinesics and Context.* Philadelphia: U of Pa Pr.

Blalock, H. M., Jr. 1970. *An Introduction to Social Research.* Englewood Cliffs, N. J.: Prentice-Hall.

———. 1972. *Social Statistics*. New York: McGraw.

Bock, P. K. 1969. *Modern Cultural Anthropology*. New York: Knopf.

Bohannan, L., and Bohannan, P. 1968. *Tiv Economy*. Evanston, Ill.: Northwestern U Pr.

Bohannan, P., and Middleton, J. eds. 1968a. *Kinship and Social Organization*. New York: Natural History.

———. 1968b. *Marriage, Family and Residence*. New York: Natural History.

Boling, E. T. 1975. Black and White Religion: A Comparison in the Lower Classes. *Journal of Social Analysis* 31:73–80.

Bottomore, T. B. 1966. *Classes in Modern Society*. New York: Pantheon.

Brislin, R. W.; Lonner; and Thorndike. 1973. *Cross-Cultural Research Methods*. New York: Wiley.

Broom, L., and Selznick, P. 1977. *Sociology*. New York: Harper.

Brown, R. W. 1965. *Social Psychology*. New York: Free Pr.

Bruner, J. S. et al. 1962. *Study of Thinking*. New York: Wiley.

Buswell, J. O., III. 1975. Creationist Views on Human Origin. *Christianity Today*. Vol. 19, no. 22: 4–6.

———. 1978. Contextualization: Theory, Tradition, and Method. *Theology and Mission*. ed. D. J. Hesselgrave. Grand Rapids: Baker.

Caplow, T. 1969. *Two Against One*. Englewood Cliffs, N. J.: Prentice-Hall.

Casteel, John L. 1968. *The Creative Role of Interpersonal Groups in the Church*. New York: Assoc Pr.

Cavan, R. S. 1969. *Marriage and Family in the Modern World*. New York: TY Crowell.

Chapple, E. D. 1970. *Culture and Biological Man*. New York: HR&W.

Clausen, J. A. 1968. *Socialization and Society*. Boston: Little.

Cohen, Y. A. 1968. *Man in Adaptation: The Cultural Present*. Chicago: Aldine.

Dalton, G. 1973. *Economic Systems and Society*. New York: Penguin.

Davis, J. A. 1971. *Elementary Survey Analysis*. Englewood Cliffs, N. J.: Prentice-Hall.

Davis, J. H. 1969. *Group Performance*. Reading, Mass.: Addison Wesley.

Davis, K. 1948. *Human Society*. New York: Macmillan.

Deng, F. M. 1972. *The Dinka of the Sudan*. New York: HR&W.

Downs, J. F. 1972. *The Navajo*. New York: HR&W.

Durkheim, E. 1897. *Suicide*. Glencoe, Ill.: Free Pr.

———. 1954. *The Elementary Forms of Religion*. Glencoe, Ill.: Free Pr.

Edgerton, R. B. 1972. Violence in East African Tribal Societies. In *Collective Violence,* ed. J. F. Short and M. E. Wolfgang. Chicago: Aldine.

Engel, J. F. 1977. *How Can I Get Them to Listen?* Grand Rapids: Zondervan.

Engel, J. F., and Norton, W. W. 1975. *What's Gone Wrong With the Harvest?* Grand Rapids: Zondervan.

Evans-Pritchard, E. E. 1951. *Kinship and Marriage Among the Nuer.* Oxford: Oxford U Pr.

_____. 1956. *Nuer Religion.* Oxford: Oxford U Pr.

Farber, B. 1918. *Comparative Kinship Systems: A Method of Analysis.* New York: Wiley.

Faron, L. C. 1968. *The Mapuche Indians of Chile.* New York: HR&W.

Fenton, W. N. 1957. *American Indian and White Relations to 1830: An Essay.* Chapel Hill, N. C.: U of NC Pr. Reprinted 1971. New York: Russell.

Firth, R. 1974. *Malay Fishermen: Their Peasant Economy.* New York: Norton.

Fletcher, J. 1966. *Situation Ethics.* Philadelphia: Westminster.

Ford, C. S., ed. 1967. *Cross-cultural Approaches: Reading in Comparative Research.* New Haven: Human Relations Area Files.

Fortes, M. 1962. *Marriage in Tribal Societies.* Cambridge: At the University Press.

Fortes, M., and Evans-Pritchard, E. E., eds. 1940. *African Political Systems.* Oxford: Oxford U Pr.

Fox, R. 1967. *Kinship and Marriage: An Anthropological Perspective.* New York: Penguin.

Frazer, J. G. 1922. *The Golden Bough.* New York: Macmillan.

Freilich, M., ed. 1970. *Marginal Natives, Anthropologists at Work.* New York: Harper.

Gergen, K. J. 1969. *The Psychology of Behavior Exchange.* Reading, Mass.: Addison Wesley.

Ginsburg, C. D. 1970. *The Song of Songs and Cohelleth.* New York: KTAV.

Golde, P. 1970. *Women in the Field.* Chicago: Aldine.

Goldschmidt, W. 1971. *Exploring the Ways of Mankind.* New York: HR&W.

Goode, W. J. 1951. *Religion Among the Primitives.* New York: Free Pr.

_____. 1961. Illegitimacy, Anomie, and Cultural Penetration. *American Sociological Review* 26:910–25.

Goodenough, W. H. 1963. *Cooperation in Change.* New York: Russell Sage.

Gough, K. 1952. Changing Kinship Usages in the Setting of Political and Economic Change among the Nyars. *Journal of the Royal Anthropological Institute of Great Britain and Ireland* 82:71–87.

Graburn, N. 1971. *Readings in Kinship and Social Structure*. New York: Harper.

Grimes, J. E., and Hinton, T. B. 1969. "Huichol and the Cora." In *Ethnology*. Vol. 8. Edited by E. Z. Vogt. *Handbook of Middle American Indians*. 16 vols. 1964—. Edited by Robert Wauchope et al. Austin: U of Tex Pr.

Grunlan, S. A. 1984. *Marriage and the Family: A Christian Perspective*. Grand Rapids: Zondervan.

———. 1985. *Serving with Joy*. Camp Hill: Christian Publications.

Grunlan, S. A., and Lambrides, D. 1984. *Healing Relationships*. Camp Hill: Christian Publications.

Grunlan, S. A., and Reimer, M., eds. 1982. *Christian Perspectives on Sociology*. Grand Rapids: Zondervan.

Hall, Edward T. 1969. *The Hidden Dimension*. New York: Doubleday.

Hammel, E. A., and Simmons, W. A. 1970. *Man Makes Sense*. Boston: Little.

Hammond, P. 1971. *An Introduction to Cultural and Social Anthropology*. New York: Macmillan.

Harms, L. S. 1973. *Intercultural Communication*. New York: Harper.

Harris, M. 1964. *The Nature of Cultural Things*. New York: Random.

———. 1968. *The Rise of Anthropological Theory*. New York: TY Crowell.

Harris, R. L. 1971. *Man: God's Eternal Creation*. Chicago: Moody.

Hawley, A. H. 1971. *Urban Society: An Ecological Approach*. New York: Ronald.

Hayakawa, S. I. 1941. *Language in Thought and Action*. New York: HarBraceJ.

Hegeman, E., and Kooperman, L. 1974. *Anthropology and Community Action*. New York: Doubleday.

Henry, J. 1963. *Culture Against Man*. New York: Random.

Hesselgrave, D. J. 1978. *Communicating Christ Cross-Culturally*. Grand Rapids: Zondervan.

Hill, Polly. 1970. *Studies in Rural Capitalism in West Africa*. Cambridge: At the University Press.

Himes, J. 1968. *The Study of Sociology*. Glenview, Ill.: Scott.

Hobhouse, L. T.; Wheeler, G. C.; and Ginsberg, M. 1965. *The Material Culture and Social Institutions of Simpler People*. New York: Humanities.

Hoebel, E. A. 1954. *The Law and Primitive Man: A Study in Legal Dynamics*. Cambridge, Mass: Harvard U Pr.

———. 1972. *Anthropology: The Study of Man*. New York: McGraw.

Homans, G. C. 1950. *The Human Group*. New York: HarBraceJ.

Horton, P. B., and Hunt, C. L. 1972. *Sociology*. (3rd ed.) New York: McGraw.

_____. 1976. *Sociology*. (4th ed.) New York: McGraw.

Horvath, T. 1985. *Basic Statistics for Behavioral Sciences*. Boston: Little, Brown.

Howard, M. C. 1986. *Contemporary Cultural Anthropology*. Boston: Little, Brown.

Hughes, C. C. 1972. *Make Men of Them*. Chicago: Rand.

Hymes, D., ed. 1964. *Language in Culture and Society: A Reader in Linguistics and Anthropology*. New York: Harper.

_____. 1974. *Foundations in Sociolinguistics*. Philadelphia: U of Pa Pr.

Jongmans, D. G., and Gutking, P. 1967. *Anthropologists in the Field*. Atlantic Highlands, N. J.: Humanities.

Keesing, R. M., and Keesing, F. M. 1971. *New Perspectives in Cultural Anthropology*. New York: HR&W.

Kenny, M. 1960. Patterns of Patronage in Spain. *Anthropological Quarterly 33:14–23*.

_____. 1961. *A Spanish Tapestry: Town and Country in Castile*. New York: Harper.

Klima, G. J. 1970. *The Barabaig: East African Cattle Herders*. New York: HR&W.

Kluckhohn, C. 1972. *Mirror for Man*. New York: Fawcett World.

Komarovsky, M. 1946. Cultural Contradictions and Sex Roles. *American Journal of Sociology* 52:185–86.

Kraft, C. 1977. Can Anthropological Insight Assist Evangelical Theory? *Christian Scholar's Review* 7:165–202.

_____. 1978. *Christianity in Culture*. Maryknoll, N.Y.: Orbis.

Kroeber, A. L. 1944. *Configurations of Culture Growth*. Berkeley: U of Cal Pr.

Ladd, G. E. 1966. *The New Testament and Criticism*. Grand Rapids: Eerdmans.

Laird, C., and Gorrell, R. M. 1971. *Reading About Language*. New York: HarBraceJ.

Langness, L. L. 1972. Violence in the New Guinea Highlands. In *Collective Violence*, ed. J. F. Short and M. E. Wolfgang. Chicago: Aldine.

Le Clair, E., and Schneider, H. K., eds. 1968. *Economic Anthropology*. New York: HR&W.

Lessa, W. A., and Vogt, E. Z., eds. 1958. *Reader in Comparative Religion*. Evanston, Ill.: Harper.

LeVine, R. A. 1974. *Culture and Personality*. Chicago: Aldine.

LeVine, R. A. and Campbell, D. T. 1972. *Ethnocentrism: Theories of Conflict, Ethnic Attitudes and Group Behavior*. New York: Wiley.

Levi-Strauss, C. 1963. *Totemism*. Boston: Beacon.

Lewis, O. 1960. *Tepoztlan: Village in Mexico*. New York: HR&W.

Lindzey, G. 1961. *Projective Techniques and Crosscultural Research*. New York: Appleton.

Lingenfelter, S., and Mayers, M. 1986. *Ministering Crossculturally*. Grand Rapids: Baker.

Linton, R. 1936. *The Study of Man*. New York: Appleton.

Llewellyn, K. N., and Hoebel, E. A. 1941. *The Cheyenne Way: Conflict and Case Law in Primitive Jurisprudence*. Norman, Oklahoma: U of Okla Pr.

Lowie, R. H. 1929. *Are We Civilized?* New York: HarBraceJ.

———. 1948. *Social Organization*. New York: HR&W.

Luzbetak, L. J. 1963. *The Church and Cultures*. Techny, Ill.: Divine Word.

McCroskey, J. C. 1972. *Introduction to Rhetorical Communication*. Englewood Cliffs, N. J.: Prentice-Hall.

Madge, John. 1965. *The Tools of Social Science*. New York: Doubleday.

Mair, L. 1962. *Primitive Government*. New York: Penguin.

———. 1969. *Witchcraft*. New York: McGraw.

Malinowski, B. 1922. *Argonauts of the Western Pacific*. London: Routledge.

———. 1927. *Sex and Repression in Savage Society*. London: Routledge and Kegan. Reprint 1955. Cleveland: Meridan.

———. 1944. *A Scientific Theory of Culture and Other Essays*. Chapel Hill, N.C.: U of NC Pr.

———. 1948. *Magic, Science, and Religion, and Other Essays*. Glencoe, Ill.: Free Pr.

Manners, R. A., and Kaplan, D., eds. 1968. *Theory in Anthropology*. Chicago: Aldine.

Martin, G. 1976. *Marriage and the Family*. Scottsdale, Ariz.: Christian Academic Publications.

Matlick, J. et al. 1974. Mission = Message + Media + Men. *Central American Mission Bulletin* 447:6.

Mayer, K. B., and Buckley, W. 1970. *Class and Society*. New York: Random.

Mayers, M. K. 1987 (2nd ed.). *Christianity Confronts Culture*. Grand Rapids: Zondervan.

———. 1976a. *A Look at Latin American Lifestyles*. Dallas: Summer Institute of Linguistics.

———. 1976b. "The Behavioral Sciences and Christian Mission." A paper presented at the Association of Evangelical Professors of Missions, Overland Park, Kansas.

————.n.d. *A Look at Filipino Lifestyles*. Dallas: Summer Institute of Linguistics.

Mayers, M. K.; Richards, L.; and Webber, R. 1972. *Reshaping Evangelical Higher Education*. Grand Rapids: Zondervan.

Mead, M. 1949. *Male and Female*. New York: Dell.

————. 1964. *Anthropology: A Human Science*. New York: Van Nostrand.

Merrifield, William. 1976. Does It Matter What They Wear? *In Other Words*. Vol. 2, no. 2:6.

————. 1976. When Is an Aunt? *In Other Words* Vol. 2, no. 2:8.

————. 1981. *Proto Otomanguean Kinship*. Dallas: Summer Institute of Linguistics.

Merton, R. K. 1957. *Social Theory and Social Structure*. New York: Free Pr.

Mickelsen, A. B. 1963. *Interpreting the Bible*. Grand Rapids: Eerdmans.

Moore, R. W., ed. 1966. *Readings in Cross-Cultural Methodology*. New Haven: Human Relations Area Files.

Morgan, C. T., and King, R. A. 1966. *Introduction to Psychology*. New York: McGraw.

Morgan, L. H. 1963. *Ancient Society,* ed. E. Leacock. New York: World. Orginally published in 1887.

Morris, H. M. 1974. *Scientific Creationism*. San Diego: Creation Life.

Murdock, G. P. 1949. *Social Structure*. New York: Macmillan.

————. 1961. *Outline of Cultural Materials*. New Haven: Human Relations Area Files.

————. 1967. *Ethnographic Atlas*. Pittsburgh: U of Pittsburgh Pr.

Nader, L., ed. 1969. *Law in Culture and Society*. Chicago: Aldine.

Nida, E. A. 1947. *A Translator's Commentary on Selected Passages*. Dallas: Summer Institute of Linguistics.

————. 1952. *God's Word in Man's Language*. New York: Harper.

————. 1954. *Customs and Cultures*. Pasadena: William Carey.

————. 1960. *Message and Mission*. New York: Harper.

————. 1961. *Bible Translating*. London: United Bible Societies.

————. 1964. *Toward a Science of Translating*. Netherlands: Brill.

————. 1968. *Religion Across Culture*. New York: Harper.

Nida, E. A., and Taber, C. 1969. *The Theory and Practice of Translation*. Netherlands: Brill.

Norbeck, E. 1964. Peasant Society. In *A Dictionary of the Social/Sciences,* ed. J. Gould and W. J. Kolb. New York: Free Pr.

Oberg, K. 1960. Cultural Shock: Adjustment to New Cultural Environments. *Practical Anthropology*. Vol. 7, no. 4:177–82.

O'Dea, T. F. 1966. *The Sociology of Religion*. Englewood Cliffs, N. J.: Prentice-Hall.

Parsons, T. 1949. *The Structure of Social Action.* New York: Free Pr.
————. 1954. The Incest Taboo. *British Journal of Sociology* 5:102–15.
Peters, G. 1972. *A Biblical Theology of Missions.* Chicago: Moody.
Pitt-Rivers, J. 1961. *The People of the Sierra.* Chicago: U of Chicago Pr.
Plog, F., and Bates, D. G. 1976. *Cultural Anthropology.* New York: Knopf.
Powdermaker, H. 1966. *Stranger and Friend: The Way of an Anthropologist.* New York: Norton.
Prosser, M. 1973. *Intercommunication Among Nations and Peoples.* New York: Harper.

Quebedeaux, R. 1974. *The Young Evangelicals.* New York: Harper.
Queen, S. A., and Hobenstein, R. W. 1971. *The Family in Various Cultures.* 3rd ed. Philadelphia: Lippincott.

Ramm, B. 1954. *The Christian View of Science and Scripture.* Grand Rapids: Eerdmans.
————. 1956. *Protestant Biblical Interpretation.* Boston: Wilde.
Redfield, R. 1947. The Folk Society. *American Journal of Sociology.* Vol. 52, no. 4:293–308.
————. 1955. *The Little Community.* Chicago: U of Chicago Pr.
Reyburn, W. D. 1959. Polygamy, Economy, and Christianity in the Eastern Cameroun. *Practical Anthropology.* Vol. 6, no. 1:1–19.
Richardson, D. 1974. *Peace Child.* Glendale, Calif.: Regal.
Rivers, W. H. R. 1910. The Genealogical Method. *Sociological Review* 3:1–11.
Rogers, E., and Shoemaker, F. 1965. *Communication of Innovations: A Cross-Cultural Approach.* New York: Free Pr.

Sahlins, M. D. 1958. *Social Stratification in Polynesia.* Seattle: U of Wash Pr.
————. 1960. Political Power and the Economy in Primitive Society. In *Essays in the Science of Culture,* ed. G. Dole and R. Carneiro. New York: TY Crowell.
Sahlins, M. D., and Service, E., eds. 1960. *Evolution and Culture.* Ann Arbor: U of Mich Pr.
Schapera, I. 1956. *Government and Politics in Tribal Societies.* London: Schocken.
Schusky, E. L. 1965. *Manual for Kinship Analysis.* 2nd ed. New York: HR&W.
Schwartz, L. 1972. Conflict Without Violence and Violence Without Conflict in a Mexican Mestizo Village. In *Collective Violence,* ed. J. F. Short and M. E. Wolfgang. Chicago: Aldine.
Sitaram, K. S., and Cogdell, R. T. 1976. *Foundations of Intercultural Communication.* Columbus, Ohio: Merrill.

Smalley, W. A. 1967. *Readings in Missionary Anthropology*. Tarrytown, New York: Practical Anthropology.
Snarey, John. 1976. *Jesus-Like Relationships*. Wheaton: Pioneer Girls.
Spindler, G. E., ed. 1970. *Being an Anthropologist: Fieldwork in Eleven Cultures*. New York: HR&W.
Spindler, G. E. et al. 1973. *Burgback: Urbanization and Identity in a German Village*. New York: HR&W.
Spradley, J. P., and McCurdy, D. W. 1972. *The Cultural Experience*. Chicago: Science Research.
Steward, J. H. 1955. *Theory of Culture Change: The Methodology of Multilinear Evolution*. Urbana, Ill.: U of Ill.
Sumner, W. G. 1906. *Folkways*. Boston: Ginn.
Swartz, M., ed. 1966. *Political Anthropology*. Chicago: Aldine.

Tax, Sol. 1953. *Penny Capitalism*. New York: Octagon.
Taylor, H. F. 1970. *Balance in Small Groups*. New York: Van Nostrand.
Tenney, M. C. 1965. *New Testament Times*. Grand Rapids: Eerdmans.
Terrance, H. S. et al. 1979. Can an Ape Create a Sentence? *Science* 206:891–902.
Tyler, S. A., ed. 1969. *Cognitive Anthropology*. New York: HR&W.
Tylor, E. B. 1964. *Researches Into the Early History of Mankind and Development of Civilization*. Chicago: U of Chicago Pr.
———— 1971. *Primitive Culture*. London: J. Murray.

Unger, M. F. 1954. *Archaeology and the Old Testament*. Grand Rapids: Zondervan.

Wagner, C. P. 1971. *Frontiers in Missionary Strategy*. Chicago: Moody.
Wallace, A. F. C. 1966. *Religion: An Anthropological View*. New York: Random.
Washington Post. 1970. Sept. 2: A–6.
Westermarck, R. 1894. *The History of Human Marriage*. New York: Macmillan. Reprint 1925. New York: Johnson Reprint Corp.
White, L. A. 1949. *The Science of Culture*. New York: FS&G.
Willowbank Report, The. 1978. Wheaton: Lausanne Committee for World Evangelization.
Wilson, M. 1951. *Good Company: A Study of Nyakyusa Age Villages*. Boston: Beacon.
Wintrob, R. 1972. Hexes, Roots. *Medical Opinion*. Vol. 1, no. 1: 55–61.

Young, E. J. 1957. *Thy Word Is Truth*. Grand Rapids: Eerdmans.

Zuck, R. B., and Getz, G. A. 1968. *Christian Youth: An In-depth Study*. Chicago: Moody.

AUTHOR INDEX

SUBJECT INDEX

SCRIPTURE INDEX